UP TO THE CHALLENGE

Teaching Resilience and Responsibility *in the Classroom*

JAY JACKSON

Solution Tree | Press

a division of
Solution Tree

555 North Morton Street
Bloomington, IN 47404
800.733.6786 (toll free) / 812.336.7700
FAX: 812.336.7790
email: info@SolutionTree.com

SolutionTree.com

Printed in the United States of America
Visit **go.SolutionTree.com/SEL** to download the free reproducibles in this book.

Library of Congress Cataloging-in-Publication Data

Names: Jackson, Jay (Jay A.), author.
Title: Up to the challenge : teaching resilience and responsibility in the
    classroom / Jay Jackson.
Description: Bloomington, IN : Solution Tree Press, 2023. | Includes
    bibliographical references and index.
Identifiers: LCCN 2022037898 (print) | LCCN 2022037899 (ebook) | ISBN
    9781954631212 (paperback) | ISBN 9781954631229 (ebook)
Subjects: LCSH: Affective education. | Resilience (Personality
    trait)--Study and teaching. | Responsibility--Study and teaching.
Classification: LCC LB1072 .J34 2023 (print) | LCC LB1072 (ebook) | DDC
    370.15/34--dc23/eng/20220922
LC record available at https://lccn.loc.gov/2022037898
LC ebook record available at https://lccn.loc.gov/2022037899

Solution Tree
Jeffrey C. Jones, CEO
Edmund M. Ackerman, President

Solution Tree Press
President and Publisher: Douglas M. Rife
Associate Publisher: Sarah Payne-Mills
Managing Editor: Kendra Slayton
Editorial Director: Todd Brakke
Art Director: Rian Anderson
Copy Chief: Jessi Finn
Production Editor: Gabriella Jones-Monserrate
Content Development Specialist: Amy Rubenstein
Proofreader: Jessi Finn
Cover and Text Designer: Laura Cox
Associate Editor: Sarah Ludwig
Editorial Assistants: Charlotte Jones and Elijah Oates

Acknowledgments

I have many people to thank for this book. First, thank you to my parents, Paul and Terry Jackson, for simultaneously pushing and supporting me, especially during my formative years. I am also grateful for my older brother and sister, Jeff and Janna, who modeled how to take on difficult challenges—I have always looked up to you both and am very proud of all your accomplishments. A huge thank you to my beautiful wife, Laurie, who is my rock and partner in crime; your caring nature and ability to keep things running smoothly at home affords me the time to pursue difficult things (like this book). I love you so much! To our sons Casey and Cameron, I appreciate how accepting and enthusiastic you are with the parenting your mother and I are doing our best to provide; watching you accept obstacles on your own inspires me daily.

Nels Larsen, thank you for being a great coworker, friend, sounding board, and generator of ideas in this book. Your contributions, while under-the-radar, were very influential in this text. Joe De Sena, you have inspired so many people (including me) to travel outside of their comfort zones—I'm not sure I would have even started this project without you challenging me to pursue it. Through challenging others, you are making the world a better place. I would also like to acknowledge two inspiring people to me who are no longer with us: Paul Auerbach and Bill Sinnott. Paul, you were my idol for taking on challenges; you were a perfect and amazing combination of hugely accomplished and humble. Bill, you were my mentor concerning positive thought and relationships—I only hope to be half the teacher and person you were. I would like to also thank the Solution Tree editorial staff. I now realize how much effort goes into making a book, and I am beyond grateful for the time the editorial staff gave to make this publication more readable and organized. Finally, I feel moved to thank the teachers, especially at the Clarksburg Children's House and the Montessori Children's House of Denver, who took the tools from this book and showed that they can make an impact in students' lives. I am humbled by your hard work and your creativity to bring the concepts to life in your classrooms.

Solution Tree Press would like to thank the following reviewers:

Dean Armstrong
High School English Language
    Arts Teacher
Melfort and Unit Comp Collegiate
Melfort, Saskatchewan, Canada

John D. Ewald
Educational Consultant
Frederick, Maryland

Colleen Fleming
Literacy Specialist
Calgary Academy
Calgary, Alberta, Canada

Kelli Fuller
Instructional Facilitator
Howard Perrin Elementary School
Benton, Arkansas

Justin Green
Third-Grade Teacher
Nanaimo Ladysmith Public Schools
Nanaimo, British Columbia, Canada

Kelly Hilliard
Mathematics Teacher
McQueen High School
Reno, Nevada

Louis Lim
Vice-Principal
Richmond Green Secondary School
Richmond Hill, Ontario, Canada

Nancy Petolick
Instructional Coach/K-5 Mathematics
    and Reading Specialist
Savannah Elementary
Aubrey, Texas

Lauren Smith
Instructional Coach
Noble Crossing Elementary School
Noblesville, Indiana

Lana Steiner
Mathematics Coach
Horizon School Division
Humboldt, Saskatchewan, Canada

Rachel Swearengin
Fifth-Grade Teacher
Manchester Park Elementary School
Olathe, Kansas

Visit **go.SolutionTree.com/SEL** to download the free reproducibles in this book.

Table of Contents

About the Author

Jay Jackson is an educator at Fremont Unified School District and has been a teacher or administrator since 2002. Before becoming an educator, he served as the assistant wrestling coach for seven years at Stanford University. His focus in education is to help students simultaneously become more successful and happier versions of themselves as they take on challenges (those chosen and those thrust on them). He accomplishes this by using simple tools that, when coupled with questions, allow him to integrate concepts of sports psychology into academic classes. These tools promote student introspection on how they, personally, can best achieve peak performance while remaining joyful.

Jackson has led conversations and modeled the tools with individual educators of all subjects, departments, schools, sports leagues, and businesses throughout the United States and Canada to share his process. Leaders working with prekindergarten through adults have successfully included his tools in their classrooms, programs, and organizations.

Jackson has a bachelor of arts in psychology from Stanford University, California, and a master of arts in education from Pacific Lutheran University, Washington.

Contributors

Jennifer Brazier is a founder and chief officer of The Clarksburg Children's House, a Montessori program that serves children ages eighteen months to twelve years old in Harrison County, West Virginia. Brazier is also lead guide for the lower-elementary program. Her various coaching and educational experiences prior to establishing the school in 2006 range from teaching grades 4–8 students in public school settings in southeastern United States, Texas, and for the Department of Defense Dependent Schools in Hanau, Germany.

In 2012, Brazier discovered a deep interest in obstacle course racing, which led her to explore the connections between physical, cognitive, and social development. After noticing the natural inclination of even the youngest children to persevere and problem solve during the junior races, she became committed to creating an in-house physical program at school that ties together the integrated movements and academic progressions of the primary Montessori materials with social-emotional learning. In 2014, she became a certified trainer and obstacle course coach through Spartan Race and was contracted to collaborate with Jay Jackson to adapt his high school curriculum for ages 6–12. During this time, Brazier also worked as part of the children's course facilitation team for Spartan Race from 2016–2018 and as an educator liaison to other schools, all while creating community training and local events to assist in developing the program. The Clarksburg Children's House continues to elaborate and expand on these concepts and grow them collectively as the school population matures.

Brazier holds a bachelor's degree in elementary education from the State University of New York at Buffalo and is completing her lower-elementary guide Montessori Accreditation Council for Teacher Education certification through the Center for Guided Montessori Studies. She resides in Bridgeport, West Virginia, with her two sons.

Stacy Howard is a social-emotional learning specialist at Montessori Children's House of Denver (MCHD) in Colorado. She is also the head of the physical education program at MCHD, where she has been teaching since 2017 and has led schoolwide transformation in the areas of physical literacy and social-emotional learning. She is also a former high school girls' basketball coach.

Howard received bachelor's degrees in communication and English from the University of Denver, Colorado. She has had continuing education as a Montessori educator, as well as through various summits in child development, social-emotional learning, and outdoor education. She is a candidate for her master's in social-emotional learning from National University in California. She lives outside of Boulder, Colorado, with her wife, two kids, and dog, Theo.

Introduction

I sat in a hospital bed in the intensive care unit with doctors and nurses whizzing around me, groggy and paralyzed on my right side from the neck down. Hours earlier, I had been climbing across the monkey bars at my school's obstacle course training. It was a program we started to take students' minds from their stressors and onto the obstacle in front of them. (It's hard to worry about an upcoming test when all your attention is needed to climb over an eight-foot wall.) The bars were usually an easy warm-up for me, but this day was different. I stopped midway and dropped down. My head and body suddenly felt light. I could hear and understand words, but they weren't important at the time and seemed to drift off into the distance. It felt peaceful and confusing at the same time, which, it turns out, is not a great combination.

I was having a stroke. An arteriovenous malformation, a cluster of blood vessels in my brain that I was born with, chose that moment to burst. Blood had started to seep into my gray matter, causing me to float away mentally while slowly weakening my right side. Soon after, an ambulance came and rushed me to the hospital.

As I sat propped up on the bed, a doctor whisked in with a scan in hand. "Mr. Jackson, you had a significant bleed in your upper-left frontal lobe," he said matter-of-factly. "I need you to know that the process of recovery is going to be long and difficult. This will be a major challenge."

When I heard the word *challenge*, I perked up and became more aware.

Challenge is an empowering word for me. I have a meaningful connection to it. It elicits a positive response (even writing it charges me up). Throughout my life, challenges have brought me emotional highs and lows and provided the times when I've felt most alive.

I've learned to be grateful for and appreciate challenge. My father is a former physical education teacher and wrestling coach who was also a Green Beret during his time in the army. As I grew up, he manufactured difficult but safe challenges for me and encouraged me to complete them. In time, I learned how I could introduce challenges into my life and take them on. Because of this relationship with challenge, my purpose for teaching has always been this: I want to share with students the same excitement of taking on challenges that my dad gave to me. From my experience, attacking challenges correctly makes a person feel in control and will lead to success and joy.

For the first several years of my teaching career, which started in Marysville, Washington, in 1999 and continued in Fremont, California, in 2005, I tried to weave my dad's lessons into my history classes; but these lessons were integrated with little preparation, research, and impact. Then, a few years into my tenure in California, the principal called me to his office and asked me to teach a sports psychology class. Since there was no previous sports psychology class in the district, no textbook, and no state (or province) standards, I got to start from scratch and create the class how I wanted. I was excited as creating this course would force me to take a deep dive and organize my thoughts about how to best teach students to appreciate challenge. I decided the class would be based on my father's influence and the work of president for the Institute for Excellence and Ethics, Matthew Davidson; vice president of the same institute, Vladimir Khmelkov; and professor of education Thomas Lickona (2008). Davidson and colleagues (2008) write about human character "as having two major parts: performance character and moral character . . . character isn't just about 'doing the right thing' in an ethical sense; it is also about doing our best work" (p. 373). The authors continue, explaining, "We describe performance character as 'mastery orientation.' It consists of those qualities . . . needed to realize one's potential for excellence in any performance environment, such as academics, extracurricular activities, the workplace, and throughout life" (Davidson et al., 2008, p. 373).

The focus of this new class, therefore, would be *performance character*. While moral character was important to me and had a necessary place in the course, performance character needed further exploration to meet the goal of changing how students view and approach challenges. With this emphasis, I knew the class would feature the work of psychologists who focus on performance character, such as Angela Duckworth (2016), Anders Ericsson (2016), and Mihaly Csikszentmihalyi (2009). Since I wanted the course to be practical and intentional for students, I began to encourage students enrolled in the class to discuss and journal why they quit in various challenges so that I could research solutions from experts that might help them keep moving forward in the future. This process helped me narrow performance character into what I felt were eight components that students needed to accept and persist in challenges in the best possible way: (1) self-awareness, (2) integrity, (3) purpose, (4) passion, (5) positive mindset, (6) courage, (7) commitment, and (8) grit. If these eight components are done well, they could lead to *flow* (which is defined as the feeling of being fully immersed, focused, and finding enjoyment in a task). Flow is a potential and powerful byproduct for the person who works well through a challenge. As flow is such an amazing feeling, it merited a unit in my class to explain how to reach flow and further establish why students should improve on the eight components.

As I started teaching the course, I felt that what I was teaching about taking on challenges in sports could also apply to an academic setting. Lessons in developing performance character could be impactful (both in accomplishment and emotionally) to students who may not understand why or how they can best take on their academic challenges. Therefore, I started to create minilessons from sports psychology material to utilize in my world history classes. I found that taking ten minutes to cover a performance character concept before a project, assignment, or assessment led to the class exerting more and better effort toward the challenge.

The year after I first started to use these lessons in all my classes, the principal came to my classroom and suggested I join the administration, putting my performance character experiment on hold for four years. As an assistant principal, however, I quickly noticed that students were coming to the office complaining about being sad or anxious because of schoolwork. Curious, I wanted to see if that sentiment permeated the entire school. Therefore, I met and collaborated with Dr. Stuart Slavin from St. Louis University medical school to conduct a survey with our students. The survey revealed that over 50 percent of the 1,400 students surveyed showed moderate to severe levels of depression, while roughly 80 percent reported moderate to severe levels of anxiety (Abeles, 2016). As a community, we felt we couldn't look at those numbers and do nothing. Therefore, we tried to get teachers to reduce workload, talked about later start times, and brought in puppies for students to pet during finals.

While these tactics may have worked on some level, I couldn't help but go back to my research with performance character. I felt that the root of many of our problems was that our students were pursuing challenges in a way that wasn't leading to success or joy. School, after all, is a series of challenges every day. Each learning experience, assignment, and assessment is a challenge. If our students didn't know why they were taking on academic challenges or how to persevere through them, that may have been the main cause why our students were experiencing negative effects. To increase production and reduce depression and anxiety, educators could think about what level of challenge might be appropriate for their students, how they could guide and coach students to understand why they're taking on challenges, and how to teach students to attack challenges in the best possible way. As teachers, if we're not intentional about these things, students may feel as if they are victims to the many challenges that hit them in school every day. We cannot control what happens to students outside of school, but if students understand the concepts of performance character, as outlined in this book, I believe they can feel more in control of educational challenges and see them more as an opportunity to learn rather than hardships they are forced to endure.

About This Book

Challenges are never easy, but emotional well-being and success hinge on why and how someone takes on the challenge. If done poorly, challenges can lead to depression and anxiety. If done well, challenges can lead to success and joy. This book aims to assist K–12 teachers with knowledge about the necessary components of performance character and tools that they can use to help their students think about the best possible way they can personally take on challenges. If students can determine the best way to navigate challenges in school, they should experience more accomplishment and positive feelings. To this end, each chapter provides research on one of the eight key components of performance character along with flow. Each chapter is described as follows.

- **Chapter 1: Self-Awareness**—While our egos try to convince us we are without flaws (making us feel better than others), *self-awareness* allows us to see ourselves as we really are without comparisons. Author Mark Manson (n.d.) says, "Self-awareness is our ability to observe and accurately identify our thoughts, feelings, and impulses, and determine whether they are grounded in reality or not." This chapter identifies the behaviors of a self-aware person and helps educators devise strategies to help students become more self-aware.

- **Chapter 2: Integrity**—Merriam-Webster defines *integrity* (n.d.) in two ways: (1) "firm adherence to a code of especially moral . . . values" and (2) "the quality or state of being complete or undivided." Putting the two definitions together, *integrity* means that we have our own unwavering virtuous and noble truths that extend to our actions. This chapter reviews why integrity, while a moral trait, is also necessary for performance character.

- **Chapter 3: Purpose**—If you have no purpose, you really have nothing to work toward. Author Simon Sinek (2019) encourages us to "Start with why" to find our direction of how we will do something and then what we will do. If you have a good why, reason, or purpose for what you want to achieve, you are more likely to feel motivated and happy. This chapter provides methods for establishing purpose in yourself and your students.

- **Chapter 4: Passion**—As people move toward a purpose, they experience all types of positive and negative emotions—challenges tend to elicit emotional highs and lows. These emotions, in turn, make life much more exciting and make us feel emotionally connected to our purpose and strongly compelled to continue toward that purpose, turning it into a passion. This chapter looks at ways to cultivate passion, find what makes your students passionate, and learn how to help them find passion in learning.

- **Chapter 5: Positive Mindset**—A positive mindset is the fifth necessary component of performance character that helps us take on obstacles. A positive mindset means that you are optimistic, grateful, and joyful while taking on challenges. This chapter looks at the research behind identifying the qualities a person with a positive mindset possesses and review strategies for helping students cultivate their own.

- **Chapter 6: Courage**—Often when taking on a challenge, your thoughts of fear will try to persuade you to stop pushing forward. Courage can get you to work *with* this fear to help you persist. To help students strive for courageousness, this chapter identifies what courage means in the classroom and provides some resources to help you integrate courage-building behaviors in your lessons.

- **Chapter 7: Commitment**—If you would like to improve and reach expertise in some area, hours and hours of focused effort will greatly help. This includes the thought it will take to come up with the best course of action along with the follow-through it will take to execute your plan; this is *commitment*. This chapter explains true commitment and helps students apply commitment to their studies and their values.

- **Chapter 8: Grit**—Grit is the final necessary component of performance character and is what all the other components build to. According to

Angela Duckworth, "Grit is passion and perseverance for long-term goals" (as cited in FAQ, n.d.). *Grittiness* is, therefore, using passion and perseverance in tandem to pursue a challenge over an extended period. This chapter builds on lessons learned in previous chapters and helps students develop a sense of grit in their work.

- **Chapter 9: Flow**—While being gritty toward a purpose, you may reach flow. Flow is not a key element of performance character, but it can be a very welcome bonus of which students should be aware. *Flow* happens when your brain is completely engrossed with the challenge to the point where you are fully immersed in the present and the ego (and comparison) completely vanishes. This chapter explores this phenomenon and locates ways for students to use it to succeed.

Beyond the research, this book offers simple tools that an educator can use to foster a discussion about various concepts of performance character with students. The tools at the end of each chapter consist of a diagram and questions for discussion and are the heart of this book. The concepts in the chapters are often abstract and difficult to grasp, making the visual aspect of these tools important. Having a visual can make it easier for students—and teachers—to access, discuss, and understand the concepts. The tools give the classroom community a common language to talk about these important topics. Please see appendix A (page 189) for instructions on how to implement these tools in the classroom.

Note that because I teach high school, much of the content in these chapters and the tools associated with them were designed with secondary students in mind; but you can use several of them with younger students as well. Throughout the book, educators Jennifer Dawes Brazier and Stacy Howard, who have each been using the tools with students for several years, offer advice, called "Elementary Teacher Tips," in which they'll share how they include the tools in their classroom for younger learners. Jennifer and Stacy coupled the tools with teaching strategies that make the tools more effective. The tools provide a way to have discussions about performance character, but teachers who weave them into their lessons and make them specific to their classes will produce much more with them. This will take effort and is a challenge, but the benefits can be great. Students should learn why and how to work with challenge in your class because it will likely lead to more self-aware, honorable, motivated, courageous, and persistent learners who may learn to be joyful in school.

Please note that not all the tools will include tips as the advice from Jennifer and Stacy is intended for elementary school students. Some of the tools can prove to be a little too complicated for younger learners. Additionally, please understand that several of Jennifer and Stacy's tips include physical activity. These movements and exercises help serve to improve brain function. As John J. Ratey (2008) writes in his book *Spark: The Revolutionary New Science of Exercise and the Brain*, "It turns out that moving our muscles produces proteins that travel through the blood-stream and into the brain, where they play pivotal roles in the mechanisms of our highest thought processes" (p. 5). The physical components of these teacher tips, therefore, should engage students further as they work to gain an understanding of the concepts. If any of these teacher tips are not feasible for your situation (like taking students to a playground), please feel free to modify them.

At the end of this book, you'll find two appendixes. Appendix A (page 189) is a guide for using the tools in this book. Appendix B (page 191) lists recommended supplemental reading for students that can either be integrated into your curriculum or read at home on personal time.

Put It Into Action

Instead of having an educator giving a lecture of what students need to do to use the eight components to motivate their learning and persevere through challenge, the tools provided at the end of each chapter may serve as a discussion point and an opportunity for students to construct their own knowledge and opinions. Teachers can alter the questions based on the class and situation. At times, students and teachers may not agree on how to best work with a concept, but that is also acceptable and may result in a productive discussion. In these instances, teachers may get to know their student better and understand where they are coming from as they deal with the challenges of school and adolescence.

While this book offers nineteen tools, I advise using only a handful throughout the academic calendar. For students to learn to apply a performance character concept, in many cases, takes several weeks. Using too many tools too quickly lessens the impact and learning. As I model in the following chapters, these diagrams and questions are meant to enhance the course curriculum and not dominate it. In my world history class, I tend to focus on only five or six tools per year. The tools I use vary with each class, based on the students I have and the challenges I am offering.

As an educator, I encourage you to take ownership of the tools by using which-ever tips and tools in this book you want to, however you see fit, in whatever order you'd like. You know and understand your class better than anyone and can determine if and where they might be effective. For each tool you choose to use, my suggestion would be to follow six steps.

1. Discuss the tool with a colleague or collaborative team. Each tool includes sample general questions to guide a peer discussion; however, you are encouraged to come up with your own questions for a deeper conversation that is more specific to your circumstances. This should prepare you before you share the tool with your students.

2. Plan a lesson that you could use to teach the performance character concept along with subject content. Teachers often find that they have preexisting lessons or projects that mesh with one of the tools. Other educators find joy in choosing a tool first and creating a new lesson or project that couples well with it. This flexibility also means that any academic discipline can use these tools to enhance their classes. Mathematics, science, English, physical education, special education, and educators from other subject areas are already using these tools successfully. (Since 2014, I have been lucky enough to lead workshops for teachers and coaches who have subsequently started using the tools. I have had teachers from all of the categories report successful results with the tools.)

3. Lead a short, ten-minute discussion about the diagram portion of the tool (when you are ready). This can be a full-class discussion, small-group discussion, or a simple think-pair-share with the sample questions that are provided or new questions that you developed with your colleague or team.

4. Teach the lesson you planned.

5. After the lesson, have students reflect on how they did with the concept. It's often the case that students will say one thing in the discussion and do something very different during the lesson or project. Even if students' behaviors did not match their intentions, they have learned something about themselves that they can use to improve. Educators offer this reflection piece in different ways: some lead a full-class discussion, others facilitate small-group discussions, while others have students write their thoughts and observations in a journal. Again, you may determine what is best for the situation and your class.

6. Refer to the diagram portion of the tool throughout other challenges in your class when it applies. Appendix A (page 189) also lists these steps for your convenience.

These tools help students determine their best way to take on challenges they will get to experience daily in school. Life, like school, is a series of challenges, and it therefore also provides numerous opportunities to practice and improve on performance character. The concepts from the tools can transfer to college or trade school, jobs, relationships, and more, meaning the ideas students learn in your class can assist them beyond the classroom and for their future lives. Often, students will say that it's pointless to learn certain things at school because they will not need those things ever again. Everything they learn through understanding performance character is applicable to their current and future challenges that they choose to undertake or have thrust on them.

Hopefully, the content and tools of this book will help you and your students determine how to personally work with challenge. Having many discussions with these tools has allowed me to think very deeply about how I can best attack challenges in life. Because of these discussions, others (even my own students) helped me evolve and decide which mental processes would make me successful and happy. As the doctor in the intensive care unit (ICU) made me aware of the challenge of stroke recovery, I had a solid idea of how I wanted to deal with this situation and felt prepared to take it on. Because of my mindset based on research and tool discussion, I appreciated and enjoyed the several-month process to a full recovery with no regrets. It certainly wasn't easy, and I encountered numerous setbacks along the way, but it was much better to be in control of that situation instead of being a victim to it. By assisting students in viewing challenge this way, we prepare them for our class and the rest of their lives.

Elementary Teacher Tip

While the tools are easy to adapt to any grade level, there are some specific approaches to conceptual tools that may cement understanding more efficiently. To enter a conversation about these tools with elementary-grade students, try the following.

- On the first day of teaching a tool, put it up on the whiteboard with no explanation and allow the students to study and perhaps draw it. On the second day, put up the words and let students figure out where they go. On the third day, teach the tool lesson.

- Provide copies of the tool precut into pieces, and have students reconstruct it. This is excellent for visual and tactile learners. For more complex tools, have students work in pairs or small groups to collaboratively complete the task.

1

Self-Awareness

What is necessary to change a person is to change his awareness of himself.

—Abraham Maslow

On top of my other obligations in my inaugural year of working in administration in 2013 as an assistant principal at Irvington High School, one of my tasks was to oversee a student's expulsion hearing. The student in question had allegedly been harassing several other students through social media by stealing their passwords and posting their report cards and grades online. It was virtual crime, but it had shaken up several students at the school (many of whom had gotten very emotional in my office when discussing the situation). Because of this and because this was a challenge, I wanted to learn and do a thorough job.

In our district, expulsion hearings are done before the director of student services and a panel of three principals or assistant principals (or a combination) from other schools that serve as the jury. My duty was to present the case for expulsion while the student, along with whomever they chose to help them, got to defend.

We both presented our sides, we both got to add and question witnesses, and then the administrators deliberated. In the end, I lost the case. The student was exonerated and could come back to school. Instead, the student chose to transfer to another school in the district.

Leaving the hearing, I felt awful. Part of it was because I had lost. The other part was because I knew that, through their actions, this student had severely and adversely affected other students. I didn't really need the student to be expelled, but I did want them to at least think about their selfish behavior. I got the feeling that the student wasn't worried about anything but winning and proving superiority over others. On the drive back to school, my immediate thoughts were to make excuses and blame others for my failure—after all, this was my first hearing and the panel of administrators must not have been paying attention when I made my points. As I returned to school, however, I gave myself a dose of humility and reality by putting the onus on myself. I called the director of student services and left a message: "I didn't do what I wanted at the hearing today. When you have time, can you share with me when and where I failed?"

As much as I wanted to make excuses and blame someone or something for not reaching my goal, I knew that those things wouldn't make me better. I had to be honest with myself and know that I could have done more and been better prepared. Therefore, I wanted to ask an expert what I could do to determine how to improve for the future. What I didn't need at that moment were justifications to make me feel better. What I needed at that moment was the truth. What I was looking for was self-awareness.

Self-awareness is the foundation of character performance. It is where we begin to see ourselves as we truly are, so we can identify where we have space to grow. Just as I sought self-awareness after the results of the expulsion hearing, students can look for moments of clarity and direction after they have encountered what they might consider a failure. Nurturing self-awareness in the classroom is an important step in ensuring your students cultivate a positive attitude about themselves, their classwork, and their temporary setbacks in learning.

In this chapter, we explore self-awareness as the foundation of the eight performance character traits and review methods of encouraging students to develop self-awareness in their schoolwork and beyond. We delve into defining self-awareness, entitlement, and the difference between the two; reviewing research on self-awareness and entitlement; and explaining how challenge coupled with self-awareness can lead to humility. The chapter also offers two tools comprising a diagram and accompanying questions to help foster discussion about these concepts.

The Definition of Self-Awareness

Most of us think very highly of ourselves and not of others, even if we don't think we do. We tend to overemphasize our successes and underemphasize or disregard our flaws. In his novel *The Little Prince*, Antoine de Saint-Exupéry (1943,

2020) writes, "It is much more difficult to judge oneself than to judge others. If you succeed in judging yourself rightly, then you are a man of true wisdom" (p. 17). This quote exposes this flaw in the human condition. To obtain true wisdom, we need to judge ourselves rightly, stripping away our biases and seeing ourselves for our strengths and our weaknesses. Those who can do this are *self-aware*.

Self-awareness is the first key element of performance character because, without it, a student really wouldn't be able to improve as he, she, or they take on a challenge and likely wouldn't be successful. To fully understand self-awareness, however, a teacher must first understand ego.

Neurologist and founder of psychoanalysis Sigmund Freud (1962) popularized the term in his book *The Ego and the Id*. Freud contends that the human brain consists of three parts: (1) the id, (2) superego, and (3) ego. The *id* is our animalistic brain; it is completely selfish, focused on satisfying our urges and desires. The *superego* is the selfless and moral part of our brain. As one is completely selfish and the other selfless, the id and the superego are continuously at odds. The *ego* is selfish like the id but understands the constructs of the real world. Therefore, the ego tries to mediate the conflict between the id and the superego, justifying to the individual why selfishness is appropriate. None of us would survive without selfishness; if we were completely selfless, we would give everything away to others and perish. Therefore, the ego is necessary to keep our sanity. Without the ego, we would find ourselves in constant turmoil and guilt every time we made a selfish decision or had a selfish thought. To help us all function and overcome our necessary selfishness, the ego uses defense mechanisms like repression or denial to make us feel better about our lack of morality.

While the ego is necessary, it sometimes gets carried away. Its purpose is to be selfish, which leads to justifications that the individual is better and more deserving than others. In *A New Earth: Awakening to Your Life's Purpose*, author Eckhart Tolle (2016) writes, "The ego tends to equate having with Being: I have, therefore I am. And the more I have, the more I am. The ego lives through comparison. How you are seen by others turns into how you see yourself" (p. 40). Tolle (2016) shares that, since the ego is the selfish part of our brain, its goal is to gain more material objects or skills to prove that we're better than others. In reality, no one person is better than another (regardless of what we've achieved or what we have), but our egos work overtime to create our own personal world to prove that we are superior and, therefore, more deserving than others. Think about how much time and effort you put into comparison with others. That's your ego at work.

When we are not accomplished or fail at something, our ego doesn't want to admit that we are lesser, so it kicks into gear to make us feel better. If our ego takes charge of our thoughts, it will not accept a failure; rather, it will make excuses and blame people or situations for lack of competency or lack of improvement—it's all out of our control, and someone or something else is to blame. Those who succumb too much to their ego and have unrealistic expectations of their abilities are *entitled*. Their egos have convinced them that they deserve outcomes and improvement, but they do not look to themselves for how to get it. In other words, entitled people are victims who believe they cannot change their circumstance, yet they still feel that they deserve positive outcomes.

To use other terminology, entitled people are *ego-brittle*. Ego-brittle people are less able to control their ego's desire for false superiority. The opposite of ego-brittle is *ego-resilient*, those who can better combat their ego's justifications for failure. David Farkas and Gabor Orosz of the Institute of Cognitive Neuroscience and Psychology in Budapest (2015) study the concept of ego-resiliency (ER) as psychologist Jack Block conceptualized. They write:

> Block defined ER along a continuum: ego-resilient persons have the flexibility to adapt to changing contexts and to coordinate their behavior with situational demands and behavioral possibilities. In contrast, ego-brittle individuals cannot resourcefully respond to the dynamically changing requirements of the environment and they tend to perseverate. (p. 3)

Ego-resilient people, therefore, understand they are not above failure. Therefore, they can adapt their thoughts and behaviors to own their failures and improve. For ego-brittle or entitled people, this is not the case. Their ego has convinced them that failure has nothing to do with them. There is nothing they can do so they do nothing, and learning stagnates.

Farkas and Orosz then take Block's idea to a different level, breaking ego-resiliency into three parts: (1) repertoire of problem-solving strategies, (2) active engagement with the world, and (3) integrated performance under stress. Those who are entitled and succumb to overpowering ego will not pay attention to what they can improve. However, those who have ego-resiliency will pay attention to what is around them, thinking of different ways to work through their failures to obtain multiple positive outcomes.

Ego is a very difficult and involved concept to explain (especially for younger students). As the intention of this book is to teach the concepts of performance character while taking minimal time away from class content, the tools at the end of the chapter will bypass ego by referring to an ego-brittle person as *entitled* and an ego-resilient person as *self-aware*. From the students' perspective, *self-awareness* should be the ability to completely understand yourself—warts and all. The self-aware person will recognize what they do well and celebrate that, but also be cognizant of where to improve. While failure has a nasty stigma, self-aware people view it as a positive and an opportunity to learn how to grow. Failure, then, is not final. Instead, it is a necessary part of everyone's journey to identifying what they can work on to grow. All of us can be amazing and get better at everything we do; the way to do this is to be aware of both our successes and our failures.

I will add that it is important to not belittle students for their selfish and entitled behavior. Because the ego is inescapable, we are all entitled at times (even as teachers). If you think you're not entitled, you're entitled about not being entitled. Social science author, doctor, and researcher Jeremy E. Sherman (2014) writes for *Psychology Today* that we all deal with ego and entitlement:

> It happens to the best of us. Our lives get shaken; our grooves get broken. We get a little disoriented or maybe a lot. It's all we can do to keep it together and every little further perturbation; real or perceived is a threat. So we circle the wagons, hyper-vigilant against attacks, challenges, feedback or questions. We get prickly and rigid, insistent that we're on top of things, precisely because we're not. To those around us it can look like the height of arrogance but it's actually vulnerability. We don't think more of ourselves, but less and are grasping for the self-certainty we've lost.

This certainly happened to me after the expulsion hearing. I failed, and my first reaction was to be upset, make excuses, and blame others before I caught myself in ego justifications. Because ego is part of us, we all struggle with the battle against entitlement.

Moving from entitled to self-aware is a process. The good news is that the shift from ego-brittle to ego-resilient seems to improve for school-aged children. In the *International Journal of Environmental Research and Public Health*, psychologist at the Center for Psychological Studies Application at South China Normal University Qishan Chen and colleagues (2021) discuss a study that shows that school children's ego-resiliency improves over time. Among other factors that help students improve, they highlight their "frequent interactions with teachers and peers in school may promote their ability to solve a variety of problems" (p. 8). This shows that educators and the school system are important to usher students from entitlement to self-awareness.

Entitlement and Self-Awareness

As educators, we've probably witnessed students being self-aware in the classroom. The self-aware students are a joy. They are teachable and coachable, taking all feedback as an opportunity to improve. When self-aware students turn in a paper, they are more interested in the teacher feedback rather than the grade at the top as the comments can give them insight on what they do well and how they can get better. On the other hand, ego-brittle or entitled students look only at the grade. If it's a good grade, they're satisfied. If it's not a good grade, they tend to blame the teacher or make excuses. They either do not look at the comments, or they try to use them as ammunition to prove the teacher wrong. The entitled view causes teacher-student friction, and the student does not grow. See the following scenario for a possible solution to students' focus on grades.

This is why middle school English teacher Mrs. Mangiardi writes comments but never initially puts a score on the top of papers. The first time she did this, some students responded adversely, asking what their score was. Mrs. Mangiardi explained, "You'll get your score after you respond to all my comments. If it's feedback that you need to improve, I want you to fix it and improve. If it's positive feedback, you can respond with 'Thank you.' Once I get these back with responses to every comment, I'll put a score on your paper." Using this method, Mrs. Mangiardi puts the focus on self-awareness instead of opening the door to entitlement.

It may be wise to counteract ego-brittleness as an entitled mindset can lead to some major psychological issues for the students. According to professors of psychology and researchers J. B. Grubbs of Bowling Green State University and Julie J. Exline of Case Western Reserve University (2016), *entitlement* is "pervasive feelings of deservingness, specialness, and exaggerated expectations." Grubbs and Exline (2016) say that entitled people feel that they deserve something and expect that thing to come to fruition either with or without effort. As they think this way and realize unmet expectations, emotional distress follows closely behind with anger and depression. Grubbs and Exline (2016) write that to counter these emotions and feel better, entitled people will bolster their entitled beliefs, convincing themselves that they are even more deserving without changing anything. Because they don't change anything, they will encounter more unmet expectations and even more anger and depression, creating a dangerous cycle that grows on itself. Keep in mind that, as they are young and working on ego reduction, students are likely not conscious or aware of this behavior. Instead of viewing this as intentional and malicious, educators can see this as an opportunity to educate students and assist them in being more ego-resilient.

Students with low scores aren't the sole parties experiencing these downward spirals. You may think that the students who do better in school have more self-awareness, but this isn't always the case. In his podcast *Against the Rules*, bestselling author Michael Lewis (2019) talks about the Golden State Warriors basketball team. The team was very successful, having made the NBA Finals in five straight years from 2015–2019, but they also led the league in complaining to referees. Because they are used to winning, they feel, more so than other teams, that referees' calls should go their way. When they don't, they complain and blame the officials for doing a poor job. Some of our better students may think the same way. Since they're great students who are used to getting *As*, I've observed that some tend to blame and make excuses when they don't receive a top score. Entitlement may be harder to see in top students but be aware. Even they may need to think about self-awareness and entitlement from time to time.

Further, entitlement is not something that is the exclusive domain of students. Teachers can be just as prone to feelings of entitlement and in just as much need as their students to build capacity for self-awareness. The following sections explore the push and pull between entitlement and self-awareness for students and teachers, respectively.

Student Self-Awareness and Entitlement

It may be important to identify entitlement in your classes and discuss it directly with students when you see it. Whether it's a conversation with an individual or a group discussion with an entire class (the tools in this book can help with this), it's important to be intentional with students about the distinction between entitlement and self-awareness. When you see students blame and make excuses, first understand that this is natural behavior, especially for school-aged children. Then, talk with them about accountability, helping them through the natural progression from ego-brittleness to ego-resiliency. For example, if two students get into a fight, their immediate response is to get you (or anyone else) on their side by building a case against their adversary—everything was the other person's fault. Instead of that, you can find out what happened and ask, "What could *you* have done better in the situation?" Trust me; ego will ensure you'll have plenty of opportunities to have these discussions no matter what grade you teach.

Sinek (2016) contends that instant gratification is a root cause of entitlement in young people. In modern life, most can get what they want right away. You can order something online and get it within a day. The media we consume (video, audio, and print) are almost universally accessible on demand. *Knowledge* is available on demand, though so is misinformation. These are not universally bad things. But for students who have never known a world where the information or media they need isn't instantly accessible, it can be hard to grapple with the notion that acquiring critical knowledge and skills often requires struggling to overcome challenge.

Additionally, Sinek (2016) says that the environment plays a role. He contends that, when people enter the workforce, they find themselves working for companies that care more about numbers than the person—work is typically more about making money than personal growth (Sinek, 2016). It could be argued that this happens to young people long before they go to work or college. Schools and parents may also value numbers (promotion, grades, test scores, and so on) rather than making our students more knowledgeable with improved character. With this, students could learn that it's more important to simply complete tasks than learn.

If, as a teacher, you emphasize learning above grades, the entitled student loses their power. They have little to argue when there is no tangible expectation to argue about. If a student comes in with a paper that they feel deserves an *A*, they'll want to argue that you did something wrong. If you change the conversation to, "Let me show you why you didn't quite get an *A*, and let's talk about how you can fix it," the discussion switches from entitlement to self-awareness. Time is better spent with a student who wants to learn than one who simply wants to argue about a grade change. (A standards-based grading system could greatly help students make this process much easier—more on that in chapter 3, page 41.)

According to Sinek (2016), these causes of entitlement are all happening to millennials—it's no fault of their own. If parents are telling students that they're special and removing obstacles for them, they've grown up with instant gratification as the norm, and they're learning that their worth is based on a result rather than a learning process, they have a much better chance of being entitled. With all of this going on, it's understandable that millennials show fairly high levels of entitlement.

Others aren't quite so sure millennials (and subsequent generations) are any more entitled than any of their predecessors. Author and researcher from Stanford Clara S. Lewis along with Breanna Della Williams, Minkee Kim Sohn, and Tamara L. Chin Loy (2017) conducted in-depth interviews of twenty-nine students at elite universities to ask questions pertaining to entitlement. They found that most of the students showed tendencies toward self-awareness. Lewis and colleagues (2017) report that the "vast majority of the students we interviewed expressed a strong preference for learning and growth over and above what they term 'easy A's'" (p. 3001) and "Our participants overwhelmingly expressed a preference for being challenged. They connected feelings of satisfaction and reward with achieving high marks in difficult courses" (p. 3002).

The authors share this sentiment:

> Our results show that consumerism and the entitlement associated with it is not a fixed generational attitude so much as a conditional sentiment that

> grading practices can either disarm or inflame. It seems that despite being characterized as demanding consumers, some students want exactly what every other generation of college student has wanted: the challenge of enacting transformative intellectual, personal, and professional growth. (p. 3006)

According to the interviews, students in 2017 wanted the same thing as previous generations—to learn important concepts in challenging courses. The students added that what would be helpful to achieve this thing were professors who could create a classroom environment that allowed them an opportunity to push themselves academically. The authors continue with (Lewis et al., 2017):

> further, students explained how each ideal learning experience was contingent on excellent teaching performed by an instructor with enough time and sufficient training to design clear, compelling assignments; to offer growth-oriented, critical feedback; and to carefully manage the classroom environment in ways consistent with clearly stated learning objectives that meaningfully reflect the nature of the subject being studied as it operates in the world beyond the campus. (p. 3007)

Whether you believe the burden of responsibility lies with the educators or the students, the time when millennials reached high school and college en masse seemed to coincide with a rash of studies on academic entitlement. In perhaps the seminal paper on the subject, developmental psychologist at the University of California Irvine Ellen Greenberger along with Jared Lessard, Chuansheng Chen, and Susan Farruggia (2008) define academic entitlement as "a construct that includes expectations of high grades for modest effort and demanding attitudes toward teachers" (p. 1). In that study, the experimenters created an academic entitlement scale, asking college students how strongly they agreed or disagreed with statements like "course prerequisites are for people not as smart as me" and "all classes should offer extra credit." The survey yielded some interesting results: 66.2 percent of students agreed that "If I have explained to my professor that I'm trying hard, I think he/she should give me some consideration with respect to my course grade" and nearly 25 percent felt that "A professor should be willing to lend me his/her course notes if I ask for them" (p. 5). These statistics show that not all students are academically entitled in various areas, but a number are.

In a more recent study, Debra Lemke, Jeff Marx, and Lauren Dundes (2017) replicate Greenberger's study with 384 undergraduate students, finding that academic entitlement rates are decreasing. They say this:

> We did not find evidence that academic entitlement is increasing. In fact, our evidence suggests entitlement as traditionally defined has generally decreased

from 2009 to 2017, a difference largely driven by the drop in the propor-
tion of males who felt academically entitled in 2009 (50 percent) compared
to 2017 (34 percent), a much larger change than for females (from 34 percent in 2009 to 27 percent in 2017).

While academic entitlement does appear to be on the decline, the thought of
one in four undergraduate men and one in four undergraduate women showing
signs of academic entitlement is still alarming.

Perhaps of most paramount importance to teachers, academically entitled
students experience more problems in school. Professor of clinical psychology
from Middle Tennessee State Mary Ellen Fromuth, Jeffery Bass, David Kelly,
Teresa Davis, and Kin Leong Chan (2017) find that "higher levels of academic
entitlement were associated with lower grades. Specifically, increased academic
entitlement was related to lower self-reported high school GPA and overall college GPA" (p. 1161). This makes sense as people who believe their mistakes are
beyond their control are less likely to reflect and change to overcome those mistakes in the future. Fromuth and colleagues (2017) continue, "Higher scores on
academic entitlement were associated with a greater tendency to perceive external variables (such as too much work in the course, tests were too difficult) as
having a negative impact on academic achievement." If we want our students to
learn and have academic success, we must help them understand entitlement and
how and why it affects academic achievement.

Educator Self-Awareness and Entitlement

Entitlement is prevalent among the student population, but what about teachers? As educators, we consistently deal with the entitlement and self-awareness
battle in our heads. For example, when you give an assessment and the students
struggle greatly, which direction do you go? It's easy and natural for any teacher
to be entitled and blame someone or something else for the lack of performance.
The teacher might say that the students faltered because they didn't work hard or
the textbook doesn't cover the right things. The entitled teacher never improves
their own practice because, in their mind, it's not their fault—the only way to
get better results is for the students to change their behavior or to get a new textbook. Entitled teachers feel that they don't need to alter a thing and that change
will come only if exterior factors are fixed.

In the same situation with poor performance on an assessment, teachers can
also choose to be self-aware and look inward. While the low scores might well
be partly or mostly due to student efforts, lack of resources, or both, there are
always things that we can improve on as teachers. What could you, as a teacher,
do differently to teach the concept and motivate the students? If the textbook

doesn't cover the right things, how can you fix that? Self-aware teachers put the onus on themselves, which is difficult at times but necessary to be in control and make gains.

If you are interested in becoming a more self-aware teacher, it's not always fun or easy as you, likely, must be incredibly honest with your self-appraisal. In his book *Can't Hurt Me: Master Your Mind and Defy the Odds*, David Goggins (2018), arguably the toughest person alive, talks about how he transformed from a depressed, nearly three-hundred-pound exterminator to someone who completed special forces training for every branch of the military, became a successful ultramarathon runner, and once did a world record 4,030 pull-ups in seventeen hours. For Goggins (2018), it all started with something he called the *accountability mirror*.

Whenever he felt sorry for himself and wanted to make excuses, Goggins (2018) looked in the mirror and had a very honest self-reflection. He didn't hold back, verbalizing and exposing his flaws and failures to himself, shunning excuses, and vowing to do something about them. In his earlier life, he blamed his misfortunes on his father, asthma, a congenital heart defect, and whatever he could to make himself feel better. He was a victim who was unable to control his circumstance. With the accountability mirror, he was honest with himself and took control. How often do we look into the accountability mirror regarding our teaching practices? Do we blame exterior forces for students' poor performance, or are we self-aware and truthful with ourselves? If we are self-aware, we start to take the reins over our improvement as an educator.

Additionally, Goggins (2018) does an excellent job of not portraying himself as special—even though he has done many, many exceptional and incredible feats. Instead, he is vulnerable throughout the book, sharing his personal flaws and demons and what he does to work on them. You would expect someone this accomplished to say that he's always been special, but he is very honest and open with the reader in this regard. Goggins is not alone with this. Often, the people who have had to work incredibly hard for their success share the traits of vulnerability and humility. If they don't see their failures, they cannot improve on them to be successful. Renowned research professor Brené Brown (2015), who specializes in shame, vulnerability, and leadership, says, "Vulnerability sounds like truth and feels like courage. Truth and courage aren't always comfortable, but they're never weakness" (p. 38). While some might view being vulnerable as weakness, it's a superpower. It's the only way to keep perfecting your craft. As teachers, we can realize that we can all improve. The day we think we have reached the pinnacle of teaching is also the day when we stop improving. The best teachers (and the happiest) seem to be the ones who are always looking for ways to better their craft. Complacency does not breed joy.

Some teachers want their students to view them as infallible and perfect while others will share with students the difficulties they had and have when taking on challenges. The latter educator models for the students that no one is perfect and the road to mastery is a productive struggle fraught with difficulty. This could very well be the most important lesson for students to understand. To help educators teach this, Stanford University created the Stanford Resilience Project (YouTube, n.d.). This program consists of over fifty videos (and growing) of Stanford students and faculty sharing "personal narratives, programming, and coaching to motivate and support students as they experience the normal academic setbacks that are part of a rigorous education" (YouTube, n.d.). According to its YouTube channel, the goal of the project is to

> emphasize the importance of failure in the learning process and seek to instill a sense of belonging and bravery in students to ultimately change the perception of failure from something to be avoided at all costs, to something essential to a meaningful education. (YouTube, n.d.)

It may be important for students to understand that those considered some of the best and brightest have failures, and those failures help them learn and become better.

Students often view teachers like we're academic machines that must've been born with abilities that allowed us to be exceptional at our chosen subject. The truth, however, is that, like them, we all struggled at one time or another. We had failures along the way that we had to work through. If we share our personal stories with students, they may understand that these things happen to everyone and that they are important and necessary regarding learning and growing.

The Entitlement Versus Self-Awareness Tool

Entitled people are those who, when they fail, convince themselves that they would have been successful if it were not for external factors; therefore, they blame others and make excuses. On the other hand, a self-aware person takes responsibility for failures. Use the tool in figure 1.1 (page 23) to serve as a springboard for a rich class discussion about entitlement and self-awareness.

After reviewing the tool with the class, your peers, or on your own, please use the following questions to discuss and reflect. See appendix A (page 189) for the complete instructions on using the tools in this book.

Questions for Educators and Their Colleagues

These are questions to help you discuss the entitlement versus self-awareness tool with colleagues to gain a more personal and broader understanding.

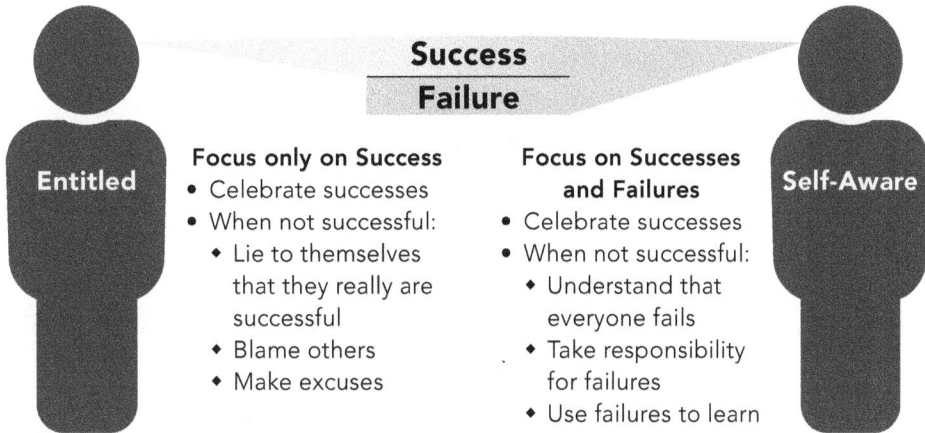

Figure 1.1: Entitlement versus self-awareness tool.

*Visit **go.SolutionTree.com/SEL** for a free reproducible version of this figure.*

- If students do poorly on an assessment in your class, how much of your response is entitled about it and how much is self-aware? In other words, how much do you blame students, and how much do you look at what you can fix? How much of the failure do you think is the students' responsibility?

- How might mistakes and failures be a bad thing? How might they be a good thing?

- How has your relationship with self-awareness changed in your lifetime? Reflect on when you were in elementary school, middle school, high school, and college, and as a teacher.

- How do you feel in the short term and long term when you catch yourself behaving with a sense of entitlement? How do you feel when you demonstrate self-awareness?

Questions to Prompt Class Discussion

These are questions to promote class understanding about the entitlement versus self-awareness tool. You can complete the following within small- or large-group discussion or by quietly reflecting in a journal.

- Think of a time you failed or lost at something. It could be something big or something small. Did you take responsibility for it (using self-awareness), or did you blame others or make excuses (exhibiting entitlement)? Why did you behave that way? How does blaming others or making excuses make you feel?

- Think of a time you got caught misbehaving or breaking a rule. It could be at school, at home, or anywhere else. Did you take responsibility for your actions (self-awareness), or did you lie, blame someone else, or make excuses (entitlement)? How did you feel about the way you handled it?

- What could you do in your daily life to be more self-aware? Would that be hard or easy for you?

- How happy do you think entitled people are in the long and short term? How happy are self-aware people in the long and short term?

- At this point in your life, how entitled and how self-aware are you?

Questions for Student Reflection

After a content-specific lesson that is also an opportunity to assess entitlement and self-awareness, the following questions can assist students in evaluating their thoughts and behavior during the lesson as they pertain to the concept.

- Do you think you were entitled or self-aware during the lesson? Why do you think this? (Provide examples of your behavior.)

- What did you do well during the lesson? What could you improve on? If you made a mistake of some kind during the lesson, did you blame others or make excuses, or did you look at your actions honestly and take responsibility?

- Think of a time when you've worked on a group project, and it didn't go well. Who do you consider responsible? What could you, specifically, have done to make it go better?

Elementary Teacher Tip

Read *Wolfpack* by Abby Wambach (2019) aloud to students. Wambach's book is an encouraging self-development guide for women to recognize their strengths and support fellow women. At the point in the book when Abby tells about her reaction to her soccer coach cutting her from the next camp, pause and ask questions such as the following.

- Was Abby's first reaction (feelings of anger, defensiveness, and devastation) a self-aware reaction or an entitled reaction? Why?

- What do you think about the email Abby wrote to her coach? Does it show self-awareness or entitlement?

- What do you think Abby learned from this failure?

- Think of a time you failed. Were you self-aware or entitled? How did it feel? What was the result?

- Why do you think people feel entitled? What do you think is the perceived motivation or benefit of such feelings?

- Think of a time you acted entitled. When was it? Why do you think you chose to be entitled instead of self-aware? How does being entitled make you feel?

- Think of a time you used self-awareness. When was it? How did you feel?

Self-Awareness and Humility

Those who are entitled might know about a subject, concept, or skill on a surface level and think that they understand it completely. However, true comprehension takes a lot of questioning, effort, failure, and self-awareness. As a student travels through this uncertainty and adversity, he, she, or they start to see that understanding takes a lot of hard work, mistakes, and self-reflection. This journey through adversity helps students move from entitled (thinking they understand) to humble (knowing that understanding is a difficult process). Consider the following scenario in which Mr. Hodgins, an educator, leads a discussion on inherent selfishness and selflessness.

Mr. Hodgins is a mathematics teacher at his high school, where he was pulled from his prep to act as a substitute for the Advanced Placement government class. He read the detailed lesson that the teacher left for the students and asked the class to get to work. Instead, students roamed out of their seats, chatting about anything but the assigned task. At least two balls of paper flew across the room while many students pulled out their phones. After fifteen minutes of observing, Mr. Hodgins brought the class together.

"As an AP government class, have you studied Hobbes and Locke?" A student responded, "We know all about Hobbes and Locke. That was the first thing we learned last semester."

"Then you know that Hobbes felt that people were naturally selfish. He thought that, in a natural state, people would be brutish, fighting and killing each other. Because of this, Hobbes felt that people needed a strong ruler to keep them in line, so he preferred a monarchy."

"Yeah," said a student. "That's basic."

"And can you tell me what Locke thought?"

"Sure," answered another student. "Locke thought that people were naturally good and would eventually make decisions that would benefit the whole group. That's why Locke thought a democracy works best for a government."

"Good answer," said Mr. Hodgins. "Who do you think is right?" All hands went up for Locke.

"Okay, Locke it is. But do you really believe and understand that? I just gave you all the challenge for the day left by your teacher, and what was happening? Were people being naturally selfish or were they doing what was best for the group? For this class to work today, do you need a strong ruler to force you to do the right thing, or can you govern yourselves to be productive? What would be the best way to proceed for the rest of the period?"

Like these AP government students, young people (and adults) often think that they fully comprehend something when they have only a rudimentary understanding of it. In a paper for the *Journal of Personality and Social Psychology*, Justin Kruger and David Dunning (1999), social psychologists and professors at the NYU School of Business and the University of Michigan respectively, identify that, when people know little about a social or intellectual area, they tend to overestimate their abilities, whereas those who know more tend to underestimate themselves on the given task. In their study, Kruger and Dunning (1999) assessed participants on humor, grammar, and logic, then asked them how well they felt they did. Those who scored in the lowest group, on average, overestimated their test scores, while those who scored the highest, on average, underestimated theirs. For example, subjects who scored in the twelfth percentile felt that they scored in the sixty-second percentile. The experiment shows that, when we only have a basic understanding about something, we are entitled, thinking we know more than we do. Those who are more skilled in an area realize there is much more to learn and underestimate their abilities, making them humble.

This Dunning–Kruger effect gained momentum over the years since its introduction into the field, but it is not without detractors. Economics professors and researchers Jan R. Magnus and Anatoly A. Peresetsky (2022) highlight over ten studies that support the theory and agree that it has a psychological explanation. However, they also offer trepidation about Dunning and Kruger's reasoning behind their finding. They cite Krueger and Mueller (2002) whose approach to explaining the Dunning–Kruger effect is based on two things. The authors write, "First, it is well-known that people tend to overestimate their performance . . . Second, the slope in the linear regression of estimated performance on actual performance is not equal but less than one" (p. 2). What they're saying is that most people tend to overestimate their performance, regardless of how knowledgeable they are. They also add that the effect occurs because of the symmetry of relation to the mean. In their study, Magnus and Peresetsky (2022) agree with this, saying that the Dunning–Kruger effect does not include any psychological explanations.

Either way we look at the Dunning–Kruger effect, many of our students and we tend to overestimate our capabilities.

As teachers, we will likely run into students who falsely believe they are competent without fully understanding a concept. They can answer the question and complete the problem and think they've got it, but maybe they're simply plugging in numbers and words without getting to higher-level thinking. If a teacher gives a student a project, the entitled student will try to get it done as quickly as possible. The student who wants to get more out of it will put more thought and effort into the project, challenging themselves to learn more. Helping students become aware of their entitled behavior may convince them to put in more effort which will lead to better understanding.

Entitlement and humility can be something teachers deal with too. If we're being vulnerable and honest with ourselves, many of us can likely relate to the following fictitious story of an educator's first year of teaching (exaggerated for full effect). We'll call this educator Reynolds, but Reynolds is reflective of the mindset many new teachers have as they enter the profession. Certainly, I see elements of my own experience and thinking in this story, and very likely, you will too: Before Reynolds even starts teaching in the classroom, they think that they are different from other teachers, that they're special. They assume that because they went to school as a student and finished their certification program, they know everything about being a teacher. With this, Reynolds is positive they're going to be so good that the students will all revere them, act perfectly in class, and learn more from them than in their other courses. Because Reynolds is so amazing and different, students will all be motivated and respectful; they will all love and adore them. They think they know what it takes to be a good teacher, but it's all a prediction; they haven't yet faced the adversity that all teachers do in their first years.

Now, reflect on your own lived experiences in your first few days of instruction. Very likely, it quickly became clear that you may not be the gift to teaching that you originally thought. It may have gone well, but there are always unexpected issues and hardships that you didn't expect. As you drove home, did you think about the things that went wrong? Did you feel a compulsion to blame the students for any issues? There is no judgment if you did. You're a human being. The question is, did you eventually catch yourself and peek into your own accountability mirror? Even if you're reading this as a veteran teacher, it's important to recognize that for all the things you're doing right, there are still many aspects you can improve.

Adversity exposes areas of improvement. Accountability for your mishaps and failures may look like you talking to other teachers about their best practices and even being vulnerable enough to ask the students and parents how you can better yourself as an educator. (Be careful, however, with student and parent feedback. Because they went to or go to school, both groups may feel that they understand what it takes to be a teacher when they might be entitled about it.) With feedback from others and self-feedback, you can identify how you can improve and start working toward that. Once you start to work on those things, you become humble, realizing that being an excellent teacher is not given or magical. Rather, it is a long and challenging process of repeated adversity identifying areas of improvement that includes self-awareness and learning. That's precisely why teaching is so great. It's doubtful that any of us left school after a day of teaching saying, "Everything went perfectly today. I have nothing to improve." Teaching is a challenge; we always have something to work on. With new information, new ways of teaching, and new students yearly, education is never boring and always an exciting journey.

As nonteachers might feel entitled and think that teaching would be easy without having gone through a school year as a teacher, we, as educators, need to be careful about not being entitled as well when viewing students. You might think that you understand what a student is going through, but you can't ever be sure unless you are in their shoes every day. If a student doesn't turn an assignment in on time, you might make a snap judgment, thinking you know exactly why that student failed on the challenge. This is especially tempting when such behavior represents the continuation of a pattern. You may even be correct in your assumption but be mindful that you may not understand the reasoning behind the behavior. Having a relationship with a student and trying to further understand their situation can help you move away from entitled thoughts.

The Humility Tool

Use the tool in figure 1.2 (page 29) to serve as a springboard for a rich class discussion about entitlement and humility. This tool uses the concept of a bridge to show that if you are self-aware about your failures and mishaps when traveling through adversity and do something to remedy it, you have a good chance of achieving humility.

After reviewing the tool with the class, your peers, or on your own, please use the following questions to discuss and reflect. See appendix A (page 189) for the complete instructions on using the tools in this book.

Source: Created by Nels Larsen. Used with permission.

Figure 1.2: Humility tool.

*Visit **go.SolutionTree.com/SEL** for a free reproducible version of this figure.*

Questions for Educators and Their Colleagues

Use the following questions to help you discuss the humility tool with colleagues to gain a more personal and broader understanding.

- What role does self-awareness play in getting across the adversity bridge?

- How could you use the tool to explain the career of an educator?

- How might an educator stay entitled through their entire career?

- Where would you put your students on this diagram when it comes to academics?

- Where do you think you are on the diagram with teaching? Why? Are you entitled or humble when it comes to understanding the lives of the students you teach? What is the evidence for your answer?

- How can you move yourself across the bridge? Can you ever fully get across the bridge?

Questions to Prompt Class Discussion

Use the following questions to promote class understanding about the humility tool. This can be done with small- or large-group discussion or by quietly reflecting in a journal.

- What do the words *entitlement*, *self-awareness*, *adversity*, and *humility* mean to you?

- How much adversity should you face to become skilled at something? What would happen if you faced adversity and weren't self-aware?

- Think of an adversity you've had to go through to achieve something. What was it? What did you think about it before you faced the challenge? What did you think afterward?

- Come up with a skill you've never had before. How easy or difficult do you think that skill would be to acquire? How accurate do you think your assessment of the acquisition of the skill is?

- Give an example of someone going through a challenge. How happy is that person if they are entitled? How happy is that person if they are self-aware?

Questions for Student Reflection

After a content-specific lesson that is also an opportunity to assess entitlement and humility, the following questions can assist students in evaluating their thoughts and behavior during the lesson as they pertain to the concept.

- During the lesson, how far did you get across the bridge? In other words, how much did you challenge yourself?

- If you failed during the lesson, were there times when you were entitled (blamed others or made excuses) or times when you were self-aware (took responsibility)? Explain.

- Did this assignment make you humble? In other words, did you travel across the adversity bridge, experience failure, and become self-aware about it? Explain.

- In school, do you challenge yourself or not? Why? When you fail because you've challenged yourself, what do you do? What should you do?

Summary

As we've learned in this chapter, to be self-aware means taking the time to see your actions with an unbiased view, to understand what you do well and what you would need to fix to improve. Entitlement, on the other hand, is when you are only focused on success. When entitled people fail, they make excuses, blame others, or convince themselves they didn't fail. In other words, everything is beyond their control; nothing needs fixing. Reframing failures as opportunities to grow addresses this kind of mindset. The path to improvement is littered with failures. If students can learn to be more self-aware in class and less entitled, they will take ownership of these failures, seeing them all as opportunities for improvement. If the student understands that improvement comes from a combination of adversity, failure, and self-awareness, they learn humility, realizing that growth takes a great deal of effort and refinement. In chapter 2, we develop students' sense of self-awareness by introducing the concept of integrity.

2

Integrity

We learned about honesty and integrity—that the truth matters . . .
that you don't take shortcuts or play by your own set of rules . . . and
success doesn't count unless you earn it fair and square.

—Michelle Obama

During my time as an assistant principal, an obviously frustrated English teacher burst into my office and tossed four student essays on my desk. It took just a quick online search to discover what had upset her: all the papers were plagiarized, yet all had passed through the online originality-checking program that our school used. How could this be?

After a few days of sleuthing, we noticed that the first lines of all the papers were indented one space more than the other lines in the papers that were also indented. We found that all four students were putting a quotation mark at the very beginning of the paper and one at the very end. Then, they changed the font color of the quotation marks to white, leaving only what looked like a simple one-character space in front of the first line of their essay.

At the time, the program did not read sentences in quotation marks as plagiarism, looking at them as legitimate citations where a student would give credit to the author of the quote. By putting their entire paper in quotation marks (which were invisible to a teacher) the students were able to take advantage of a loophole in the program such that it did not register any plagiarism red flags in the papers.

When I called the students into my office individually, they all denied any wrongdoing—one quite vehemently, threatening parental and legal action. After I pulled up their papers on the program and highlighted their invisible quotation marks, all confessed—even the fervent denier who suddenly didn't want parents or a lawyer involved. The main excuse students gave for plagiarizing was that they didn't have enough time. They were all in multiple honors classes and activities and said that they were unable to keep up. One student told me, "Sometimes, I have to cheat to survive."

There are numerous reasons students feel overwhelmed by the volume of schoolwork they receive and the need to balance that with their realities and responsibilities outside of school. Some of these factors are legitimate, and some are not. When I asked these students why they didn't sign up for a reasonable schedule with fewer activities, they all said the same thing, "If I want to get into a good college, it's what I have to do."

I can understand where these students are coming from. Pressures from self, peers, parents, and others may lead to the challenge of getting into what they deem a top-tier university. If that is their goal, they are doing what they think they need to do to obtain that goal that might include signing up for more than they can handle and cheating when they fall behind. The question they will eventually have to ask themselves is this: Am I at peace with pursuing a goal through partial or total lack of integrity?

I don't know if one of them came up with this quotation marks idea on their own or if they got the idea from the internet, but it was admittedly ingenious. Nonetheless, we want our students to question whether being dishonorable and trying to beat the system is the best method to obtain their goals.

All these students had a goal. At some point, they also had a decision to make. If they didn't have time or weren't going to get a grade that would get them into their university of choice, were they going to be honorable and risk lack of success or be dishonorable and improve their chances of success but risk being caught? In other words, when taking on a challenge, which is more important: success or integrity? This is not to say that you can't have both; but if it came down to a choice between the two while taking on your challenge, which should students pick? In this chapter, we define integrity to explore the idea of success achieved through honorable means, embodying integrity, and avoiding cheating. We will investigate research on integrity and its relationship with success and offer one tool to help you better understand this concept along with tools to bring this important topic to your classroom.

The Definition of Integrity

Integrity is the ability of a person to be honest and make more selfless choices. Someone without integrity is selfish, being dishonest by looking for shortcuts so that they can feel more accomplished and superior to others. A lack of integrity is very ego-driven as cheating only focuses on a desired outcome to prove worthiness. A person who doesn't cheat seems to be more interested in the process and improvement.

As mentioned in the introduction (page 1), integrity is a moral character trait rather than a performance character trait. However, it is essential in guiding how someone works through a challenge, and so, for the purposes of this book, we treat it as a performance character trait. If someone attacks a challenge by cheating or uses the challenge to prove supremacy over others rather than seeking to deepen their own knowledge and skills, they are veering back into ego. On the other hand, if someone undertakes a challenge with integrity, it shows that they are more interested in learning than an outcome. As discussed last chapter, learning is a difficult and often messy process lined with failures. The person with integrity understands this and embraces it. The person who cheats simply wants to get the challenge done with the outcome they want with the least amount of effort. Learning doesn't figure into their process.

Students need time to learn how to deal with their egos. Their egos may justify that cheating is appropriate in certain situations, which may be true. However, most situations where students use a lack of integrity will bypass challenge and lead to a lack of learning.

Success and Honor

In *The Prince*, Niccolò Machiavelli (2020) famously writes, "The end justifies the means" (p. 22). Machiavelli is saying that it doesn't matter how you acquire something as long as you do acquire it. For some students, academics can be a Machiavellian endeavor, focusing more on obtaining success than acting with integrity. Some will lie, cheat, and steal to obtain their goal—often without thinking about it.

In *ScienceDaily* (2015), professor of psychiatry and pediatrics at the Pitt School of Medicine Beatriz Luna explains why students might make a snap decision to cheat. She says:

> Our findings indicate that the teen prefrontal cortex is not much different than in the adult, but it can be easily overruled by heightened motivation

centers in the brain. You have this mixture of newly gained executive control
plus extra reward that is pulling the teenager toward immediate gratification.

These heightened motivation centers often override the part of the brain that understands the lengthy process of learning. This is completely normal for adolescents. If we can get them to think about what is more important to them before they make an impulsive choice, we are helping them learn to make more mature choices in terms of integrity.

I will admit my bias in this chapter is against Machiavelli and for honorable actions, but I've had discussions that have challenged my beliefs. When I worked with some students from New York City, I asked which was better: Success with dishonor or failure with honor? The entire group of sixteen agreed that, between the two options, they would choose success with dishonor. Because I had discussed this with many groups prior and never had a group admit to that answer, I was curious why they decided on that. One student shared, "Mr. Jackson, I live in the projects. I will do whatever I need to do to get out, even if I have to cheat. When I get out, I'll think about being more honorable. But, for now, I'll choose success over honor." The rest of the group nodded. Because I can never fully understand their lived experience (I haven't driven across their same adversity bridge), I can't argue with their opinions and tell them what is right and wrong. I just want students to be aware of this decision so that they can make the most educated choice on how to deal with integrity for themselves. Helping students discuss this concept of success versus honor could help them make these decisions.

It seems that many high school students choose success over honor at one time or another. Donald McCabe, one founder of the International Center for Academic Integrity (ICAI), studied more than seventy thousand high school students in 1990 (a team of ICAI researchers updated and confirmed this research with a follow-up study in 2020), revealing that 64 percent admitted to cheating on a test, 58 percent said that they were guilty of plagiarism, and a whopping 95 percent said that they have cheated in school at one time or another (as cited in Facts and Statistics, n.d.). So, students are cheating at alarming rates, but why?

Professor of educational studies at Ohio State Lauren Hensley (2013) offers several reasons why students make the decision to be dishonorable, including that they want a good grade at any cost, they are struggling and want to show competence, they lack effective time-management skill, and they want to assist a peer. Researchers Eric M. Anderman, Tripp Griesinger, and Gloria Westerfield (1998) add, "Some students may feel compelled to cheat in order to . . . participate in athletics; others may cheat in order to please their parents; still others may cheat because they find the subject matter to be uninteresting" (p. 4). In their book on cheating in college, authors Donald McCabe, Kenneth Butterfield, and Linda Klebe Trevino (2017) note that 60 percent of students surveyed saw digital plagiarism as trivial. This means that well over half of college students surveyed had no problem going to the internet to steal someone's work and didn't even see it as being dishonorable.

Cheating betrays a lack of self-awareness in students. It is not always a direct result of a lack of self-awareness, but those who are self-aware have the presence and potential to understand the consequences of cheating more effectively. In the following sections, observe the relationship cheating has to both a student's self-awareness and the human body.

Cheating and Self-Awareness

Cheating in school is an inherently selfish act. It is all about how the student can get the best possible benefit by doing the least amount of work. If the student is ego-brittle, they will create justifications that their behaviors are acceptable and appropriate. The more ego-resilient student is self-aware; they understand that cheating is immoral and will start to feel guilty if they make a dishonorable decision.

Sociologists Jan Stets and Ryan Trettevik (2016) ran an experiment where subjects could win tickets to win prizes in a drawing. If they received more tickets, subjects had a better statistical chance to win. Subjects received numerous chances to cheat and earn more tickets, although not everyone partook. Those who did cheat initially reported that they were still good, honest people; however, when experimenters discussed with them how others might view their behavior and see it as dishonorable, they started to become more self-aware, and their happiness plummeted. The experiment shows that, when someone cheats and realizes others are aware of their transgression, the less happy they become.

While it could be that subjects in the study felt guilty and unhappy when they realized that they had done something selfish, subjects also might have experienced sadness because they thought that others knew of their misdeeds. Social shame regarding selfish behavior can foster guilt, but self-awareness and ego-resilience implies that the student will make the honorable and selfless choice even if no one is looking.

Perhaps the most interesting reason for cheating that surfaces is the classroom environment. Anderman and colleagues (1998) find that cheating is more prevalent in a results-focused classroom. If the teacher or peers in the classroom value grades over process, students are more likely to cheat. If the environment in the classroom is geared toward improvement where mistakes are part of the process, it might lessen the likelihood of cheating. Anderman and colleagues (1998) say this:

> If a student sees the goal of an academic task as either (a) getting a good grade, or (b) demonstrating one's competence, then the student may see cheating as a means to achieving the goal. When the goal of an academic task involves mastering the task and truly learning the material for intrinsic reasons, then cheating may not be a viable means to achieving a goal of task mastery; in contrast, when the primary goal is to earn a good grade or to demonstrate ability, some students may perceive cheating as a logical and justifiable strategy for achieving that goal. (p. 5)

These findings indicate it might be worthwhile to create an environment in your classroom focused on process rather than results, therefore reducing potential incidents of cheating. To accomplish this, a standards-based approach could be an option. With this grading method, a teacher or collaborative teacher team determines the essential standards for what students will learn and how to best assess learning of those standards. Instead of a set and final written assessment, students can prove that they comprehend each standard in multiple ways, such as through a performance (a demonstration of knowledge like a lab or class presentation) or even a one-on-one conversation with the teacher to verbalize acquired learning. Additionally, students who don't understand the standard right away are allowed to continue to work on the standard until they show competence. In this way, teachers gather assessment through more than one format while also ensuring mistakes are a formative part of the learning process rather than solely a summative measure of learning.

Northwestern College researcher Kayla Veenstra (2021) studied several teachers implementing a standards-based approach and found that, eventually, it created an environment that led to more focus on learning and less cheating:

> The other notable theme that emerged was related to teachers' instructional strategies where teachers had to figure out different ways to encourage desirable behaviors from students such as taking responsibility, completing work on time, and not cheating or plagiarizing. Although one of the consequences from students included them demonstrating less accountability in the beginning, over time the teachers noticed students taking more responsibility and adopting mindsets more focused on growth. (pp. 20–21)

Pay particular attention to the progression this study finds: cheating did occur with a standards-based approach—especially at the beginning. However, after students realize that they can have second chances and an assessment is not final, the frequency of cheating lessens. When the school environment changed to put more emphasis on the process of learning (which includes self-awareness), students similarly learned to prioritize that same learning process rather than the grading outcomes.

Dishonesty and the Body

It turns out, improved learning outcomes aren't the only reason for teachers to instill the value of academic integrity in the classroom. Cheating, quite simply, is bad for one's health. Researchers Leanne ten Brinke, Jooa Lee, and Dana Carney (2015) find that dishonesty is positively related to testosterone and cortisol release and increases in arousal and heart rate, leading to negative outcomes like stress, high blood pressure, and inability to access parts of the brain which deal with emotional regulation. Interestingly, these reactions aren't just for people who lie; those who witness dishonesty also share these physiological effects (ten Brinke et al., 2015). The more a person experiences these effects, the more potential negative health outcomes will arise. Even the recurring thoughts of dishonesty may trigger these negative bodily reactions.

We have all likely seen this play out in a classroom. If you catch a student lying or cheating, they might physically react to the discovery. Their heart pounds, blood pressure rises, and they're completely stressed. For the other students and the teacher who didn't cheat, you don't fare much better—everyone has more stress. If dishonesty is consistent and rampant it takes a toll on all.

A student's lack of integrity in a class can affect the teacher in other ways as well. If a student cheats and a teacher does not confront them about it, the student (and all others paying attention) will assume that cheating is acceptable. Therefore, the teacher will usually approach the student about their behavior. This direct conversation could lead to the student denying wrongdoing, parents getting involved, yelling, or crying. It's a mess. When a student cheats, the educator didn't partake in any wrongdoing, but they may feel guilty because of the reaction from students or parents, particularly if it impacts a student's chances of success. The aftermath of cheating is destructive for everyone involved.

Finally, studies have shown that dishonesty in school leads to dishonesty in the future. Looking closely at several studies regarding this subject, researchers from Bucharest Octavian Rujoiu and Valentina Rujoiu (2014) write, "In this paper, we insisted on the relationship between academic dishonesty and workplace dishonesty because there is a very high probability that those who adopt misconduct behaviors in college will also do this later in their workplace" (p. 934). In other words, and this is probably no surprise, students who learn to gain success by cheating in school have a solid chance of using dishonesty to improve their standing as adults.

Deciding whether to cheat is something that many students will confront. Based on their brain make-up, they may make rash decisions; however, teachers can help them make a more informed choice. It may be important to have students think deeply about cheating, why they're cheating, and if it's ever appropriate. To do this, a teacher can use the success and honor tool in the following section to lead a class discussion.

The Success and Honor Tool

When taking on challenges, we will succeed or fail. If students are failing at something, they have a choice to be honorable or dishonorable. Being dishonorable might lead to completion of the challenge but may have implications. Being honorable is the morally correct thing but may not help us finish the task successfully. Use the tool in figure 2.1 to promote a rich class discussion about success and honor.

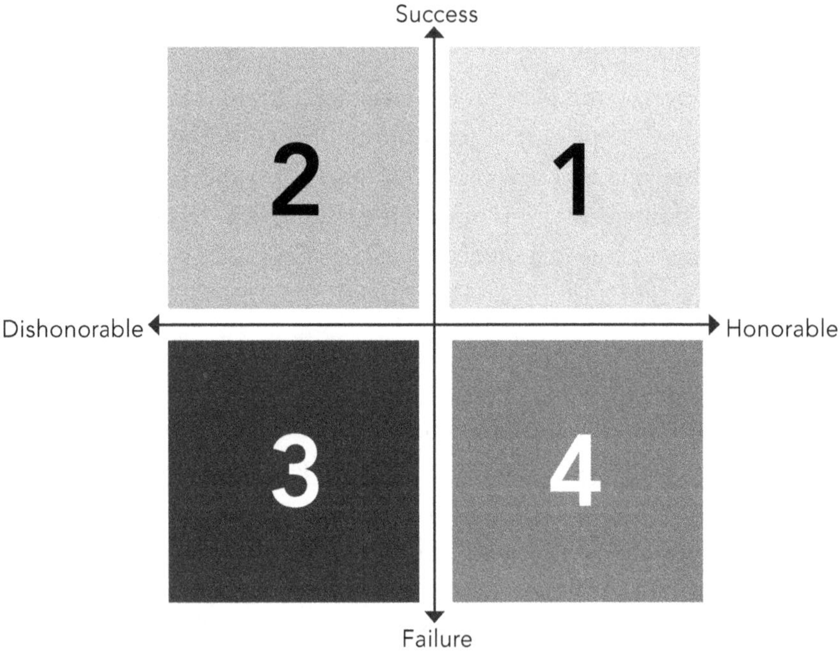

Figure 2.1: Success and honor tool.

*Visit **go.SolutionTree.com/SEL** for a free reproducible version of this figure.*

After reviewing the tool with the class, your peers, or on your own, please use the following questions to discuss and reflect. See appendix A (page 189) for the complete instructions on using the tools in this book.

Questions for Educators and Their Colleagues

These are questions to help you discuss the success and honor tool with colleagues to gain a more personal and broader understanding.

- Everybody wants to be in quadrant 1 where you are honorable and successful. Nobody wants to be in quadrant 3 where you are dishonorable and fail. Which do you think is better: quadrant 2 or quadrant 4? Why?

- Given the same question, do you think your students would choose quadrant 2 or 4? What do you think their parents would pick for them? Why?

- Think of a time when you made a quadrant 2 choice. How did you feel? How do you think students feel when they cheat?

- Why do you think students cheat? Are there any reasons where it might be appropriate for a student to cheat?

- How does cheating relate to ego and entitlement?

- If a person equates success with improvement instead of grades, does that change the tool?

- Where does a person go on the tool if they are in quadrant 2 and get caught cheating? If they wanted to get to quadrant 1 after this, what would they need to do?

- If you had to pick one of two candidates for a job, and one was very quadrant 2 while the other was very quadrant 4, how would you decide on who got the job? How might different jobs affect your decision?

Questions to Prompt Class Discussion

These are questions to promote class understanding about the success and honor tool. This can be done with small- or large-group discussion or by quietly reflecting in a journal.

- Define *honorable* and *dishonorable*. What do they mean to you?

- Everybody wants to be in quadrant 1 (to feel and be seen as honorable and successful). Nobody wants to be in quadrant 3 (to feel or be seen as dishonorable and a failure). Which do you think is better: quadrant 2 or quadrant 4? Why?

- Between quadrant 2 and quadrant 4, which do you think your parents would want you to be in? Why?

- Why do students cheat in school?

- Is it OK to cheat if everyone else is doing it? Why or why not?

- Think of a time when you've made a quadrant 2 choice. How did you feel?

- Are there times when it is OK to cheat? Explain.

- If you cheat in school, do you think you'll cheat in your job? Why or why not?

Questions for Student Reflection

After a content-specific lesson that is also an opportunity to assess success and honor, these questions can assist students in evaluating their thoughts and behavior during the lesson as they pertain to the concept.

- What is success for you?

- During the lesson, what quadrant were you in? How do you know?

- During the lesson, which quadrants were your classmates in? How did you know? For school, if you had to choose between quadrant 2 and quadrant 4, which would you pick? Why?

Elementary Teacher Tip

Play the game Heads Up Seven Up. In this game, seven students will be "it" while all other students put their heads down on their desks and put one thumb out, facing up (as if giving a thumbs up to someone). The seven students will quietly touch the thumb of one of the classmates before returning to the front of the room. Once the seven have finished, the other students will put their heads up. Those who had their thumb touched will attempt to guess who it was that touched them. If they guess correctly, they get to be "it." Afterward, ask students if it was tempting to peek (which is cheating). If you have established trust within the classroom culture, ask students to share whether they indeed peeked and, if they were able to resist peeking, how they did it.

Summary

Integrity is doing what you know is right. While integrity is a moral character trait, it does drive performance character. If a student pursues a challenge in school without integrity, their improvement is compromised, and they didn't really earn their success. Nevertheless, many students will cheat. As young people have overpowering motivation centers in their developing brains, the rash decision to cheat is a natural one. Additionally, students can rationalize many other reasons to cheat. As opportunities for students to cheat are plentiful, students should make a self-aware and informed choice of whether being dishonorable or successful is the best option in both the short and long term.

3

Purpose

Goals transform a random walk into a chase.

—Mihaly Csikszentmihalyi

Two days after my stroke, I was moved from the ICU in one hospital to a rehabilitation facility in another. My entire right side from my neck down was still paralyzed. The goal was to recover full function, and I was in the right place to achieve it. This wing of the new hospital boasted experienced physical, occupational, and speech therapists; a rehab pool; a weight room; and all manner of equipment to assist people with brain injuries on their path to recovery. I had the necessary staff and facilities, but I needed the best mindset.

To do this, I knew that I couldn't focus simply on the desired outcome. If that happened, I would be frustrated until I reached the goal—in other words, I wouldn't be happy until I had full use of my right side. Additionally, I might look at failures along the way as impediments to my progress; those failures would keep me from accomplishing the goal. Instead, I knew that I needed to focus on the process. With this mindset, I could celebrate any improvement, something that happened daily. Failures became events that I could use to help me improve as they helped me identify where I was and what I needed to work on.

Between therapy sessions, I started to work on raising my right arm while I rested in bed. At first, I only moved my index finger. Then, I started to move all five digits. At times, I would think hard about moving my hand only to have the reaction happen thirty seconds after the thought (which was super weird). Within a few days, I could lift my arm a few inches at the same time I was thinking about it. After a week, I was able to raise my arm over my head. Initially, it felt as if someone else was raising my hand for me. After several months, I was able to reach full movement.

Had I focused only on the outcome, I would still be frustrated because, even though I was improving, I was still short of the goal as my lower body was not doing as well. However, focusing on the process and improvement made each day a celebration. Perhaps more importantly, I was happy and motivated throughout the process, and I felt that way because I had a good purpose. My purpose drove me to focus on what I wanted, how I was going to get it, and how I needed to think about it to sustain my motivation until the end.

Students, too, can learn to find and use purpose this way. In fact, their success and happiness depend on it. Knowing what they want and how they are going to get it, as I did, is the first step in finding purpose in their learning. Finding purpose in school will help them find motivation to complete the daily, weekly, and monthly tasks that comprise their education. Students without purpose have no reason to try hard. Some students will find a purpose, which leads to motivation but also to depression and anxiety. If it's a good purpose, students will remain joyful through the process as they pursue academic challenges.

This chapter will discuss what a good purpose that drives students while allowing them to be happy might look like. Also, once students find purpose, how should they pursue it? To think about these principles, we will look at three concepts that will drive our understanding and application of purpose: (1) growth mindset, (2) sacrifice and reward, and (3) event, response, and outcome.

The Definition of Purpose

Purpose is a very difficult concept to define and even harder to teach. Purpose is our reason for doing something. If a student doesn't have a purpose, they find themselves complacent, unwilling, and unable to move forward. When a friend of Hunter S. Thompson asked for advice on life's purpose, Thompson replied with these words (as cited in Usher, 2017):

> And indeed, that IS the question: whether to float with the tide, or to swim for a goal. It is a choice we must all make consciously or unconsciously at one time in our lives. So few people understand this! Think of any decision you've ever made which had a bearing on your future: I may be wrong, but I don't see how it could have been anything but a choice however indirect— between the two things I've mentioned: the floating or the swimming.

But why not float if you have no goal? That is another question. It is unques-
tionably better to enjoy the floating than to swim in uncertainty. So how
does a man find a goal? Not a castle in the stars, but a real and tangible
thing. How can a man be sure he's not after the "big rock candy mountain,"
the enticing sugar-candy goal that has little taste and no substance? (p. 64)

In the excerpt, Thompson identifies two kinds of people: (1) those who don't
have a purpose (floaters) and (2) those who do (swimmers). While floaters drift
through life aimlessly, swimmers have a direction to move toward. If our students have a purpose for why they are in school, it may help them understand
why they are showing up every day and give them a reason and a direction to
swim. Thompson also includes his thoughts on choosing a good purpose. In his
mind, a purpose should be something meaningful instead of something with
"little taste and no substance." Should we, as teachers, assist students in finding
a purpose; and how can we do that? As important, how can we help them think
about a good, tangible goal?

Research shows that students who are swimmers do better in school (Marshall,
2012). Members of the John Templeton Foundation (2018) and the Claremont
Moral Development Lab write that students with purpose "perform better academically and report that their schoolwork is more meaningful" (p. 13). They add
that "the presence of purpose is associated with positive psychological states" (p.
10). The paper also suggests that, for some, purpose may lead to negative effects:

[I]n some instances, the pursuit of purpose can be difficult and stressful, and
individuals who pursue meaningful purposes may actually be less happy than
individuals who do not. For instance, studies find that being a parent can be a
highly purposeful experience, but it is not always an easy or happy one. (p. 11)

The shift from happiness to anxiety may have something to do with how students respond to stressors that arise while pursuing a purpose. Author Jackie Swift
(2021) interviews Cornell researcher Anthony L. Burrow, who conducted a study
having subjects reflect on purpose for three weeks. He found that those who rated
higher on purpose showed more emotional stability. Burrow explains, "It's not
the absence of stress, it's how we react to it . . . That's potentially the explanatory
mechanism that affects health. Purposeful people can mitigate stress that would
otherwise derail them" (Swift, 2021).

In other words, pursuing a purpose involves challenge and failure. If a student can understand that those things are inherent and necessary to reach their
goals, they will have more opportunities to work through them and emotionally

regulate them. This may be a process, but Burrow contends that those with purpose, for the most part, learn how to deal with stress.

Students may more positively work through this if they think of purpose as a process rather than a result. Those who view purpose in terms of a result are pursuing a set outcome. Students focused on a result may tend to do just enough to reach their set outcome (it wouldn't make sense to put in any more effort), and they may cheat to get their goal. Likely, they will not be happy until they reach their result; and if they don't get it, it may make them bitter. Plus, if they reach their result, they may be happy for a while, but they may also move on to a new purpose to obtain. If you're having students work in groups to complete a puzzle, for example, and their goal is to win, the following will likely happen: they will try hard until they see that another group wins or is going to win; then, they'll give up. They may also cheat to obtain the outcome or accuse others of cheating.

On the other hand, students who focus on the process have a purpose of improvement and learning. If this is the case, they are less focused on completion of assignments and grades and more interested in bettering themselves. These students can also work hard with that purpose, but there is no cap or limit as they can always learn more. Additionally, students with this focus don't cheat—it wouldn't help them learn or improve. They also seem to have a better chance at being happy as they can reach their goal much more often (improvement toward a goal happens more often than completion of a goal). If a student has a purpose of improvement, that is something that, with sacrifice, the student can achieve daily. If the group of students working on solving the puzzle is focused on process instead of result, they wouldn't cheat, and they would continue to work hard on solving the puzzle (even if another group has already completed their puzzle and won). Students could be aware of both types of purposes so that they can make an educated decision about which one they choose to pursue.

If students can learn to think of purpose as a process, determine what reward they want for their efforts, and put their purpose in the forefront of their thoughts, students may have a better chance at success and happiness in school. The tools in this chapter can help you lead discussions for students about these three areas.

Outcome Versus Process Goals

A student's motivation and satisfaction in school is based on the type of goal they create for themselves. To be successful and happy, should their goal be about results or improvement? Consider the following scenario. It follows Mr. Pham, a fictional educator, leading a class on the idea of purpose for the first time.

Mr. Pham had been teaching sixth grade for twenty years. Over time, he noticed a trend in his students' behaviors. When he started, it seemed that students were interested in learning. Now, students seemed to care more about completing an assignment or getting a good grade. So, he decided to ask some questions and share some thoughts.

"Students," asked Mr. Pham. "Do you want to be happy? If so, what do you need to be happy in your lives in the next fifteen years?"

Students first said that they, of course, wanted to be happy. When Mr. Pham pressed them on what it would take to make them happy, many students had similar answers: "I need to get into a good college, get a good job, make a lot of money, and live in a nice house."

"OK," he said. "Sounds like you want stuff, and those things will make you happy. Tell me, then, what you think of this analogy: let's say that there is a surfer who goes out every morning to surf. He loves it because he's appreciating being in nature, and he loves improving and trying new skills. He comes in after a session, and a guy on the beach says, 'You're really, really good at surfing. You should enter the surfing contest this weekend.'

"So, the surfer goes to the competition. He could attack it the same way he goes out every morning by appreciating the ocean and seeing the competition as a way to improve his craft. In that way, he would still be trying hard, but he wouldn't care about winning or placing—that would just be a bonus to his goal of improvement. On the other hand, he could go into the competition with the sole purpose of winning or a spot on the podium. In that case, he's not as grateful and appreciative. Instead, his focus is on how others are doing compared to him. He's thinking about what his score was on the last wave, what other people's scores were, and how he's going to end up in the competition. If he finds himself far out of placing, he might give up. After all, if you're not doing well, there's no reason to try anymore. Technically, both mindsets are versions of surfing, but the first one seems beautiful and organic. The second one is still surfing, but it seems like some twisted, impure version of the sport. Who do you think will try harder and who is happier?"

While students debated on who would try harder, most of the students felt that the first mindset would breed more happiness. Mr.

Pham continued, "Isn't this story like school? Learning is beautiful and organic. You can come here with the mindset that you're grateful for this opportunity to learn, improve, and better yourself. Or you can see school as a contest where you need to get a certain grade and be better than others. If you do this, you're still technically learning; but it's a distorted version of learning that puts a lot of pressure on you and leads to anxiety."

A student in the back countered, saying, "Life will be fun when I make a lot of money." "In that case, you won't be happy until you make a lot of money. Why not be happy now? Don't you think that all the stuff will come if you are working to improve yourself daily?"

Students were starting to talk over each other, so Mr. Pham put them in small groups to discuss, letting students talk this through before he continued with the large-group conversation. He wanted them to think about these questions: Do you have a reason for being in school? If so, what is your reason for being in school? Does it make you work hard? Does it make you happy? Is your reason for being in school about results or growth? Then, he planned to give the students a challenge to see if they took it with the pure or distorted version of learning.

Mr. Pham's questions were rooted in the concept that there are two different types of purpose: (1) outcome goals and (2) process goals. Art Markman (2014), professor of psychology and marketing at the University of Texas at Austin, describes these:

> The most typical goal people pursue is an outcome goal. It refers to a specific state that you hope to reach in the future . . . The second type of goal is a process goal that focuses on a set of actions you can perform. As a side effect of those actions, you may achieve some desirable outcomes, but your focus is on the actions, not the outcome. (p. 60)

In other words, those with outcome goals focus solely on the result while those with process goals focus on a series of steps and actions taken to realize improvement. Outcome goals include end results like completion of assessments, grades, graduation, and getting into the university of their choosing. If a student has an outcome goal, they may limit themselves. They will work as hard as they need to reach the outcome or expectation. If they focus on a standard that they can already achieve through their current abilities, they will not need to work as hard. If they set an outcome or expectation that is beyond their abilities, they may work very hard. Those with true outcome goals, however, will not be satisfied until they obtain the desired result. A great example of this is the student whose goal is getting into an elite university. Regarding their outcome, they may remain anxious and unsure throughout high school until the end of their senior year when they get their acceptance letter from the university. If they don't gain admittance, they may be debilitatingly bitter about it.

Students with process goals, on the other hand, may still have direction they are swimming toward, but they are focused on how they get there. With attention on the process, students understand that mistakes and failures are not detrimental toward obtaining a goal; rather they are necessary steps of learning. Students who put out effort to obtain a process goal will likely see gains more often, giving them pride and belief that they can keep moving toward a desired outcome, even with mistakes along the way. A process-oriented student trying to get into an elite university will not focus solely on the final goal; instead, in class, they will be the best version of themselves in the moment. If they do this, they will improve.

Outcome goals and process goals are closely related to the concept of fixed versus growth mindset, which Stanford professor of psychology Carol Dweck's (2016) book *Mindset: The New Psychology of Success* popularized. Dweck discusses an experiment in which two groups of fifth graders were offered an easy test. After their successes on the assessment, one group was praised for being "smart" while the other was praised for their engagement in the learning process. When the experimenters offered a follow-up assessment with the choice of another easy one or a more difficult one, most of the students in the group praised for being smart chose the easier option, while 90 percent of students in the process-focused group opted for the more difficult assessment. Dweck (2016) theorizes that those praised for their intelligence did not want to take the more difficult test because they had a fixed mindset—they felt that their intelligence was set, and they didn't want to do anything more difficult that might prove that they weren't smart. They felt they had no control over their level of intelligence. On the other hand, those praised for effort that chose the more difficult test had a growth mindset. They saw themselves in control of their intelligence—they could always work to improve their learning process and, in so doing, achieve their goals.

One could look at Dweck's study through the lens of outcome and process goals. The students who were lauded for intelligence had already reached an outcome of being smart. They didn't need to do anything else to prove their intelligence, and many passed on the second assessment as a mistake on the second assessment might alter the achieved result from the first assessment. On the other hand, by the experimenters praising the other students for hard work, they gave students an opening for improvement, which many took. In this case, a second assessment might show a higher climb or improvement of their skills. In other words, a fixed mindset encourages outcomes while a growth mindset encourages process.

Growth and fixed mindset in this context also affects a student's stress level. Researchers Hae Yeon Lee, Jeremy P. Jamieson, Adriana S. Miu, Robert A. Josephs, and David S. Yeager (2018) suggest a connection between happiness and the two different mindsets. The experimenters had high school students complete a survey to determine if they viewed their intelligence as a fixed entity (what they refer to as holding an *entity theory*) or as something malleable and then split them into two groups based on the results of the survey. Then, they tested cortisol levels in the two groups of students when they received a stressor (such as when their grades declined at a marking period). As cortisol is the body's main stress hormone, the adrenal glands excrete cortisol when the student feels threatened. Those with a fixed mindset show elevated cortisol levels at the moment and for days afterward and report feeling more anxiety and feeling powerless to change their circumstances. Those with growth mindsets exhibit less cortisol production and report having less anxiety and feeling capable of improving the situation.

As school will likely consist of a series of stressors and challenges, those students who feel in control of their fates may prove to be happier and more successful. Those students who feel that they are unable to change their circumstances may feel less happy and experience less success. Lee and colleagues (2018) write the following:

> Daily academic stressors may continue to loom large for struggling students who hold an entity theory, perhaps because of what everyday difficulties portend about their long-term intellectual abilities and prospects. A bad grade or an extra homework assignment may not be viewed as a temporary hassle but rather as a more global sign that the stressors that one can't handle are piling up and that one is fundamentally "not smart." (p. 14)

This suggests that student mindset ultimately comes down to how they view the act of making mistakes, which generally falls into one of two buckets: (1) adaptive perfectionism and (2) maladaptive perfectionism.

Adaptive and Maladaptive Perfectionism

How a student deals with mistakes and failures seems to be a tell-tale sign of whether a student is utilizing a growth or a fixed mindset. Students tend to fall into two different categories on this matter, adaptive perfectionism and maladaptive perfectionism. National Chengchi University researcher Shu-Shen Shih (2011) studied Taiwanese eighth-grade students and found that "adaptive perfectionism enabled adolescents to experience positive emotions and to engage in behavioral self-regulation, whereas maladaptive perfectionism was positively associated with negative emotions and self-handicapping" (p. 131). In other words, students who had *adaptive perfectionism*, in which students focus on growth and see mistakes as part of the process, experienced more happiness and joy and were able to cope with hardships and mistakes well. Oppositely, students who had *maladaptive perfectionism*, the belief that making mistakes prevents one from getting the desired result, felt more negative emotions and had more of a tendency to give up.

In the book introduction (page 1), I mentioned a survey of students at my high school done through St. Louis University medical school. When Stuart Slavin received the results of the survey, he had his statistician calculate a second and a third time—he couldn't believe the results: 79.5 percent of students showed moderate to severe levels of anxiety, 54.5 percent showed moderate to severe levels of depression, and 27.6 percent showed clinical levels of maladaptive perfectionism (Abeles, 2016). Along with these data, the survey found that the number one stressor for students (with a 3.35 on a four-point scale) is getting into a good college (Abeles, 2016). As with the students in Shih's (2011) study, the students at my high school experienced high anxiety, depression, and maladaptive perfectionism. It's very interesting that the top cause of these negative outcomes is an outcome goal (getting into a top-tier university). What would these data look like if our students' focus was learning instead of a result?

Success traditionally revolves around the ego—we understand that we are more successful when we can show superiority over things or others. If we complete something, win, get a higher grade, or get into a "better" university, we are successful. A combined process goal and growth mindset introduce an alternative definition of success for students. Instead of comparison to others, success means that you are doing your best work in the moment, which leads to gains. It's not about comparing ourselves to our past selves either; rather, it's about being in the present and focused on being the ideal version of you at that moment. I can agonize over comparing how many pull-ups I can do now to how many I could do when I was twenty years old, but if I focus my attention solely on doing my best on my current pull-ups, I know I'm being my best self *now*, which will elicit improvement. I can be satisfied and happy knowing that.

In the context of learning and grades, author of several educator guides Nathan Barber (2014) responds:

> Test scores and grades may not accurately reflect a learner's success or failure, though parents and students spend enormous amounts of time, energy, and money chasing grades and scores because they believe these things are

true indicators of learning. Hence, great teachers encouraged by great educational leaders must keep learners focused on the process, not the results. Students chasing scores and grades will lose sight of the learning process and their own growth and development. . . . When a language student, for example, focuses on mastering the language rather than making an A, the results will follow.

It seems important to acknowledge that students with outcome goals and students with process goals can both work very hard, but in my experience, those who work toward improvement seem to smile a lot more and bring more joy to both themselves and to the class.

As their attention is on learning, they are less anxious and sad when their grade takes a hit or others are getting better marks. Like Barber (2014) says, if the focus is learning, the results will follow. If a student is in class to improve, good grades, graduation, and college admissions are likely to follow. Plus, these are the students for whom I'm much more likely to write a glowing college recommendation as compared to those who are only in it for the grade.

The Outcome and Process Goal Tool

People with process goals focus on the process; their purpose is on learning and improvement. People with outcome goals focus on an end result as their purpose. In addition to indicating how the two mindsets experience success and failure, this tool in figure 3.1 (page 51) introduces the element of happiness. The happiness line in the middle signifies that, if you are above the line, you're happy, while if you are below the line, you're unhappy. Some of the discussion questions prompt consideration of whether this is true. Use this tool as a springboard for a rich class discussion about process and outcome goals.

After reviewing the tool with the class, your peers, or on your own, please use the following questions to discuss and reflect. See appendix A (page 189) for the complete instructions on using the tools in this book.

Questions for Educators and Their Colleagues

These are questions to help you discuss the outcome and process goal tool with colleagues to gain a more personal and broader understanding.

- What is this tool trying to say? Do you agree? According to this tool, what do you think is the difference between a goal and an expectation?

- Think of people who have outcome goals and those who have process goals. How much effort do those with the two types of goals put forth? How happy are those with the two types of goals?

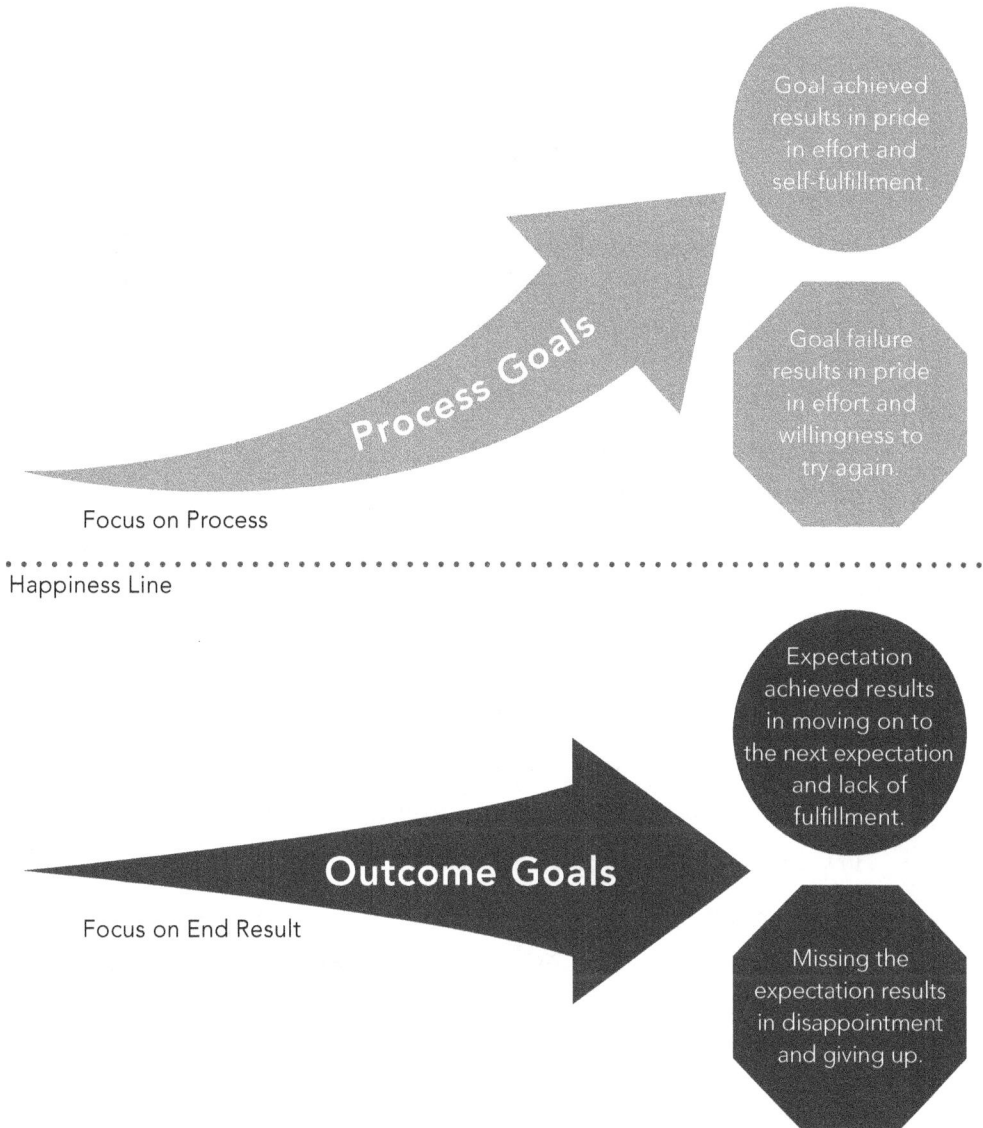

Source: Adapted from image created by Ryan Willer. Used with permission.

Figure 3.1: The outcome and process goal tool.

*Visit **go.SolutionTree.com/SEL** for a free reproducible version of this figure.*

- How do people with outcome goals deal with mistakes? How do people with process goals deal with mistakes?

- How might those with outcome goals and process goals view cheating?

- If you were to find out many of your students were below the happiness line, how could you change this in your classroom? How could your school change this?

- Could students' grades affect if they are above or below the happiness line? In other words, how might a kindergartener look at school compared to a high school student?

- If teachers find themselves below the happiness line, how could they change this? How could the school change this?

- Think of various relationships you have in your life. How might this tool be used to explain relationships with others? Does someone with outcome goals or process goals have better relationships with others?

Questions to Prompt Class Discussion

These are questions to promote class understanding about the tool. This can be done with small- or large-group discussion or by quietly reflecting in a journal.

- What do you think this tool is trying to say? Do you agree? According to this tool, what do you think is the difference between a goal and an expectation?

- How hard do people with outcome goals work? How hard do people with process goals work?

- According to the outcome and process goals tool, how happy are people with outcome goals? How happy are people with process goals?

- How do students with outcome goals and process goals view mistakes?

- How might students with outcome and process goals view cheating?

- Think of yourself in school. Where are you on the tool? How does it make you feel? If a student wanted to get above the happiness line, what should they do? How difficult would that be?

Questions for Student Reflection

After a content-specific lesson that is also an opportunity to assess the outcome and process goals, these questions can assist students in evaluating their thoughts and behavior during the lesson as they pertain to the concept.

- During the lesson, where were you on the tool? How hard did you work? How did it make you feel?

- Imagine a student who is clearly below the happiness line during this lesson. What advice would you give?

- Beyond this lesson, how might a student work to be above the happiness line in school? How possible is this?

Sacrifice and Reward

If a student is going to sacrifice and put forth effort, they do it for some reward that they wish to receive. Sacrifice and reward share an important relationship. Sacrifice of time and effort in school leading to a desired reward elicits pride and gratitude but sacrifice of time and effort that does not end with a desired goal is frustrating. What reward can a student pursue that will help them lead more toward gratitude and less toward frustration? The previous section discussed that, maybe, a process goal (instead of an outcome goal) should be the type of reward a student should seek. A reward of process is learning and improvement. To make this reward happen, a student needs a growth mindset and understanding that learning and skills are malleable and can be improved. If students can do this, they have a greater chance at gratitude as improvement is a reward that can be obtained daily with sacrifice. If a student's reward was a result, they would only need to sacrifice as much as they needed to obtain the result. Additionally, if they didn't achieve the result, that could lead to frustration.

In the introduction of this book (page 1), I referenced a program at my school where a group of certified coaches lead an obstacle course training every weekend for our students. Knowing this was available, one of the school's government teachers offered her students the following choice: they could take the regular final for the course, or in lieu of the final, they could attend seven of these hourlong training sessions by the end of the semester. She based her idea off business school professor Andrew Johnston's TEDxYouth (2015) talk where Johnston asks his students to interview business owners. Johnston offers "what business owners are telling my students the key to success has everything to do with the development of this: character, life skills, things like passion for your work, work ethic, persistence, determination, and good old-fashioned grit." To learn all these performance character traits, Johnston started a class called Change Through Challenge where, as part of the course, students are required to run a marathon. Since we had an opportunity at our school to teach character traits, this teacher wanted to use it to help her students become better people.

Several students took her up on the offer and attended the workouts, but they always stood out from the peers in attendance who were not part of the AP government class. They wanted an outcome reward (not taking the final), and they had no motivation to sacrifice more than the bare minimum to get it. For the hour, they could be found taking lengthy water breaks, talking in the shade, and spending their time at the easiest obstacles while avoiding running and the more challenging ones. The only thing that mattered to them was getting a signature from a coach at the end of the session to mark that they did, indeed, attend for the hour.

The other students who attended were there of their own accord. From the beginning, their desired reward was improved physical health or stronger mental health—they wanted to get fitter, tougher, or improve in some way. For this reason, they were more willing to sacrifice both time and energy in furtherance of that goal—they tended to push themselves harder, waste less time, take on the challenging obstacles, and seemed to be prouder of their efforts at the end. The government teacher's goal was to motivate students to improve their performance character traits, which is laudable. It's the type of risk-taking that I admire in teachers. However, the approach is flawed, and it starts with the fact that participation in the program was in no way connected to the actual course curriculum. While the goal was to improve their resilience, the students who participated did so specifically to *avoid* having to engage with curriculum content. It seemed like they weighed the amount of sacrifice for the final against seven hours of their time where they oversaw their level of challenge, and they went for the easier option. In the end, I'm not sure that these students were grateful or proud of their choice.

So, what is the bridge that will empower students to attack school with the reward of process-driven growth? Unfortunately, we know that many of our students fall prey to outcome goals. How can teachers inspire outcome-motivated students to change their default and ingrained mindset? Luckily, there are a few research-supported interventions you can use to change your mindset, which you can introduce to students when you are discussing this piece of performance character with them in class.

Changing Your Mindset

According to research, it is possible to switch mindsets with intervention—sometimes. Some interventions prove successful in changing fixed to growth mindset while others show little or no improvement. University of Oklahoma education professor Teresa DeBacker and colleagues (2018) note "modest" gains in growth mindset with a one-shot intervention—where an expert comes in for a day to teach a lesson to students. Researchers Lisa Blackwell, Kali Trzesniewski, and Carol Dweck (2007) see more positive changes with an eight-week workshop for a group of seventh graders. The authors explain the program:

> The key message was that learning changes the brain by forming new con-
> nections, and that students are in charge of this process. This message of
> malleable intelligence was presented in the context of an interesting read-
> ing, which contained vivid analogies (e.g., to muscles becoming stronger)

and examples (e.g., of relatively ignorant babies becoming smarter as they learned), supported by activities and discussions. (p. 254)

Teaching about process goals and growth mindset is a difficult task—especially when many students are focused on outcomes as rewards. The style and consistency of the method led to more understanding of growth mindset and more students buying into the concept. But is two months of creative lessons and discussions enough?

In another study, researchers Helene Zeeb, Julia Ostertag, and Alexander Renkl (2020) note that many interventions about mindset training are not as effective because they aren't woven into the regular school day. The authors offer this:

The interventions are usually isolated from regular instruction and delivered by special trainers or online programs. While the effects of educational interventions are often strongest when researchers implement the training, the isolation from ordinary lessons may be problematic in the particular case of a mindset training. The reason is that instructional practices—for example, teachers' feedback—influence students' beliefs in a vigorous and permanent manner and may thus influence whether growth mindsets actually take root in the classroom after a training.

For this reason, Zeeb and colleagues (2020) developed a lesson-integrated training on growth mindset for a physics class that the classroom teacher would administer. (They chose physics because they felt it provided significant challenge for students.) Lessons taught both physics and growth mindset simultaneously. For example, the physics teacher would lead a lesson on growth mindset. Then, the teacher would apply those lessons to challenging physics problems where the students had an opportunity to use what they learned and the teacher could coach them through concepts they learned, like they can improve if they put in the effort, mistakes are part of the learning process, and so on. In the study, students with the mindset-enhanced lessons showed strengthened growth mindsets and motivation.

The tools in this book intend to replicate the Zeeb and colleagues (2020) study. The belief is that, when teachers administer these lessons about performance character and teach them in conjunction with the class content, students will feel empowered to adjust their mindset toward that content and enhance their capacity to learn. Further, when teachers integrate performance character concepts with a content-specific lesson, they generate opportunities for students to self-assess not only their understanding of the content but also their mindset while learning that content.

Discussing Performance Character With Students

Because teachers are around students for the entire school year, they inevitably form relationships with those students. As such, few others are in a better position to mold tools to instill performance character for the needs and personalities of individual students. Nels Larsen, longtime educator and creator of the humility tool (see page 28), uses the following system to get students to think about changing their purpose to focus on process rather than result. As a physical education teacher, he asks students who seem to lack motivation what their purpose is for being in his class. If it's a result-focused goal, he asks them why they've set that goal until they get to a process goal. The following is a sample of the kind of conversation Larsen would have with one of his students.

Nels: "Why are you in this class?"

Student: "I want to pass."

Nels: "Why do you want to pass?"

Student: "So that I can graduate."

Nels: "Why do you want to graduate?"

Student: "So that I can go to college."

Nels: "Why do you want to go to college?"

Student: "So that I can get a good job."

Nels: "Why do you want a good job?"

Student: "So that I can make money?"

Nels: "Why do you want to make money?"

Student: "So that I can move out of my house and live on my own."

Nels: "Why do you want to do that?"

Student: "So that I can show that I'm responsible and, eventually, can take care of a family."

Nels: "So you want to be self-sufficient, responsible, and able to help others? Those are all things you can work on daily. Maybe that should be your reason for being in school and in this class? Isn't that better than just wanting to pass?"

Student: "Are you a wizard?"

Nels may or may not be a wizard; but he contends that, with this exercise, students will find a more meaningful and worthwhile purpose or reward. As you get deeper and deeper into the conversation, students' reasons tend to get more selfless, lifelong, and purposeful. Additionally, the process aims to change an outcome reward into a reward focused on process.

Students will sacrifice time and effort to get a reward they want whether that reward is an outcome or a process goal. The difference is that a reward that is focused on outcomes might lead to frustration if the student does not obtain the reward. The student who has a reward focused on improvement has a better chance of receiving that reward as improvement consistently happens through the process of learning. The following tool allows a teacher to lead a class discussion so students can think about what kind of reward they want, what kind of sacrifice they make, and what will help them become more successful and emotionally content.

The Sacrifice and Reward Tool

Sacrifice is spending time and effort to receive a reward. Use the tool in figure 3.2 to serve as a springboard for a rich class discussion about sacrifice and reward. According to this tool, being unwilling to sacrifice to receive a reward can result in boredom and complacency if that reward isn't received. If it is, it results in feeling entitled (an aspect of egocentric thinking). If you do sacrifice, you will become frustrated if you don't receive the reward that you were seeking and grateful and proud if you do.

After reviewing the tool with the class, your peers, or on your own, please use the following questions to discuss and reflect. See appendix A (page 189) for the complete instructions on using the tools in this book.

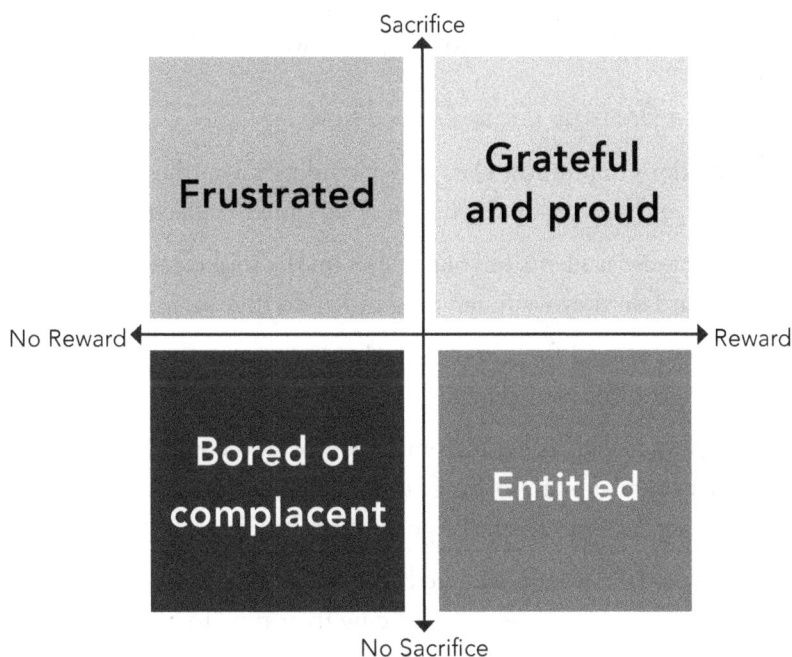

Figure 3.2: Sacrifice and reward tool.

*Visit **go.SolutionTree.com/SEL** for a free reproducible version of this figure.*

Questions for Educators and Their Colleagues

Use the following questions to help you discuss the sacrifice and reward tool with colleagues to gain a more personal and broader understanding.

- Do you think any of the words in the four quadrants should be changed? If so, what would you change them to?

- Imagine you have a student in class who is sacrificing time and effort but isn't getting the reward they wanted of an A. What quadrant are they in? What quadrant would they be in if a parent talked to the administration and got them out of your class? What quadrant would they be heading for if their parents tried to bribe you for an A? If administration refused to let them out of the class, what advice would you give them to deal with this situation?

- What do you think is the reward for most of the students at your school? Where are they on the tool?

- If you wanted more students to be in the Grateful/Proud quadrant, how could you do it? How could you change their reward to give them a better chance to get to that quadrant?

- Where are most teachers at your school on the tool? Why do you think they have ended up there?

- What is your reward for teaching? What quadrant are you in? Are there things you can change to get to where you want to be?

Questions to Prompt Class Discussion

These are questions to promote class understanding about the tool. This can be done with small- or large-group discussion or by quietly reflecting in a journal.

- Where are most students in your school on the tool regarding academics? What reward do they want and how much do they sacrifice?

- What is your reward for school and where are you on the tool? How grateful are you for your classes?

- How might a reward as an outcome goal (focused completely on the outcome or result) or a process goal (focused completely on learning and what you are doing to reach the goal) affect this tool?

- Let's say your friend is on a basketball team and their reward is getting to play in the games. They are sacrificing their time to be at practice and sacrificing effort during the practice, but they only play a few minutes in competitions. They are frustrated and come to you for advice. What would you tell them?

- What quadrant are you in for school and why? How could you change your reward and sacrifice to help you become more grateful and proud?

Questions for Student Reflection

After a content-specific lesson that is also an opportunity to assess sacrifice and reward, these questions can assist students in evaluating their thoughts and behavior during the lesson as they pertain to the concept.

- During this lesson, what quadrant were you in? How do you know? During this lesson, what reward were you looking for? Was it an outcome or a process goal? How do you know?

- In school, how much do you sacrifice and what is your reward? What quadrant does that lead to?

- Can you change anything you're doing in school to be in quadrant 1 more often?

Event, Response, and Outcome

Once you have determined your reason for doing something, it's not a purpose until you make it a priority. You can say that you have a purpose and even explain it to people, but it doesn't become official until you start and continue working toward it (more on putting well-planned and exceptional effort toward something in chapter 7: Commitment, page 119). To make this happen and ensure that your purpose is, indeed, a purpose, you can start to make decisions leading to behaviors that will feed your purpose.

The word equation *event + response = outcome* (Canfield, 2007) represents this concept as it's an effective means to set priorities. *Events* are things that happen to us every second of every day that we cannot control. We can, however, control our *response* to that event. The event, coupled with our response to it, leads to an *outcome*. If we think logically about achieving our purpose rather than emotionally, we can be outcome focused. If our purpose for school is to learn, we want that to be our outcome. As events happen, we can think of what responses we need to make to achieve the desired outcome of learning. For example, if a teacher assigns an essay to the student and the student has a purpose and outcome of learning, the student should want to attack the challenge as it will help them learn.

Consider the example of the British rowing team, which competed in the eight-man crew Olympic races in 1992 and 1996 and did not place in either. For the 2000 Sydney Olympics, they decided to do something different. According to Dr. Benjamin Hardy (2022), "With every decision or opportunity, every member of the team asked themselves: WILL IT MAKE THE BOAT GO FASTER?"

(Hardy, 2022). If the event was someone asking them if they wanted to attend an all-night party, they would ask, "Will it make the boat go faster?" (Hardy, 2022). If they determined that it would not, they wouldn't do it. If they were offered more time on the water to practice, they would ask, "Will it make the boat go faster?" If that extra time would increase their speed, they would do it. If they determined that they were already training too hard and this extra time on the water would decrease their speed, they wouldn't do it. Event. Response. Outcome. With this simple method, the team had a process goal which was to do whatever would improve their time, and they made decisions based on this. With this direction on their purpose, the British eights won gold in the 2000 Sydney Olympics (Hardy, 2022).

If you have found your reason for being in education, you have the direction toward which you want to row. If you're serious about your purpose, you will make decisions based on the outcome you want. For example, if you're teaching to help students understand and find joy in mathematics, you will look up or create lessons that will engage and excite them. If the opportunity of going to an innovative mathematics lessons conference comes to your attention, you may want to attend. If it will make the boat go faster, it might be worth the choice. Event. Response. Outcome.

It's the direction and the action of the rowing that really determines the purpose, not the intention alone. Those who have a legitimate purpose have goals, while those who don't have a real purpose have wishes. A wish is something that you want to do, but instead of taking the time to make it happen, you're just hoping that it will come true. On the other hand, someone with a goal has a purpose and makes decisions to move toward it. Unlike a wish, a goal is comprised of a series of decisions that will get you closer to the desired outcome. A goal motivates, making the effort to back up the decisions feel worthwhile.

Being motivated to make decisions based on a purpose can be explained with expectancy-value theory. Researchers from the University of Maryland and the University of Michigan respectively Allan Wigfield and Jacquelynne Eccles (2000) explain the concept, saying, "Theorists in this tradition argue that individuals' choice, persistence, and performance can be explained by their beliefs about how well they will do on the activity and the extent to which they value the activity" (p. 68). Researchers Kelvin Seifert of the University of Manitoba and Rosemary Sutton of Cleveland State (2021) explain more:

> [The model is] sometimes written with a multiplicative formula: expectancy x value = motivation. The relationship between expectation and value is 'multiplicative' rather than additive because, in order to be motivated, it is

necessary for a person to have at least a modest expectation of success and to assign a task at least some positive value. If you have high expectations of success but do not value a task at all (mentally assign it a '0' value), then you will not feel motivated at all. Likewise, if you value a task highly but have no expectation of success about completing it (assign it a '0' expectancy), then you also will not feel motivated at all.

In the case of the 2000 British Olympic eights, they had a high expectation of success (they believed that they could improve enough to be the best in the world) and strongly valued what they were doing; therefore, they remained motivated to achieve their goal of making the boat go faster. It would have been interesting if they didn't have this process goal and, instead, had a result goal of winning a gold medal. Based on the previous two Olympics, where they didn't place, some or all the members of the team might have deemed the expectation of success as too difficult and rated it low, diminishing their motivation. Because they did have a process goal of making the boat go faster, they may have increased their expectation of success (improving boat speed is something that can be achieved daily).

What if students changed to process goals as well? Let's say that, as a student enters high school, they determine that their purpose is to be the valedictorian. After a few weeks in high school, the student sees how hard this will be and starts questioning whether this is possible. This might decrease the student's motivation. If the student gets a B or sees another student with higher grades, the student might lose their expectation of success and, therefore, all motivation. On the other hand, if that same student had a purpose for school to learn or make their family proud, the student's motivation might have a better chance to stay strong. These purposes are things that make the boat go faster. They are things that, with effort, the student can achieve many times throughout a school year. A process goal makes it easier to make decisions that will lead to a desired purpose.

Students will experience situations and events that will test their dedication to their purpose and their motivation. If a student says they have a purpose to learn and a teacher assigns a project, the student can ask, "Will it help me understand the concept?" If the student determines it will and makes the decision to engage in the project to feed their goal, the student either has or is on their way to a solid purpose. Event. Response. Outcome.

The Event-Response-Outcome Tool

Use the tool in figure 3.3 (page 62) to serve as a springboard for a rich class discussion about setting priorities in line with your purpose.

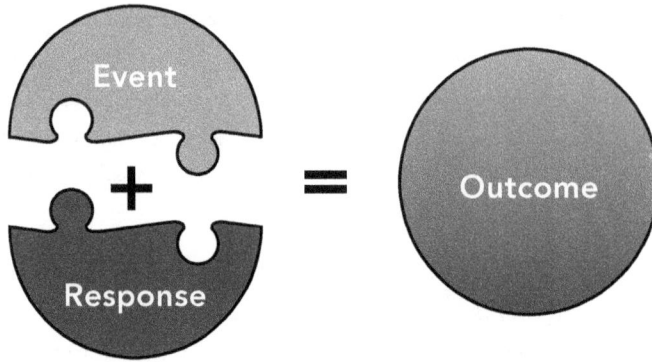

Figure 3.3: Event-response-outcome tool.

*Visit **go.SolutionTree.com/SEL** for a free reproducible version of this figure.*

After reviewing the tool with the class, your peers, or on your own, please use the following questions to discuss and reflect. See appendix A (page 189) for the complete instructions on using the tools in this book.

Questions for Educators and Their Colleagues

Use the following questions to help you discuss the event-response-outcome tool with colleagues to gain a more personal and broader understanding.

- Look at the following scenarios that could happen to you in teaching. What responses could you make to them? What outcomes might come from those responses? Consider the following examples.

  - Seventy percent of your students fail an assessment.

  - A student sasses you in front of the class.

  - Another staff member is rude to you.

  - Your principal tells you that you're going to teach a different grade level or course.

- What is your purpose or reason for teaching? If that is your desired outcome, how would you respond to the aforementioned events?

- How often are your responses based on emotion and how much are they based on logic? Which one is better? Can you have both?

- How might your life be different if you always thought about the outcome you wanted before you responded to events? How do you think that would make you feel?

Questions to Prompt Class Discussion

These are questions to promote class understanding about the tool. This can be done with small- or large-group discussion or by quietly reflecting in a journal.

- Look at the following events. What responses could you make to them, and what outcomes would come from those responses?

  - ◆ You fail an assessment.

  - ◆ Someone writes something bad about you on social media.

  - ◆ You find a wallet on the ground with $200 in it.

  - ◆ Your teacher assigns you a ten-page paper.

  You may want to think of the outcome you want before making a response. If you wanted an outcome to be a person who always works to improve (both in school and as a person), what responses would you make to the aforementioned events?

- Are most of your responses to events based on emotion or logic? How often do you take the time to think logically? How can emotional responses harm or help you?

- What do you want your outcome or purpose for being in school to be? Does your purpose motivate you and make you happy? How serious are you about that purpose? How do you know?

Questions for Student Reflection

After a content-specific lesson that is also an opportunity to assess event-response-outcome, these questions can assist students in evaluating their thoughts and behavior during the lesson as they pertain to the concept.

- What outcome did you want for this challenge? How did your responses lead to that outcome?

- How much control do you have over your responses?

Elementary Teacher Tip

Put students into groups of three to four students and provide each group with a large piece of blank paper and a handful of colored pencils, markers, or crayons. Limit the colors so that some groups only have primary colors, some have all the colors, and one group has only gray, black, brown, or white. Give the class a set time to complete a drawing. When time is up, discuss how groups responded to their limited options and what the outcome was.

- Do you have a consistent outcome you want for school? How important is it to you? How often do you make responses that lead to the outcome you want?

- If you could do this lesson over again, would you respond differently? Why or why not? How would you like to respond to difficult challenges in your life?

Summary

A person without purpose has no direction and, therefore, no reason to put forth effort. A person with a purpose has a goal to strive toward. Two major types of purpose are outcome and process goals. Outcome goals are end results while process goals focus on the actions you are taking to reach the goal. For students, outcome goals may be grades, completion of assignments, graduation, and getting into a specific university. Students with process goals might have an outcome to head toward, but their attention is on the journey and how they are getting there. Outcome goals can get students to work very hard, but these students can experience anxiety and depression when they fail along the way or don't reach their goal. Students with process goals may work hard as well, but they understand that failures are necessary on the journey to improvement. They can also be proud of their improvements even if they don't reach their desired outcome. If a person has a purpose that is important to them (whether it's an outcome or process goal), they will make decisions in life that will help them move closer to that goal.

4

Passion

Passion is energy. Feel the power that comes from focusing on what excites you.

—Oprah Winfrey

Every educator has a story of how they came to be in the classroom. My path to education started with a very intense incident when I was twenty-three years old that sparked my interest in and my journey toward becoming a teacher. A word of caution first: if you've personally endured a trauma, you may find the following account challenging to read.

As I was just drifting off to sleep on a Friday night, a noise made me glance toward my bedroom door. As it slowly creaked open, a hand from outside felt through the dark for the light switch. I jolted up as the light turned on to see a man with a revolver pointed directly at me. Adrenaline coursed through my body. This was the type of thing that happens in movies, I thought; this couldn't be happening to me. But it was.

Within minutes, the intruder tied my hands behind my back, lashed my feet together with rags and shoelaces, and blindfolded me with a pillowcase. I found out later that he had been stalking me for over a year, but that wasn't important in the moment. My immediate purpose at the time was to find a way out of this terrifying situation.

After three hours of negotiation, I tricked him into putting a blanket over me, got my hands undone beneath the covers, and mumbled something to get him to come closer. When he did, I lunged at him, grabbing his wrists with my hands to control him. Although my eyes were still covered, I felt confident that I had the upper hand. When I was in high school, my dad had me wrestle blindfolded on occasion to change my frame of reference. Learning how to wrestle without seeing would make an actual match seem much easier. I would have never guessed that my father's lesson would have such a direct connection to a challenge; however, at the time, I was glad that my dad had gifted me that experience.

As my legs were still tied together, I focused on controlling him and keeping him on the ground as I didn't know where the gun was. After twenty minutes of struggling on the floor, we had moved to the other side of the room where the phone was. Since this was 1996, when we all had landlines, I took the phone cord and wrapped it around his neck, holding it with my left hand. Then, I held his arms down with my elbows, grabbed the phone with my right hand, and dialed 911. Soon after, the police arrived and took him away, leaving me to sit and ponder what had just transpired.

I hope you never do; but, if you have a near-death experience, the aftermath is an interesting process. I was absolutely not okay for weeks and had to work through some very strong emotions. However, because something like this teaches that existence is precious, it offered me the opportunity to reevaluate my life and what I wanted to do with it.

At the time, I had decided on a career in advertising. It seemed like a fun job that would put my psychology degree to work. I was interning at an agency where, the week prior to the false imprisonment, I had been working on a menu for a local barbeque joint where I needed to locate and add interesting facts about armadillos (which, in the internet's infancy, was no easy task). In looking at this career path with a new lens after my incident, I questioned whether I could do more with my life and make a bigger impact. I don't say this to demean the advertising profession; I just didn't feel that my job putting armadillo facts on menus was helping society much. I simply wanted a different purpose, so I decided to pursue education. I didn't want to be a teacher to win awards; instead, my purpose was (and is) to help young people learn lessons like my dad had taught me (namely, to learn to appreciate and take on challenges), which I felt had recently saved my life. I applied to get my master of arts in education degree and teaching credential, enrolling in school the following fall.

The attempted kidnapping added an entirely new layer of emotions to this mix, which had turned my purpose into a full-fledged passion. This passion still gets me up in the morning excited to help students be better versions of themselves. It's even driving me to write this book. If I ever find my purpose waning, I can summon the emotions that I felt throughout the incident and the process that ensued afterward. While anger and fear are two of the emotions I still feel when reliving this event, the emotion that affects me the most is the overwhelming gratitude I feel for the father I had who pushed and supported me until I understood the importance of taking on challenges on my own. That emotional charge helps maintain a passion, refocusing me and compelling me to continue toward my purpose. Introducing students to the idea of passion and helping them learn to find theirs, too, will help them stick to their sense of purpose just like I did.

This chapter covers how emotions might spark intense connection and longevity with our purpose so that it becomes a passion, and how we might regulate our emotions in high-pressure situations while preserving appropriate passion in our daily life.

The Definition of Passion

As is often the case, there are several perspectives on what it means to have passion. According to the Online Etymology Dictionary, the root of the word *passion* (n.d.b) comes "from Late Latin passionem (nominative passio) 'suffering, enduring,' from past-participle stem of Latin pati 'to endure, undergo, experience'. . . The notion is 'that which must be endured.'" Merriam-Webster's defines *passion* (passion, n.d.a) as "a strong feeling of enthusiasm or excitement for something or about doing something." While Merriam-Webster's definition seems more accurate, the etymology and older definitions can still help.

If you are passionate about something, it's not always sunshine and roses. In his book *Missing Pieces: 52 Vital Lessons Our Kids Should Be Learning at School (But Aren't)*, former teacher and author Jaime Richards (2016) discusses passion, noting the difference between pleasures and passions: *pleasures*, he says, make you feel good and do not require effort. *Passions*, on the other hand, are enjoyable but take a great deal of work. Richards (2016) writes:

> The truth is, a lot of time we hate our passions. Even though they can provide massive joy, they are equally capable of causing searing pain. A passion causes an intense emotion but not always an enjoyable one. Rage, frustration and sorrow are generated by passion. (p. 25)

Passion can bring us our most emotional highs, but it can also give us our lowest lows. Sports fans understand this—they are jubilant when their team does well and demoralized when it doesn't. Also, you can potentially develop passions through joy, anger, or other emotions. If learning to play piano better makes you joyful, that could spark and maintain a passion. Similarly, seeing a documentary about children who are food insecure could make you sad or angry, creating a fire within you that fuels a purpose to help those children or others like them.

Challenge is inherent with purpose, and emotions (the root of passion) are inherent with challenge. If you are pursuing a purpose, you will have to challenge yourself, sacrificing time and effort to make that purpose happen. If the challenges are difficult enough, you will likely ride a roller coaster of emotions—joy, for example, when you figure something out and frustration when you can't learn how to conquer the challenge in the moment. These emotions are important and make life exciting. Without challenge and effort, there are fewer or no emotions. This is another great reason for a teacher to issue appropriately challenging lessons for their students—you elicit emotions that can spark and cultivate passions.

The Productive Power of Passion

Passion is tricky but cultivating it in students could lead to a new level of motivation. If students can couple emotion with their purpose, they will work harder through more and more difficult challenges. Consider the following vignette in which Janna is a senior in high school who navigates the ups and downs of her passion.

Janna was not entirely sure where her passion for science started; it might have been when, in elementary school, she put a lot of time and effort into a weather cycle project. She received a lot of praise from her teacher, peers, and parents; but she mostly remembered the joy and pride that came along with figuring something out and understanding it enough where she could demonstrate her newfound knowledge.

Janna's passion for science stayed with her, but it wasn't always joyful. She challenged herself inside and outside of class with science to test her limits and learn more. There were times when she struggled and got frustrated, wanting to give up. In these times, she reminded herself that what made the journey of learning so incredible was that it had obstacles and challenges in it; and she thought about the feeling she got when she finally figured out the weather cycle several years prior. With these two tactics, she could turn her anger and frustration into a smile, turning her negative emotions into positive ones.

Science was something Janna planned to continue to pursue through college and beyond. It was something she loved, but it didn't define her. She spent a lot of time with science, but she was mindful about how much time she spent. Most important, science challenged Janna and provoked both positive and negative emotions that excited her. She felt alive.

Emotions are a necessary part of passion. You may have a purpose for your life or an activity; however, if that purpose is devoid of emotion, you may have a difficult time being passionate about it. Robert J. Vallerand (2012), an expert on motivational processes and professor of social psychology at University of Quebec at Montreal, defines *passion* as "a strong inclination toward a self-defining activity that people like (or even love), find important, and in which they invest time and energy on a regular basis" (p. 1). In other words, passions are activities that we have a meaningful and involved relationship with. It would be very difficult to have a meaningful and involved relationship without emotion.

Emotions are difficult to describe and discuss because they come from a different part of the brain than our logic and language centers. There are several theories of emotions like James-Lange theory (Cherry, 2020), Cannon-Bard theory (Nickerson, 2021), Schachter-Singer theory (Hopper, 2019), and others that attempt to explain how and why we have emotions, but none of these theories are certain. Many of them have rightly received criticism for overgeneralizing the complicated subject of our feelings. What we do know, however, is that emotions are a very crucial part of our lives. Looking at emotions in a positive sense, they keep us alive, they give us power, they motivate, and they can make life more purposeful and exciting. However, life can be a mess if we experience too many negative emotions.

We all have emotions when we experience something meaningful. We don't know when they'll hit or how they'll make us feel, but emotions could kickstart a passion. In his book *Can't Hurt Me*, David Goggins (2018) describes how watching the movie *Rocky* sparked his passion, specifically the scene of round fourteen of the boxing match between Rocky Balboa and Apollo Creed (Avildsen, 1976). In that scene, Rocky, who Creed battered for thirteen rounds, gets knocked down yet again. Though his coach is telling him to stay down, Rocky gets to his feet again. Apollo, who is in the opposite corner, just shakes his head; he can't believe that someone would keep coming forward after the pounding he's taken. Apollo shaking his head along with the Rocky theme music in the background stirred something in Goggins. That emotion sparked his passion to be someone who was always going to keep coming regardless of how many times the world knocked him down. This feeling drove Goggins to challenge himself by participating in events that would challenge even the toughest people on the planet.

This mindset translates well to classroom learning. As an educator, you can help create these moments for students. For example, if a student is legitimately working hard on a difficult task and they improve, you can give them praise, telling them how proud of them you are. However, make sure you are not simply applauding students for effort alone. Christine Gross-Loh (2021) interviews Carol Dweck about misunderstandings of her growth mindset. Dweck shares that parents and educators with only a rudimentary understanding of her concept started to praise any effort in their children or students, which does not promote growth mindset. Dweck says:

> Teachers were just praising effort that was not effective, saying 'Wow, you tried really hard.' But students know that if they didn't make progress and you're praising them, it's a consolation prize. They also know you think they can't do any better . . . When you focus on effort, [you have to] show how effort created learning progress or success . . . A lot of parents or teachers say praise the effort, not the outcome. I say [that's] wrong: Praise the effort that led to the outcome of learning progress; tie the praise to it. It's not just effort, but strategy . . . so support the student in finding another strategy. Effective teachers who actually have classrooms full of children with a growth mindset are always supporting children's learning strategies and showing how strategies created their success. (as cited in Gross-Loh, 2021)

If you are praising student effort that is helping them further their learning process, it can lead to an upwelling of pride in the student. Some students may ignore this, but it also may elicit positive emotion that sparks a passion toward the subject, school, or taking on difficult tasks.

As a teacher, you can also summon negative emotions in students to spark passion. For example, you may expose students to some injustice going on in the world. Again, some students will not connect with it; but others might have an emotional reaction. Even though the emotion might likely be perceived as negative (like anger or sadness), it may kickstart a passion in certain students to want to help others.

Once a passion has begun, students must pursue it. Again, passions are not the same as pleasures; they entail a lot of time and effort. If that time and effort is starting to feel fruitless and empty, it may be wise for students to feel the initial emotion again that got you to be passionate about the activity in the beginning. As teachers, we could be aware of this. Many of us have a purpose for teaching and an emotional attachment to that purpose. In times when you feel that your passion is lacking, you may want to relive that emotion that helped spark it in the first place. It may rekindle that feeling and reignite your passion.

Emotional Regulation and Passion

While pursuing passions, students will feel emotions. Vallerand (2012) shares that people experience positive and negative emotions while pursuing a passion. As you follow your passion, you will experience joy and face hardships. "The absence of psychological stressors does not ensure thriving in one's life. It merely reduces the likelihood of suffering" (Vallerand, 2012, p. 1). If students are going to fully immerse themselves into a passion and they are going to thrive in it, they will experience failures, stressors, and suffering. These things will likely elicit negative emotions, but students can turn them into positive ones.

Being able to alter which emotions you have, when you have them, and how you experience them is called *emotional regulation*. Stanford psychologist James Gross and UC Berkeley psychologist Oliver John (2003) argue that two methods of regulation exist: suppression and reappraisal. *Suppression*, as you can imagine, is when you take an emotion you are actively feeling (mostly negative) and try to push it back down and repress it until it goes away. The problem is that it doesn't go away. You can suppress it for a while, but it will fester and find ways to get back at you for ignoring it (more on this in chapter 6: Courage, page 99). With *reappraisal*, you look at your situation and try to view it from a different vantage point to see if you can change the emotion. For example, if you are taking care of an infant, you might be up at all hours with a crying baby. Because of all this work and lack of sleep, you might feel sad or frustrated. If you reappraise the situation and tell yourself that you've always wanted children and you get to spend more time with this little, beautiful baby, you might be able to change your emotion to joy or adoration. Students may receive a difficult assessment in class that leads to multiple failures, which starts to bring out negative emotions like anger and frustration. However, if the students reappraise, they can find joy in knowing that only the best challenges include multiple failures that will lead to learning and a worthwhile amount of pride.

Gross and John (2003) add, "Reappraisers experience and express greater positive emotion and lesser negative emotion, whereas suppressors experience and express less positive emotion, yet experience greater negative emotion" (p. 348). In other words, students who can reappraise experience positive emotions while they take on challenges and should be happier and more joyful. While negative emotions can lead to passion, positive emotions should lead to passion and happier students. Researchers Ariane St-Louis, Maylys Rapaport, Léandre Chénard Poirier, Robert Vallerand, and Stéphane Dandeneau (2021) add even more reasons to lean toward reappraisal:

> [Our] findings underscore that individuals who use cognitive reappraisal tend to be more satisfied with their lives, be more optimistic, show higher levels of environmental mastery, autonomy, and personal growth, reveal greater self-acceptance, have more positive relationships, have a clearer sense of purpose in life and show fewer symptoms of depression. (p. 1794)

Students who find their passion for something will, eventually, run into some negative emotions. It seems to be a much better solution for them to reappraise the situation and alter emotion than to shove it down and pretend it doesn't exist. While reappraisal looks to be a viable option for students, teachers can also use it to experience motivation and satisfaction in their profession. See the following scenario for an example.

> *Mr. Wold's purpose for teaching is to help students get closer to their potential. He's had days where he'll see a student increase their efforts and try very hard on a class challenge, which makes him happy and elated and feeds his purpose. He's also had days where certain students are clearly and purposely off task and trying to pull others down with them. In those situations, his initial reaction is anger. All he wants to do is yell at the student. He thinks to himself, "Why would they do this to me when I'm just trying to help them and make them better?"*
>
> *He could suppress his anger and stay calm in the moment, but in this case, he knows he'll probably take it out on his family when he gets home. Instead of these responses, he regulates his anger, looking at the situation in a different way. Mr. Wold tells himself, "My purpose is to help students get closer to their potential, and no one said that was going to be easy. In fact, it'll be good for me to try to work with this student. I'm grateful that this student is acting this way so I can learn how to help this student and future students who demonstrate similar behavioral challenges improve. I love the challenge! Let's do this!" Instead of anger, Mr. Wold reappraises his emotion as excitement and approaches the student with a new attitude.*

For teachers, this is a good beginning, but remember that the goal is also to instill passion and skills of reappraisal. If a teacher assigns a complicated paper, an automatic emotional reaction for students may be anger or fear, knowing that the paper is going to take effort and time and lead to an evaluation. If the student has a solid purpose for school (say, learning), they can potentially reappraise this emotion, looking at their goal instead. If they truly want to learn, this paper is a challenge that can help them do that. If they look at the situation in this way, they can react emotionally in a very different and more positive way.

Passion affords all people more opportunities to work on and improve their emotional-regulation skills. Ariane C. St-Louis of the University of Quebec and colleagues (2021) say, "because passionate individuals experience positive and negative emotions while engaging in the activity that they deeply care about . . . it was proposed that they should be more likely to make use of emotional-regulation strategies" (p. 1791). Every time you see students display a negative emotion during a challenge, you should encourage them through guidance and modeling how they might rethink the situation—turning that emotion into a positive one. This, unto itself, is a great reason to take on challenges and experience negative emotions.

Harmonious Passion and Obsessive Passion

Helping students find their passion by designing engaging activities to explore their interests during class might not just help them improve their efforts in school; it may also be good for their mental health. Vallerand (2012) says, "having a passion for an activity represents an important type of high involvement in activities that may lead to sustainable positive effects on psychological well-being" (p. 1). If you have a passion, you are likely to experience more challenges to feed that passion. If you experience more challenges, you will likely feel more emotion. If you can reappraise that emotion, you have a good chance of being happier. Those without passion don't tend to push themselves and don't challenge themselves, leading to fewer emotions and fewer opportunities to experience joy.

It's important to be aware of which type of passion you are striving toward to remain happy with passion. Vallerand (2012) offers a dualistic model of passion which consists of *harmonious passion* and *obsessive passion*:

> The model proposes the existence of two types of passion: harmonious and obsessive. Harmonious passion originates from an autonomous internalization of the activity into one's identity while obsessive passion emanates from a controlled internalization and comes to control the person. Through the experience of positive emotions during activity engagement that takes place on a regular and repeated basis, it is posited that harmonious passion contributes to sustained psychological well-being while preventing the experience of negative affect, psychological conflict, and ill-being. Obsessive passion is not expected to produce such positive effects and may even facilitate negative affect, conflict with other life activities, and psychological ill-being. (p. 1)

Harmonious passions are part of the individual's life that they choose to pursue—they are the things they get to do. Those with harmonious passions also can garner joyful emotions during and after challenges associated with their passion.

Vallerand (2012) adds that "people with a harmonious passion should be able to fully focus on the task at hand and experience positive outcomes both during (e.g., flow, positive affect, concentration) and after task engagement (e.g., satisfaction, general positive affect)" (p. 4). (We get into flow in chapter 9, page 171, but know for now that it's a wonderful way to take your mind off ego and experience joy.) If you've had a joyful experience through challenge, you will likely be satisfied and grateful when it's over. Even if you had a negative emotion during a challenge, you are likely to look back on the experience with positive emotion for a couple of reasons: (1) you are no longer suffering as you did during the challenge, and (2) you are proud of yourself and satisfied with your efforts (especially if you pushed yourself during the challenge).

Conversely, obsessive passion controls the person. They become their passion, and their self-worth is tied to success or failure within the passion. It's not something they choose to do; it's something they must do. Obsessive passions lead to several negative outcomes because the person neglects or puts to the side all other parts of their life to pursue the passion. They may experience negative emotions during a task associated with their passion and afterward.

An example of the dual passions might be a student who is a softball player. If that softball player has an obsessive passion, they only see themselves as a softball player. How they do at practice and games reflects how they feel about themselves. If they do well and win, they feel good. If they make mistakes and lose, they feel poorly. They feel that they must train; it's not a choice. Because they must do softball, they neglect their relationships, school, and other important aspects of their life. In other words, they are a victim to their sport. They may be sad or angry when they are not doing well, and they may remain that way afterward, thinking about the things that weren't right or perfect.

On the other hand, a softball player with a harmonious passion looks at the sport differently. They love to play softball, but it's just one part of their life. They feel compelled to practice, but they are in control. They may find joy during practice or games because they are choosing to do what they love to do. After competition, they can be pleased with their efforts and equally pleased with identifying areas to grow.

If a student begins to form a passion in something and show success, many peers and adults may want to pigeonhole them into that interest or activity. Fellow students might only want to talk with the student about the passion and introduce the student as "Jennifer the softball player." Parents might create social media pages to display their child's skill at something and post about the child's successes and triumphs. This treatment may make the student think that their passion is now their identity, and thus base their self-worth on whether they are successful or not. That's a lot of pressure, and it could lead to a deleterious effect. As an educator, it is important to understand that students will have passions; but we must be aware that their passions do not define who they are. Again, let's make sure passions are something students get to do rather than must do and their self-worth is not completely tied up with their passion. If you notice a student in class who is miserable and sad as they pursue something important to them, it might be important to have a talk with them to learn if they are in control of their passion or their passion controls them. You may explain harmonious and obsessive passions to them and suggest that they take a break from the activity.

The Emotion and Challenge Tool

We experience more emotion through challenge than we would if we didn't challenge ourselves. Emotions may be different before, during, and after a challenge. If challenges elicit negative emotions before, during, and after a challenge, we can reappraise these emotions to something positive. Use the tool in figure 4.1 to serve as a springboard for a class discussion about using and altering emotions.

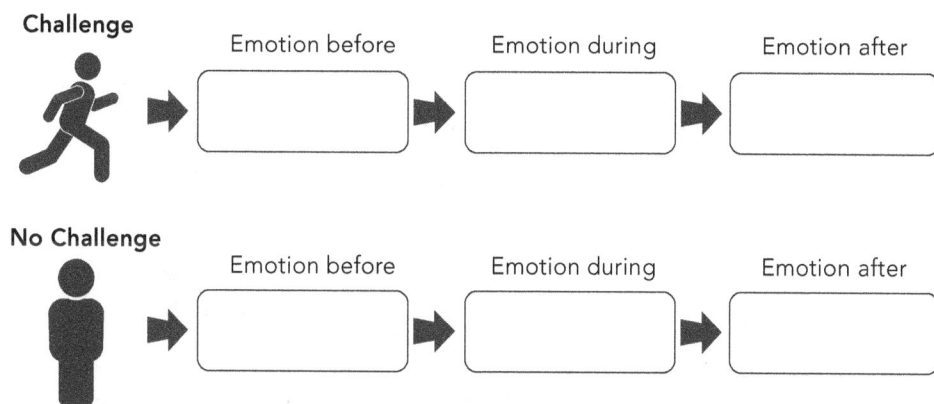

Challenge   Emotion before   Emotion during   Emotion after

No Challenge   Emotion before   Emotion during   Emotion after

Figure 4.1: Emotion and challenge tool.

*Visit **go.SolutionTree.com/SEL** for a free reproducible version of this figure.*

After reviewing the tool with the class, your peers, or on your own, please use the following questions to discuss and reflect. See appendix A (page 189) for the complete instructions on using the tools in this book.

Questions for Educators and Their Colleagues

Use the following questions to help you discuss the emotion and challenge tool with colleagues to gain a more personal and broader understanding.

- Are emotions a good thing or a bad thing? How do they make life more interesting or less interesting?

- Think of a time in your teaching career when you challenged yourself. What emotions did you have before, during, and after the challenge?

- Think of a time unrelated to teaching when you challenged yourself. What emotions did you have before, during, and after the challenge?

- What kind of emotions do you have when you don't challenge yourself?

- If you have a negative emotion (anger, sadness) before, during, or after a challenge, can you reassess the situation and turn it into a positive emotion? If so, how do you do that?

- If an unruly student is your challenge, what emotions do you have? If it is a negative emotion, can you reassess that situation to change it to a positive emotion? What could you tell yourself to make that happen?

- Think of something that you're passionate about (something you spend several hours a week on that takes a lot of effort). How are emotions related to this endeavor?

Questions to Prompt Class Discussion

These are questions to promote class understanding about the tool. This can be done with small- or large-group discussion or by quietly reflecting in a journal.

- Are emotions a good thing or a bad thing?

- How many emotions do you have when you challenge yourself versus when you don't challenge yourself? How much more interesting is life with challenges than without? If you challenge yourself in school, is it more fun? Why or why not?

- Think of a time when you really challenged yourself outside of school. What emotions did you have before, during, and after the challenge?

- Think of a time when you really challenged yourself in school. What emotions did you have before, during, and after the challenge?

- What kind of emotions do you have when you don't challenge yourself?

- If you have a negative emotion (anger, sadness) before, during, and after a challenge, can you look at the situation differently and turn it into a positive emotion? If so, how do you do that?

- Do you have a passion (something you choose to spend at least six to eight hours per week on)? If so, how are emotions related to it?

Questions for Student Reflection

After a content-specific lesson that is also an opportunity to assess emotion and challenge, these questions can assist students in evaluating their thoughts and behavior during the lesson as they pertain to the concept.

- What kind of emotions did you have before, during, and after a challenge? Why do you think this is?

- Do you have more emotions if you challenge yourself or if you don't challenge yourself? Explain why it is better to have emotions or not have emotions.

- If you have negative emotions, is it possible to turn them into positive emotions? If so, describe how.

- What is a passion? What is the connection between emotions and passion? If someone wanted advice on how to become passionate about school, what would you tell them?

Summary

Everyone has emotions. This can be a good thing when taking on challenges. When a student pursues a purpose, they challenge themselves. The effort students exert on a challenge leads to both negative and positive emotions before, during, and after the challenge. When students experience negative emotions, they can either suppress them or reappraise them. By reappraising, students can turn negative emotions into positive ones. Whether positive or not, these emotions make life more exciting. A life without emotion would be boring. Additionally, passionate students doggedly pursue their purpose because their emotional connection to it pushes them. It's important to note that a passionate student will fall into one of two categories: (1) obsessive passion or (2) harmonious passion. Those who are obsessive feel that their passion is their

Elementary Teacher Tip

Give students an academic task that is difficult or new and let them struggle through it. For example, ask elementary-grade students to write a complete paragraph with a topic sentence and supporting details for the first time with no additional guidance from you. You might want to set up a designated space in the classroom for students who are overwhelmingly frustrated to do jumping jacks or other physical activity to take a break from the task. In the middle of the task, ask students what emotions they are feeling. If their emotions are negative, ask students how they might reassess their emotion to something positive. Students who are enjoying the difficult task may even begin helping other students. Do not move on until every student completes the task in whatever way they can and celebrate everyone's success.

identity that they must pursue. Students who are harmonious understand that they are someone who chooses to participate in their passion and that their failures and successes in it do not define who they are.

5

Positive Mindset

Nothing can stop the man with the right mental attitude from achieving his goal; nothing on earth can help the man with the wrong mental attitude.

—Thomas Jefferson

As I stared down the two-hundred-pound tire, I didn't think it was going to be a positive outcome. It had been about a year since my stroke, and I'd returned to our school's obstacle course to get back in shape. I had been to the course twice in the previous two weeks, but I purposely skipped the tire.

For the tire portion of the workout, the racer is supposed to flip a heavier-than-most tractor tire twice. If done correctly, you work as many fingers as you can underneath, bend your knees, and lift straight up. At that point, most people will slide one knee under the elevated side of the tire to hold it up. Then, you work your palms underneath to extend your arms and legs to shove it over.

Before my stroke, this was always a difficult but doable task for me. Now, I wasn't too sure. I thought about all the things going against me: I just had a stroke less than a year ago. The tire is too heavy. I haven't been training. I can't do this.

As I sidled up to the tire with these thoughts in mind, I assumed correct lifting position but lacked confidence. I tried to lift, but it was a sad attempt; my muscles fired but with little to no force behind them—as if they were being restrained. I didn't even move it an inch off the ground.

I backed off, vigorously shook my head to clear it, and then flipped my negative thoughts. Instead of "I can't," I started telling myself, "You've got this! You're super tough for taking this on based on the recent past. You're going to dominate this thing!"

The second time, I approached the tire with positive thoughts and newfound confidence. This time, I lifted it easily. The sole difference was a matter of positive mindset.

If curriculum you teach is a two-hundred-pound tire, how are your students approaching it? If they're consumed with fear of not doing well (perhaps based on previous experiences or a mindset they have fallen into out of habit), your students' mindset may negatively affect their work in class. If students approach their problems with more optimism using an intentional mindset, it'll reframe the challenge as something that will bring them valuable experience. In this chapter, we'll review research and studies on optimism, gratitude, joy, and an overall positive mindset to find out how students can use positive thinking to achieve great things. This chapter includes two tools that will help you and students determine how positive they would like to be and how they might do that.

The Definition of Positive Mindset

While a positive mindset is highly personal to the individual, there are commonalities that those with intentionally positive mindsets share. Students who may have fallen into the pattern of thinking negatively or fearfully may not even know they are experiencing the effects of their own mindset. Simply alerting them to the fact that they can change how they think about things can be revolutionary. Author and expert on leadership psychology Tony Robbins (n.d.) says:

> Positive thinking is an emotional and mental attitude that focuses on the good and expects results that will benefit you. It's about anticipating happiness, health and success instead of expecting the worst . . . This mindset creates a positive feedback loop that brings even more good into your life.

A positive mindset includes thoughts of optimism, gratitude, and joy. These things will help you believe that you can do something, see the purpose or the reason in doing it, and create positive, happy feelings respectively. These are not guarantees of success, and too much optimism, gratitude, and joy could lead to problems; but not enough of a positive mindset can lead to giving up, seeing no reason in pursuing something challenging, and depression. The following sections explore two facets of a positive mindset: optimism and gratitude.

The Definition of Optimism

Optimism, the belief that everything is going to work out well, is crucial in taking on challenge. A student must believe they can do something, or they won't even try. While working toward a difficult challenge, students may have doubts. They'll convince themselves that it's too hard and it can't be done, leading them to quit before they start. In my tire example, my negative thoughts held me back. I may have assumed the lifting position and "attempted" to lift the tire, but my thoughts doomed me from the start. Like that situation, students may look at a subject, teacher, or school as hopeless. If a student, instead, is optimistic about their chances of success, they will likely persist more. To help students become more optimistic, you can share stories of others dealing with similar or greater challenges who gained success, you can write inspirational quotes on the board and discuss them, you can have them repeat a positive mantra, or you can lead them in a visualization exercise where they productively struggle with a particular challenge to a successful outcome.

Optimism is not a cure-all. Researchers Elizabeth Tenney, Jennifer Logg, and Don Moore (2015) ran several experiments using age tests, mathematics tests, and the book *Where's Waldo?* to learn whether optimism leads to success (Handford, 2012). Most subjects tend to overestimate optimism's relationship with success: "People may misattribute success to optimism, or at least attribute more of the variance in success to optimism than it deserves" (Tenney et al., 2015, p. 394). In the experiment where subjects must find Waldo, a specific character in a scene with a lot of people and action going on, Tenney and colleagues (2015) contend, "Experiencers in the high optimism condition spent longer looking for Waldo on the *Where's Waldo?* test than experiencers in the low optimism condition. However, their persistence did not lead to a drastic performance on the test" (p. 389). Optimism can lead to more effort, but it doesn't guarantee success.

A student, for example, may vary in levels of optimism regarding a mathematics test. If they're too optimistic, they may not put in the necessary effort to understand the content, thinking the test will be too easy. If the student is too pessimistic about a test, they may find themselves giving up, thinking the test is going to be impossible. The level of optimism could be somewhere in the middle or tilted toward optimism, where the student is confident but not too confident. To help students find a balance, educator Ginna Guiang-Myers (2019) suggests teaching realistic optimism by positive reframing (reappraising pessimism as optimism), selective focus (having students turn their attention toward positive "thoughts and events that lead to action-oriented solutions"), averting catastrophizing (not allowing students to go to the worst-case scenario), and using humor to counteract negative thoughts.

The Definition of Gratitude

Gratitude is seeing the good in every endeavor. Any challenge a student takes on will have both positives and negatives. Working through challenges toward a goal will help students learn, but it also takes a lot of effort and sacrifice. If students are thankful for these challenges and see them as opportunities, they see the good in them. If students see the good in a challenge, their likelihood of persevering is amplified. Not seeing a positive reason for doing something leads to a lack of effort.

Researchers Gloria Bernabé-Valero, José Salvador Blasco-Magraner, and Carmen Moret-Tatay (2019) study the effect gratitude has on young musicians' motivation. They observe that "individuals that regard the opportunity to study music as a gift, and therefore feel grateful, will be those that dedicate the most effort to music" (Bernabé-Valero et al., 2019, p. 5). In this study, those who were grateful and thankful for the experience of practicing music tended to also be more motivated. If your students view your class with gratitude, they will see it as an opportunity and should put forth more effort because of it.

Finally, the *APA Dictionary of Psychology* (joy, n.d.) defines *joy* as an emotion that elicits "a feeling of extreme gladness, delight, or exultation of the spirit arising from a sense of well-being or satisfaction." Students may think that joy and school are mutually exclusive, but they don't have to be. Teachers can help with this by making lessons more interesting, meaningful, and fun. Students can also take control of their learning, creating joy for themselves by challenging themselves and making their learning journey entertaining.

Positivity, Optimism, and Gratitude

How long your students are willing to work through a challenge or struggle can depend significantly on their ability to feel positive about their chances. In 1957, Curt Richter led a rather morbid but powerful study with Norwegian rats. He took both domesticated and wild rats, forcibly holding them so they couldn't move to corral them before putting them in eight-inch-diameter and thirty-six-inch-deep glass cylinders filled with water and no means of escape. Then, he timed how long it took them to drown. All thirty-four of the wild rats that researchers perceived as the better swimmers drowned within one to fifteen minutes. Three of the twelve domesticated rats drowned within minutes as well, while the other nine swam between sixty and eighty hours before they gave up.

The difference between a few minutes and eighty hours was significant, so Richter tried to hypothesize a reason. In his opinion, the answer was hope (or lack thereof). He explains:

> The situation of these rats scarcely seems one demanding fight or flight—
> it is rather one of hopelessness; whether they are restrained in the hand or
> confined in the swimming jar, the rats are in a situation against which they
> have no defense. This reaction of hopelessness is shown by some wild rats
> very soon after being grasped in the hand and prevented from moving; they
> seem literally to "give up." (Richter, 1957, p. 196)

Richter was saying that the nine long-lasting domesticated rats were optimistic—they felt that, if they tread water long enough, a human might save them. Wild rats who were captured only a day before, on the other hand, had only a negative experience with humans and had no hope that they would be saved. They were hopeless, and they gave up. Based on its cruelty, this experiment should never be replicated. But it does show a stark distinction that I believe equates to the human experience: People who feel their circumstances are hopeless are unlikely to fight through adversity, while those who feel a sense of hope will continue striving much, much longer (Smith, 2021b).

Children and teens are certainly not rats; however, this phenomenon can potentially parallel the way students think in school. University of Houston researcher Matthew W. Gallagher along with Susana C. Marques and Shane J. Lopez (2016) studied self-efficacy, engagement, and hope in college students to see if they positively affected success in college. Of the three traits, the authors said, "Hope uniquely predicted the number of enrolled semesters, whether students returned for the second semester of college, whether students graduated in 4 years, and students' GPAs across 4 years of college" (Gallagher et al., 2016, p. 341). The study shows that, with college students, hope leads to better grades and more persistence in college, the academic equivalent of treading water longer than others.

If students believe they can't do something, they give up. If students believe they can, they persevere. As a teacher, it may be your biggest role to instill hope in students and get them to believe that, with effort, they are capable of much more than they think. This belief is called *optimism*.

Optimism

In the world of psychology, Martin Seligman is the one who popularized the word *optimism*. Like Richter, Seligman and his colleague Steven Maier (1976) became interested in this area through an experiment on two groups of animals involving electric shocks that was, at best, marginally less cruel than the rat experiment. One group of dogs experienced an environment where shocks were present but avoidable, and one did not. As both groups became acclimated to their respective environments, the second group soon stopped trying to escape the shocks.

The animals simply laid down and accepted their fate, even after the researchers enabled a safe (shock-free) zone in the environment. Maier and Seligman (1976) called this acceptance of a negative fate *learned helplessness.*

Learned helplessness is not just a phenomenon specific to canines. Many studies discuss learned helplessness among students in school and what causes it. For example, University of Messina researcher Pina Filippello along with Neil Harrington, Sebastian Costa, Caterina Buzzai, and Luana Sorrenti (2018) study the impact of a mother's behavior on learned helplessness. Looking at 214 high school students, the researchers find that "maternal psychological control positively predicts frustration intolerance, and that in turn, frustration intolerance positively predicts school learned helplessness" (p. 360). This is one potential cause of learned helplessness in students; there are many more.

Unfortunately, you will have students whose lived experiences have conditioned them to feel learned helplessness. Maybe a student initially tries to solve mathematics problems but can't complete them fast enough to keep up with the class. Instead of persevering, they put their head down on the desk during mathematics lessons and simply give up. Maybe they try to run the mile for the first two times in physical education and find that they can't finish without walking. They could continue to practice on and improve in the mile, but they see completing it without walking as impossible. Therefore, they give up and choose to walk the entire mile or make an excuse to not participate. The thinking usually goes, "Why try when I will never be able to do it?" As teachers, we might experience learned helplessness as well. Think of a time when you tried to teach a concept or work with a student or class who continually struggled to grasp it. Did you continue to persevere to find a way? Or did you conclude it simply can't be done and stop trying? For how long did you continue the effort?

Seligman (2018) understood that some people experience learned helplessness, and he wanted to counteract it:

> The optimists and the pessimists: I have been studying them for the past twenty-five years. The defining characteristic of pessimists is that they tend to believe bad events will last a long time, will undermine everything they do, and are their own fault. The optimists, who are confronted with the same hard knocks of this world, think about misfortune in the opposite way. They tend to believe defeat is just a temporary setback, that its causes are confined to this one case. . . . Such people are unfazed by defeat. Confronted by a bad situation, they perceive it as a challenge and try harder. (p. 5)

In 1998, as president of the APA, Seligman's studies on optimism led him to issue a plea to the organization to favor positive rather than negative experiments and studies (as cited in Achor, 2018). This sparked an entire field, called *positive psychology*, which *Psychology Today* staff (n.d.c) defines as "a branch of psychology focused on the character strengths and behaviors that allow individuals to build a life of meaning and purpose—to move beyond surviving to flourishing." This outlook shifts the focus from looking at what's wrong to seeing what people do right so that it can be replicated.

It wasn't long until the school community found benefit in positive psychology. Ohio State researcher Wayne Hoy along with C. John Tarter and Anita Woolfolk Hoy (2006) study academic optimism, a schoolwide belief from students, faculty, and parents that the students will succeed. In studying ninety-six U.S. high schools in the Midwest, the researchers narrowed academic optimism into three categories: (1) academic emphasis, (2) collective efficacy, and (3) faculty trust. To test these three categories, the researchers had teachers rate how important academics are to the school community, how much an entire school staff feels they affect student learning, and how much parents and students trust the faculty. Those schools who rated higher also showed higher standardized test scores. Interestingly, this correlation was the same for schools at different socioeconomic levels. The study shows that if a school staff makes academics important, believes that they can assist all students in learning, and gains the trust of the school community, the school will be academically optimistic and see gains in student learning.

This can also play out in your individual classroom. When teachers think that students aren't capable of learning, when they see a hopeless situation, the temptation to give up grows and that affects students' own mindset toward their learning, making it easier for them to give up too. But as a teacher, if you believe that all your students can improve and adopt instructional practices that demonstrate that belief, you will gain the trust of your class and have a higher likelihood of student gains. Optimism matters here because, through genuine optimism, your students will know that you are authentic in your desire to focus on process-driven learning and in their ability to learn. Through the resulting collective success of effective instruction and student gains, you will find that putting more effort into teaching doesn't require quite so much . . . well, effort. Likewise, your infectious belief in students helps them believe in themselves.

Gratitude

Gratitude also has a significant impact on this cycle. Every event that happens to students can produce both positive and negative thoughts, giving them either gratitude or ungratefulness. Like optimism, gratitude can determine how much effort a student will put forth. For example, a sophomore might be enrolled in a mathematics class after they failed it freshman year. They could look at the negative potential of this situation and be ungrateful for a class that they think will be another waste of their time. If they focus on this, they may not even try— it's a lost cause that doesn't warrant their time and effort. Instead, if they look at the situation with gratitude, they can view this course as a challenge and an opportunity to improve their mathematics skills and perseverance. With these thoughts, they can be thankful for this situation, seeing the good in it. It's not an easy sell but, if students focus on the positive instead of the negative, they may put more effort into the course and be grateful for the challenge. See the following scenario for an example of an educator leading a class on reframing situations through optimism.

> Mr. Fern knew that every event had both positive and negative associations, but he felt that many students in his class seemed to focus too much on the negative. He noticed that, whenever he introduced a project, paper, or assessment in class, his students greeted him with a chorus of groans. Therefore, he decided to play the Eternal Optimist Game to try to shift their focus to more positive thoughts and gratitude.
>
> "OK, class, let's play a game. I'm going to give you a situation, and you're going to be an eternal optimist. I want you to see if you can find the good in anything. To this end, you'll start every response with 'That's great because . . . .' I want you to see something to be grateful or thankful for in every event. Who wants to give it a go? I'll pick a card."
>
> Mr. Fern pulled out a stack of cards with his students' names on them. He shuffled the cards, drew one from the deck, and invited that student to play.
>
> Mr. Fern started, "We're going to have a party this afternoon."
>
> The student responded, "That's great because we all get to have fun."
>
> Mr. Fern: "Your parent is going to have you start to go to bed at 9:00 p.m. every night."
>
> "That's great because I need more sleep, and I'll be more awake during class. Also, I don't really need to be on my phone at night."
>
> "We're going to start exercising every day."
>
> "That's great because I get to be in better shape and healthier."
>
> "We have a ten-page paper this unit."
>
> "That's great because I get to learn more about something, I get to learn how to write a paper, and I'll be proud of myself when I'm done."

"Great! I'm going to use the cards to put you in groups of four. I want you to play this game to see if you can stump each other. When we're done, I want to ask you these questions: Is there any situation that you can't look at positively and with gratitude? How positive or negative are you with situations that come up in your life? Can you change how positive you are (and is it even worth it)?"

A student with a positive mindset is going to be a student who sees the good in most situations. This takes self-awareness and practice but being more positive, optimistic, and grateful can, potentially, make a student happier and elicit more effort. If someone is negative, pessimistic, and ungrateful, they don't see a reason for trying (it's just going to end badly and isn't worth my time), and they give up.

The Positivity Meter Tool

A positive mindset includes both optimism and gratitude. Optimism is thinking that everything will work out in the end. Gratitude is seeing the good in something so that you appreciate it. If you aren't optimistic for a challenge, you don't think you will ever succeed, and you end up quitting. If you aren't grateful, you see no good reason for persevering in a challenge. Both optimism and gratitude together are the foundation of positivity and can help you and your students start and persist on a challenge. Use the tool in figure 5.1 to serve as a springboard for a rich class discussion about gratitude and optimism.

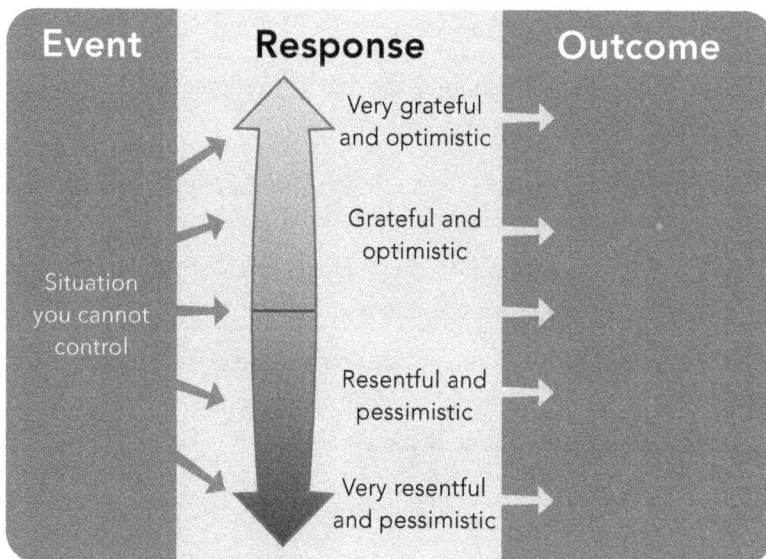

Event	Response	Outcome
	Very grateful and optimistic	
	Grateful and optimistic	
Situation you cannot control		
	Resentful and pessimistic	
	Very resentful and pessimistic	

Figure 5.1: Positivity meter tool.

*Visit **go.SolutionTree.com/SEL** for a free reproducible version of this figure.*

After reviewing the tool with the class, your peers, or on your own, please use the following questions to discuss and reflect. See appendix A (page 189) for the complete instructions on using the tools in this book.

Questions for Educators and Their Colleagues

Use the following questions to help you discuss the positivity meter tool with colleagues to gain a more personal and broader understanding.

- Explain the difference between optimism and gratitude. How are they related?

- If the event is that your principal moved you to a different classroom, how would you respond with the different levels on the positivity meter? How optimistic would you be? How grateful would you be? What outcomes would those responses lead to?

- For the following events, how might a teacher react with the different levels of positivity and what outcomes might come from that positive or negative reaction?

  - Eighty percent of the students in the class did poorly on an assessment.

  - A teacher couldn't deal with a student, so the student is transferred into another teacher's class.

  - Based on student numbers, the teacher needs to teach a new class or grade level the following year.

- Think about something in your life that you're grateful for. How does that impact your actions and attitudes?

- Think about something in your life that you're optimistic about. How does that impact your actions and attitudes?

- How hard do people work on the different levels of the positivity meter? How happy are people on the different levels?

- If you wanted to, how could you become more grateful and optimistic? Is it worth it? How positive should someone be? In other words, how optimistic and grateful should someone be?

Questions to Prompt Class Discussion

These are questions to promote class understanding about the tool. This can be done with small- or large-group discussion or by quietly reflecting in a journal.

- How are optimism and gratitude different? How are they related? If the event is that you did poorly on a test, how would you respond with the different levels on the positivity meter? What outcomes would these different responses lead to?

- For the following events, how might a student react with the different levels of positivity and what outcomes might come from that positive or negative reaction?

  - The physical education teacher has them run a mile in class.

  - They are picked to work on a group project with someone they don't really get along with.

  - They forgot to complete a homework assignment.

- Think about something in your life that you're grateful for. How does that impact your actions and attitudes?

- Think about something in your life that you're optimistic about. How does that impact your actions and attitudes?

- With school in general, how do most students react on the positivity meter? Why do you think this happens?

- How hard do people work on the different levels of the positivity meter? How happy are people on the different levels?

- If you wanted to, how could you become more grateful and optimistic? Why might it be worth it or not worth it to be more grateful and optimistic?

- How positive should someone be to be successful and happy? In other words, how optimistic and grateful should someone be?

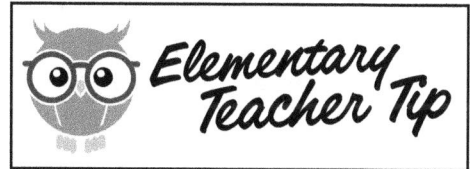

Questions for Student Reflection

After a content-specific lesson that is also an opportunity to assess the positivity meter, these questions can assist students in evaluating their thoughts and behavior during the lesson as they pertain to the concept.

Elementary Teacher Tip

Ask students to make a list of all the *people* in their life that they are grateful for. Prompt them to reach beyond their immediate family and friends and start to think about the people who stock the groceries at the store, the person who farms the food we eat, the person who keeps the bathrooms at the airport clean, and so forth. A few days later, ask them to make a list of all of the *things* they are grateful for. Again, try to get them to reach beyond the basics and think about things such as running water, electricity, a safe home, and so on. Teachers can repeat this exercise with any additional categories that make sense.

- During the lesson, how did you respond on the positivity meter? How optimistic and grateful were you?

- How did your responses with optimism and gratitude on the positivity meter affect how hard you worked and how happy you were?

- When you receive a challenge, what do you think is the optimal level of gratitude and optimism on the positivity meter?

- If one of your friends was resentful and pessimistic about school, how would you convince them to be more grateful and optimistic?

Joyful Learning

You may have been skeptical until now about the idea that students can enjoy themselves while learning, create personal goals that include learning, or change their mindset about school. It is quite a leap to suggest students just change their minds without teacher intervention; luckily, *joyful learning* offers a solution to this very issue. Consider the following scenario in which an educator, Mrs. Jensen, implements a lesson in class to engage students in joyful learning.

Mrs. Jensen had been teaching five-paragraph essays for years; however, she wanted to try something different. So, she purchased some envelopes and stamps, spreading them around on desks before class started to heighten the students' interest. When the bell rang, she introduced the lesson: "Students, I want you to think of a food item that you love and why you love it. Now, pull out a piece of paper. I want you to write the item at the top along with three reasons why you love that product."

Mrs. Jensen gave students a few minutes to discuss ideas and finish the task. Then, she continued:

"For this assignment, you are going to write a letter to the company who makes the product you just wrote about. The letter is going to be in five-paragraph essay form, with your thesis being that the product you picked is amazing. Your three body paragraphs will explain your reasons why you think it's amazing. In the conclusion, you can add that your teacher will give you full credit on the assignment if the company sends something back for you or the class. Write a rough draft first; then, share it with someone else for feedback. Once you've done that, turn it in to me so that I can assess it. After corrections, you may start on the final draft. I'll also teach everyone how to address an envelope and send them. Once you know how to address and stamp, you can start to help others."

Students excitedly started drafting their letters, thinking about who they would send to and what they might get in the mail. The students seemed to enjoy the writing, and it was the first time that Mrs. Jensen got 100 percent submission on a paper. Over the next two months, she received envelopes and boxes—some with informational material and others filled with products. One student got four boxes with over sixty bags of dried apple chips in each—enough for the entire class to share for the week. Whenever a package arrived, she had the student who wrote the letter open the package in front of the class. Every time, the student got an ovation from their peers as they got to showcase their favorite product.

Without knowing it, Mrs. Jensen was teaching with practices that constituted something called *joyful learning*. Some teachers, parents, and students might think that the only way to learn is to put your head down and grind through concepts. It conjures learning and progress, but it's set in an environment of drudgery. With this mindset, school is a workhouse and devoid of joy. Joyful learning goes against this idea, saying that learning and joy can coexist. The Joyful Learning Network (n.d.; www.joyfullearningnetwork.com) describes joyful learning as "engaging, empowering, and playful learning of meaningful content in a loving and supportive community. Through the joyful learning process a student is always improving knowledge of self and the world." In Mrs. Jensen's project, students supported each other to learn how to write a five-paragraph essay in a creative and fun way. They were improving and having fun at the same time.

Before she started teaching middle school, joyful education pioneer Judy Willis practiced neurology, studying and working on the brain and its functions. Willis (2007) notes that the brain reacts positively in a classroom environment when it is challenged, doesn't feel threatened, and is engaging in fun and meaningful activities:

> A common theme in brain research is that superior cognitive input to the executive function networks is more likely when stress is low and learning experiences are relevant to students. Lessons that are stimulating and challenging are more likely to pass through the reticular activating system (a filter in the lower brain that focuses attention on novel changes perceived in the environment). Classroom experiences that are free of intimidation may help information pass through the amygdala's affective filter. In addition, when classroom activities are pleasurable, the brain releases dopamine, a neurotransmitter that stimulates the memory centers and promotes the release of acetylcholine, which increases focused attention. (p. 64)

Armed with this information, we may look at our lessons to see if we can impact students' brains in a more positive way. As teachers, we can potentially lower student stress by being positive with our students about lessons and projects. The difference between introducing an assessment as, "You need to do well on this or else you'll fail the class" and "This is going to be a great opportunity for you to show how much you've learned," matters. Also, to lower stress, it is worthwhile to think about offering re-takes on assessments if the student doesn't understand the concept quite yet. If students know that they'll always have an opportunity to learn and address mistakes in their learning, it can lower potential negative thoughts that could cause anxiety and suck the joy out of learning.

Having good relationships with students is a key to helping them feel joy in their learning. Students will be at ease if they know you support them, that the person leading the classroom is looking out for their best interests. If they don't feel stressed in your classroom, information will pass through the amygdala unfazed. If students do feel stress from being in your class, the amygdala will process activities and assessments as a threat. When it does this, it floods the body with stress hormones that could put a student in a fight, flight, or freeze mode (Cannon, 1915). No aspect of a student yelling at us, running away, or staring at us like a deer in headlights when we offer them a challenge leads to learning.

Remember, lessening stress in students in class does not mean that we don't issue challenges. Joy does not come from prioritizing activities totally unrelated to learning. The process of learning should be the joy (more on this in chapter 9, page 171). In fact, new challenges and experiences could benefit positive brain function as well. Willis (2007) says that novel experiences stimulate the reticular activating system. The reticular activating system promotes arousal. Students should be more alert if, as a teacher, you provide students with challenges and concepts that are different and new. If you provide your students with an array of different activities, you could increase how awake they are in class.

Finally, fun and pleasurable activities that students are excited about provide a release of dopamine in the brain. Mental health reporter Hope Cristol (2021) writes:

> Dopamine is a type of neurotransmitter. Your body makes it, and your nervous system uses it to send messages between nerve cells. . . . Dopamine plays a role in how we feel pleasure. It's a big part of our unique human ability to think and plan. It helps us strive, focus, and find things interesting.

If fun and interesting activities help students release dopamine, they should help retain student focus and perseverance. It's rare to hear a student rave about a slew of worksheets in which they simply go through the motions to complete it and move on, but they'll think fondly of an open-ended, challenging, and relevant project where they got to collaborate to make something that kicks dopamine production into gear.

Author and professor in the department of curriculum and instruction at the University of Wisconsin-Madison, Alice Udvari-Solner (2012) agrees with Willis that, to create joyful learning, a teacher could provide choice and work to create assessments that don't lead to too much anxiety but also includes that teachers should make learning relevant, provide breaks, give students choices, and have students collaborate. It's typically not easy to create relevant group projects that offer choice while remembering to provide appropriate break times; but if you do, the positive centers of students' minds might fire, making them more interested, awake, and feeling good while they learn. If this happens, student perseverance should go up, and discipline problems should go down; but does it work in practice?

Doctor of education Subuh Anggoro, professor Wahyu Sopandi, and researcher Muhammad Solehuddin (2017) ran a study in which they placed fourth-grade science students in two groups—one control group and one group where the teacher used joyful learning. According to the study:

> The data showed that the gain scores of the experimental group students' attitudes toward science were significantly higher than the gain scores of the control group. In addition, the experimental group made significantly greater progress in their cognitive, affective, and conative experiences. (p. 1)

In this case, students in the joyful learning group not only seemed to learn more but also appreciated and enjoyed science more than their counterparts. If a student enjoys a subject, they should be much more likely to work hard and persevere compared to the student who does not enjoy a subject.

Someone who seems to agree with joyful learning is author Tony Wagner (Wagner & Dintersmith, 2015), who writes:

> Most lecture-based courses contribute nothing to real learning. Consequential and retained learning comes from applying knowledge to new situations or problems, research on questions and issues that students consider important, peer interaction, activities, and projects. Experiences, rather than short-term memorization, help students develop the skills and motivation that transforms lives. (pp. 7–8)

Again, some teachers, parents, and students might believe that more traditional academic rigor is necessary to persevere. To these people, rigor looks like more lecture, more homework, and more nose-to-the-grindstone memorization. When looked at through another lens, rigor can take a different form. Students can work hard and persevere while also enjoying that. As teachers, can and should we provide them with those opportunities?

Fun coupled with learning is not solely the teacher's responsibility. Regardless of the lesson, students can work to create joyful learning for themselves. If they focus on process over results, they can experience less stress. Students also can challenge themselves and create enjoyment, especially in open-ended projects and activities. See the following scenario for an example.

Joel and Vivek were juniors in Mr. Nicholl's Spanish class. In a unit titled Things Around the Kitchen Mr. Nicholl asked students to create a script where students used all the key words from the section. When they completed their scripts, Mr. Nicholl asked students to present their dialogues in front of the class, offering for students to try without their written dialogue but allowing those who needed them to scaffold. When Joel and Vivek went to the front of the room, they had completed their lines and started to perform. After the first few lines, however, Joel went away from their script, asking, "¿Para qué más podrías usar un tenedor?" ("What other uses are there for a fork?").

As this wasn't planned, Vivek was surprised but decided to play along. He tried his best to say, "You can comb your hair with it" (channeling from a previous unit) in Spanish while acting it out. Then, he countered with an off-script question of his own, "Esto es un cuchillo ¿no? ¿Lo uso con un coche?" ("This is a knife, right? Do I use it with a car?").

Now, it was Joel's turn to scramble, trying to answer Vivek's question while coming up with a question that might stump him using his limited knowledge of the Spanish language. While it was totally appropriate for students to write and read from a script, Joel and Vivek took the challenge of ad-libbing in front of the class. It certainly wasn't perfect Spanish, but the two students were taking control of learning and fun by turning the lesson into a game that was more exciting than reading a predetermined script in front of the class. Instead, they were providing themselves a challenge that engaged their reticular activating system, which increased their focus. Moreover, Mr. Nicholl loved it. He admired the two students' courage and loved that they were having fun and learning Spanish at the same time. In fact, he lauded their efforts to the class to emphasize the learning can be both spontaneous and joyful.

The Productivity and Fun Tool

Joyful learning is when students can be productive and joyful simultaneously. Some students will approach school focused solely on what is easy and fun—they will resist challenges and, instead, do whatever is pleasurable in the moment. Other students will focus solely on production and approach schooling by deemphasizing enjoyment. These students can be very productive, but school for them is a grind and not joyful. Use the tool in figure 5.2 to serve as a springboard for a rich class discussion about joyful learning. This tool shows three ways students can approach a challenge, with joyful learning in the center.

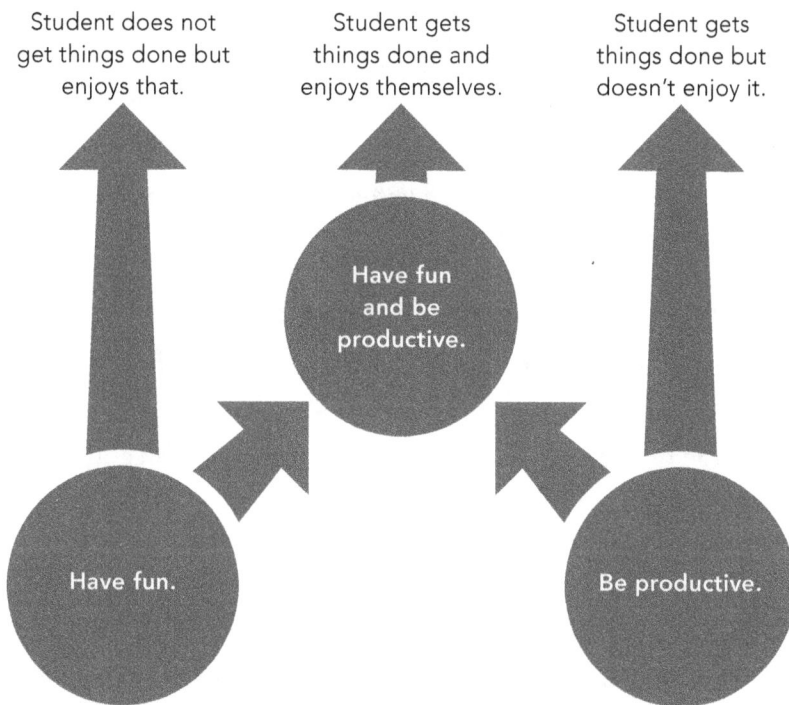

Student does not get things done but enjoys that.

Student gets things done and enjoys themselves.

Student gets things done but doesn't enjoy it.

Have fun and be productive.

Have fun.

Be productive.

Figure 5.2: Productivity and fun tool.

*Visit **go.SolutionTree.com/SEL** for a free reproducible version of this figure.*

After reviewing the tool with the class, your peers, or on your own, please use the following questions to discuss and reflect. See appendix A (page 189) for the complete instructions on using the tools in this book.

Questions for Educators and Their Colleagues

The following questions help you discuss the productivity and fun tool with colleagues to gain a more personal and broader understanding.

- What is your philosophy when it comes to teaching? How does it relate to production and joy?

- Where do most students in your class or school fall under on the tool: Have fun, be productive, or have fun *and* be productive?

- Do you have any lessons or projects where students are having fun and being productive at the same time? What would a class be like if you could have those kinds of lessons every day? How would that affect the class? How difficult would it be to make that happen?

- How much is having fun and being productive the teacher's responsibility and how much is it the student's responsibility?

- What is the best way to create a lesson where students are both being productive and having fun?

Questions to Prompt Class Discussion

These are questions to promote class understanding about the tool. This can be done with small- or large-group discussion or by quietly reflecting in a journal.

- How can someone in school be productive and have fun at the same time?

- When it comes to academics, where are most students in your school on the tool?

- Have you ever been in a class or had a lesson where most or all the students are being productive and having fun at the same time? If so, what did the teacher or the students do to make that happen?

- As a teacher, how would you get students to have fun and be productive at the same time? If you want to have fun and be productive, how much would you challenge the students?

- As a student, how responsible are you for having fun and being productive while you learn?

- If your teacher gives a lesson that most people wouldn't have fun with (for example, a worksheet or a lecture), how could you make it fun and productive at the same time?

Questions for Student Reflection

After a content-specific lesson that is also an opportunity to assess production and fun, these questions can assist students in evaluating their thoughts and behavior during the lesson as they pertain to the concept.

- During the challenge, which route on the tool did you take? How do you know? For others in the class, which route did you notice them taking? How do you know? Which route do you typically take in school? How does it make you feel?

- If your friend looks like they are sad, frustrated, or bored in class, what advice would you give your friend to make school more entertaining while staying productive?

- How could a teacher increase student productivity?

Summary

A student with a positive mindset views a challenge optimistically, with gratitude, and with joy. Optimism is when a student sees themselves as capable to accomplish a task. A grateful person will emphasize the good that comes from the challenge. Finally, someone with a positive mindset will find a way to be joyful when taking on a challenge. A student who is pessimistic, ungrateful, and miserable when they receive a task is neither happy nor productive. To help students be more positive, a classroom could include joyful learning. Joyful learning is when students are enjoying the learning process because lessons are meaningful and challenging in an environment without too much anxiety. Joyful learning is both the teacher's and the student's responsibility. For example, teachers can create challenging open-ended group projects that allow students autonomy to be creative. To make this assignment joyful, however, students need to put forth effort, work well together, push themselves, and take risks. If students think about why, how, and when to be optimistic, grateful, and joyful in school, it should help them be more successful, happier, and more enjoyable to be around as they pursue challenges.

Elementary Teacher Tip

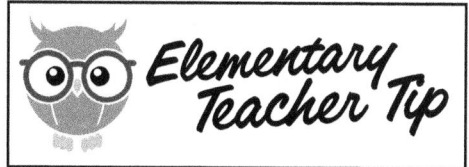

To promote joyful learning, write things students need to learn, such as basic mathematics facts and vocabulary words, on a set of Jenga® blocks and tell students to solve the problems (or define the words) as they play the game. After playing, discuss the idea that when we are learning joyfully time passes faster, we learn without even noticing, and many times we retain the information even better.

6

Courage

The secret to happiness is freedom . . . . And the secret to freedom is courage.

—Thucydides

My cell phone rang while my wife was driving me back from the hospital. I had been home from the rehab facility for a couple of weeks, and I needed to go in for some follow-up tests. Near the end of an angiogram, after they weaved a catheter into my femoral artery, through my heart, and up to my head to release dye to get a very clear image of my brain, one doctor declared, "Everything looks clear!" I was in a fantastic mood because it seemed that no other procedures would be necessary . . . until the call.

"We found a small arteriovenous malformation in your left frontal lobe," my doctor told me. "We're going to have to plan a surgery soon before it potentially bleeds again."

As I ended the call, a wave of fear raced from the top of my head quickly down to my chest. Brain surgery? The thought of having someone saw through my skull and fiddle with my cerebrum seemed barbaric and dangerous. How do they even do that? What if something went wrong?

Surgery was scheduled for me two weeks from the phone call. During that time, negative thoughts kept popping into my brain, and I started to focus solely on horrible outcomes. When this happened, I would question the irrationality of my thoughts: internet searches told me that well over 90 percent of arteriovenous malformation (AVM) surgeries are safe and successful, my AVM was in a good location for removal, and I had some of the best brain surgeons in the world working on my procedure. Finally, after the AVM was removed, I wouldn't have to worry about future strokes. If I didn't have the surgery, it might rupture at any time. I decided to embrace the surgery rather than resist it.

Over the next two weeks, negative thoughts continued, but I tried to always replace them with two positive thoughts. My fear started to turn into something different. On the day of the surgery, when the nurse wheeled me into the operating room, I said out loud, "I'm excited. Let's do this!" I was in a much better place than two weeks prior. I had developed courage. With a smile on my face, the anesthesia kicked in, and I faded off to sleep.

The fears students face in their lives and in our classrooms can come from any number of places, some obvious, some hidden. As teachers, we can help students understand and work with fear by helping them develop a sense of courage, or at least the self-sufficiency to know where to find courage in themselves when they need it. This chapter defines what courage looks like in the classroom, reviews research on fear and courage, and provides two tools that can help us understand and introduce these concepts to our classes.

The Definition of Courage

The *APA Dictionary of Psychology* defines *courage* (n.d.) as "the ability to meet a difficult challenge despite the physical, psychological, or moral risks involved in doing so." As courage always involves risk, danger and fear are necessary for courage to manifest. So, how can we be courageous in the presence of fear? Nelson Mandela said, "I learned that courage was not the absence of fear, but the triumph over it. The brave man is not he who does not feel afraid, but he who conquers that fear" (as cited in Cable News Network, n.d.). I believe Mandela is correct that all of us experience fear, even the bravest of the brave. However, I advocate that we as educators can use this emotion to help us better manage the forms of fear that manifest as anxiety.

For many students, school is fraught with fear—assessments, workload, performances, and presentations are stress-inducing situations where students have an opportunity to be courageous. This is to say nothing of students who may have genuine anxiety disorders, sometimes undiagnosed. Unfortunately, many students don't know how to work with this fear. According to her Yale Center for Emotional Intelligence and the Yale Child Study, Brita Belli (2020) reports that, when students were asked if they felt stressed, 79.83 percent responded affirmatively. While that number may be shocking to many, it may not be surprising to teachers. We all see some students show fear on various assessments and in certain social situations—even if we provide the most supportive of environments.

As students experience various fears throughout their school day, it's not unusual for them to view fear negatively and exaggerate the potential bad outcomes of stress-inducing situations. Part of courage is realizing that, often, we compound fears in our heads, making them much bigger obstacles than they are. Taking courage to a higher level, students may be able to see fear as a positive, using it to provide energy and focus to take on stress-inducing events.

Irrational Fears

We've all seen various levels of student interaction with fear. Any difficult challenge a student receives is a chance for the student to work with fear or to be a victim to it. Please see the following scenario for an example of a student being controlled by fear. It's a story that most of us can relate to on some level.

> Jayce was in PE class when her teacher announced that students would receive a challenge of running a mile in under eight minutes at semester's end. Jayce felt fear immediately through a tingling in her head and neck. She had never been able to run a mile in eight minutes before; how was she supposed to do it this time? She wasn't an athlete, and she'd never run a mile without walking. It's just too hard! She was going to fail. Now, she wouldn't pass the class, which would hugely affect her grade point average. Because of this, she wouldn't get into a good college. This, in turn, would make it so she wouldn't ever get a good job. She had to find a way out. Maybe she could get her parents to write a note to get out of the challenge. Why did her teacher do this?

Jayce's story, while exaggerated, may not be far off when it comes to how students' minds react to a difficult challenge. When confronted with something difficult, it's natural for students to have a fear response. If taken negatively, fear will get students to think only about poor outcomes and students will try to find a way out of the situation causing the fear.

As it is an emotion, fear is very difficult to describe with words. Merriam-Webster (fear, n.d.) defines *fear* as "an unpleasant often strong emotion caused by anticipation or awareness of danger," which seems ambiguous at best. Fear is a necessary emotion that arrives to assist us when we encounter a dangerous situation where the outcome is not a certainty. When a threat enters, fear triggers several reactions in our body to protect us. Tim Newman (2018), a journalist for *Medical News Today*, explains, "Breathing rate increases, heart rate follows suit, peripheral blood vessels (in the skin, for instance) constrict, central blood vessels around vital organs dilate to flood them with oxygen and nutrients, and muscles are pumped with blood, ready to react." All these reactions are to prepare us to either battle the threat or run away from it to survive. At times, this works; other times, it puts us into freeze mode where we cannot function.

In *The Art of Fear*, Kristen Ulmer (2018) discusses fear and our relationship with it. Ulmer (2018) should know quite a bit about fear as she held the title of top female extreme skier in the world for several years. She routinely pushed fear down when she would drop into one death-defying run after another. Overcoming fear by ignoring it allowed her to complete the challenges, but her relationship with fear soured. Her fear felt unappreciated and unwanted. The book is about how she fixed these issues by learning to honor fear and work with it instead of against it.

Rational and Irrational Fear

Ulmer (2018) likens us all to a corporation where fear is one of ten thousand employees. Every employee plays a vital role in the corporation, but fear is one of the most critical and necessary workers. Ulmer notes that, as such a vital employee, we should honor fear and its importance to the corporation. It should have a seat at the board of directors' table. However, she writes that many people view fear negatively, wanting to denigrate it and push it away. About this, Ulmer (2018) says:

> How do you feel about fear? Is it a bad emotion? When it shows up, when you just hear the word "fear," what happens? Do you get tense, wait to change the subject, try to leave the room? In noticing your reaction to fear, you can begin to get a sense of your own personal judgment or belief of what fear is.
>
> Are you among the billions who have determined fear to be "bad" and seek to shut it down? Do you deem it unnecessary, uncomfortable, and unwelcome? Do you want to protect yourself from it? Do you buy into the rampant belief that it needs to be controlled or overcome? (p. 24)

Ulmer (2018) adds that, because we tend to view fear negatively, we want to lock it up in a closet instead of honoring it for the important work it does in our corporation. She says that, when we repress and try to overcome fear, it will come back to haunt us with headaches, insomnia, worry, injuries, and more. It doesn't make a difference if that fear is real or something we have created and are cultivating and growing in our heads.

Students all have fears, and they come in two forms: (1) rational and (2) irrational. *Rational fears* are a direct threat that is very likely to cause harm in the immediate environment. *Irrational fears* represent a threat that is unlikely to occur as we may have overemphasized its ill effect in our minds. Writing for the Health Research Policy, Andrew Walden (2019) explains the difference between rational and irrational fear of water and drowning:

> If you're on a rickety boat in the middle of an ocean and get caught in the storm, your fear of drowning is rational. But if you're in your shower and are afraid to turn on the water because you're afraid of drowning, then that becomes an irrational fear. . . . Irrational fears aren't just the absurd fears. What separates these fears from rational fears is that the amount of fear or reaction you have is exaggerated, as what you fear is highly likely to be harmless or has a low risk of occurring.

In other words, irrational fears are those that students build up in their minds, amplifying and focusing on negative predictions for the future. Students might look at a situation with an outcome that isn't definite. If they start to ruminate on how badly it might turn out, they may experience fear every time they think about it. If we try to repress any fear we're feeling, it may lead to long-term anxiety and the ailments Ulmer (2018) writes about.

Self-Concept and Self-Criticism

Most fear of failure in school is an irrational fear that can lead to long-term anxiety. Some students may experience fear based on where they or others want their academic standing to be. It is irrational because it is not a direct threat to their safety—if a student fails a single test, their life is not over. However, a student may catastrophize the situation in their imagination. For example, a student may experience fear with an upcoming mathematics assessment. They may think that failing the assessment will lead to them not graduating or getting into their preferred college which, in turn, would keep them from getting and leading a comfortable life. It would be rare for a single test to lead to this scenario, but this focus on negative potential outcomes of their academic standing can create worry and anxiety. Repressing this fear and locking it away can wreak havoc on student health.

Along with fear of failure, author Dan Millman (1999) offers two other major causes of irrational fears: (1) limited self-concept and (2) destructive self-criticism. Like all of us, students will fall prey to all three. Genetic and environmental factors can also contribute to the development of an irrational fear or phobia (Watts, 2014). With *fear of failure*, a student will be concerned about making a mistake or not meeting their own or someone else's expectations. Even if they put in the practice time necessary to succeed, they may focus too much on potential negative outcomes of failure. With *limited self-concept*, the student might think the task is too difficult for them or that they will not be able to keep up with their peers. They might dwell on this too much instead of seeing potential success and improvement. Finally, *destructive self-criticism* comes from past mistakes. Students might tell themselves that they've failed before, so they are destined to fail again. All three are based on focusing mostly or solely on potential negative outcomes.

Logically, many scenarios that involve these three things, especially if a student has put in ample practice time, can produce positive outcomes, making these thoughts irrational. However, if students dwell mostly or fully on the negative, anxiety follows. See the following scenario for an example of what it looks like to let a limited self-concept and destructive self-criticism guide your actions and perception of yourself.

> *Mariah was a student in Mr. Strout's class. Mr. Strout had just offered the class the challenge of giving a five-minute individual presentation for the following Friday. Mariah had an immediate fear reaction to this. She then started to ruminate on what could possibly go wrong: she wasn't a good public speaker, and she had fumbled over her words before. Would she forget what she was saying? Would she say or do something embarrassing? What if she didn't pass the assignment and failed the class? The presentation was more than a week away, but Mariah had already begun showing fear responses (increased heart rate, clammy hands, and other symptoms) whenever she thought about it. Even though Mariah tried to work diligently on the speech, most of her time spent working on it included negative outcomes that led to a poor usage of her practice sessions. Additionally, her anxiety kept her up at night and gave her headaches. Because of all of this, Mariah didn't do well on her speech. Immediately afterward, she said to herself, "I'm horrible at speeches. I messed up this one, and I'll mess up again," possibly contributing to a downward spiral for her future speeches.*

Like Mariah, other students will have irrational fears about what they feel are high-stress and high-stakes situations like assessments and presentations. Again, most of these are not rational fears; but they can cause all-too-real fear-related issues. If a student has an irrational fear of failure, they might dwell on this assessment or project, worried that they won't do well or pass. Walden (2019) explains:

Take the [fear] of failing at work or school. You work hard to excel, but if you see a sudden decrease in your grade, it's rational to fear it will affect your grades. But at the same time, in the greater scheme of things, your grade for one term of school or a quarter of the work year won't really make a bump in your life, so it's also an irrational fear.

Irrational fear seems to be a major issue with many students. These fears can be based on pressures that come from several different areas. According to a Pew Research Center study Juliana Horowitz and Nikki Graf (2019) conducted, academic pressure tops the list, but several other pressures are close behind:

When it comes to the pressures teens face, academics tops the list: 61% of teens say they feel a lot of pressure to get good grades. By comparison, about three-in-ten say they feel a lot of pressure to look good (29%) and to fit in socially (28%), while roughly one-in-five feel similarly pressured to be involved in extracurricular activities and to be good at sports (21% each).

If seen through a lens that might include fear of failure, destructive self-criticism, limited self-concept, looking good, fitting in socially, and doing well in sports can potentially lead to a great deal of suffering—again, even if the fear is irrational.

Fear and Anxiety

This irrational fear manifests itself as anxiety. A direct fear response is sudden and hits very hard. For example, if a bear enters the room you're in, you will likely have an immediate fear response. This response to a rational fear is meant to protect you from the threat in that exact moment, giving you the strength to potentially fight or run from the bear. Anxiety works differently. It may not have the same punch as a response to direct fear, but it lasts much longer. For example, if a student has an irrational fear of failing an upcoming assessment, the fear response can start long before they take the assessment, worrying about what might potentially happen. In *Psychology Today*, associate professor emeritus of health economics Shahram Heshmat (n.d.) says, "In general, fear is seen as a reaction to a specific, observable danger, while anxiety is seen as . . . a kind of unfocused, objectless, future-oriented fear." A bear in the room leading to direct focus on a specific thing in the present is fear. Worrying about what might happen on an assessment next week is anxiety. Fear happens quickly and is over when the threat is gone; anxiety is an uneasy and unstable feeling that can linger for a long period of time.

Anxiety can also lead to a lack of success. If a student's thoughts focus solely on what might potentially go wrong, they may focus less on the task at hand. University of Jyvaskyla researcher Riikka Sorvo and colleagues (2017) study mathematics anxiety in second to fifth graders. They identify two types of mathematics anxiety: (1) anxiety about failure and (2) anxiety in mathematics-related situations. The former deals with a student's fear of failure in mathematics, while the latter deals with limited self-concept in mathematics. In those studied, one-third show some form of mathematics anxiety. The experimenters also note that these mathematics anxieties lead to lower mathematics scores among the students, saying, "Our results suggest that anxiety about mathematics-related situations and anxiety about failure in mathematics are separable but correlated. Both aspects were negatively related to basic arithmetic skills, the former more strongly than the latter" (Sorvo et al., 2017). If students with anxiety don't perform well with the cause of their fear, what, if anything, can students do to remedy this?

Ulmer (2018) might answer the question with the following word equation: "Suffering = Discomfort × Resistance" (p. 101). Fear is inherently uncomfortable. According to Ulmer (2018), we can't really control that. However, we can control our resistance to the fear. You reduce your suffering if you accept fear. If you can, somehow, not resist fear at all (making resistance tantamount to zero in the equation), your fear doesn't go away, but your suffering does. Let's say that a student has anxiety due to an irrational fear of assessments. Every time the teacher assigns an assessment, students have a great deal of resistance and don't want to participate in it. Multiplying that resistance with the discomfort brought forth by the fear that something bad will happen leads to suffering. Instead, if the student learns to not resist the fear, they would, according to the equation, suffer less.

Teachers can use several methods to get students to resist less. First, a teacher could lead a discussion about irrational fear to help students personally understand the concept and how they can use the knowledge to be more courageous with classroom challenges (the tool at the end of this section can help with this). For example, if a student worries about failing an assessment, they must understand that the chance of that happening, especially if they are prepared, may be much lower than they think. A teacher can also lessen student resistance to fear by making them feel comfortable and prepared for any assessment that comes their way. Additionally, a teacher can speak positively about assessments. Instead of saying, "If you don't pass this, you'll fail the class," a teacher could present assessments with positivity, saying, "This will be a great opportunity for you to showcase what you know." A teacher could also decrease resistance with reassessments. Students may resist an assessment less and have less anxiety if they know that they have a safety net and a way to recover if they didn't learn the concept quickly enough.

Reassessments allow students to focus on learning rather than outcomes. In the chapter on purpose (see page 41), this book discusses process and outcome goals. Many students focused on outcomes will home in on negative potential results, experience anxiety about not reaching their goal, and will want to resist the fear. As there is typically a set due date for assessments, the challenge turns into a high-stakes, high-anxiety, and high-resistance event. On the other hand, having a standards- or skills-based approach will afford students the ability to make mistakes and opportunities to fix them. Students will understand that failure is part of the process, and they'll have extra time to learn if necessary.

Most or all our students will experience irrational fears through challenges they receive in school. These irrational fears will cause anxiety, which leads to resistance, making the student not want to tackle the challenge. If educators can reduce irrational fears of students that challenges cause, students should resist less—leading to more perseverance, more success, and more courageous students.

The Irrational Fear Tool

Fear is an important and necessary emotion we all have that keeps us alive. Rational fear builds on a direct threat to your safety. Irrational fear is less direct, and something that we have exaggerated in our minds. Fear happens when we are unsure about an outcome of an event. With irrational fears, we overemphasize potential negative outcomes when we experience fear, leading to anxiety. By learning to think more logically and less emotionally about potential outcomes and accept fear without resistance, we can relieve stress and lead to better performance. This tool includes two diagrams to emphasize a distinction between those who have irrational fears and those who do not. Use the tool in figure 6.1 (page 108) to serve as a springboard for a rich class discussion about irrational fears.

After reviewing the tool with the class, your peers, or on your own, please use the following questions to discuss and reflect. See appendix A (page 189) for the complete instructions on using the tools in this book.

Questions for Educators and Their Colleagues

Use the following questions to help you discuss the irrational fear tool with colleagues to gain a more personal and broader understanding.

- How do you define *fear*? How does your body react when you experience fear? How is irrational fear different than rational fear? How much of each do you see at your school with students and teachers?

Rational Fear

Irrational Fear

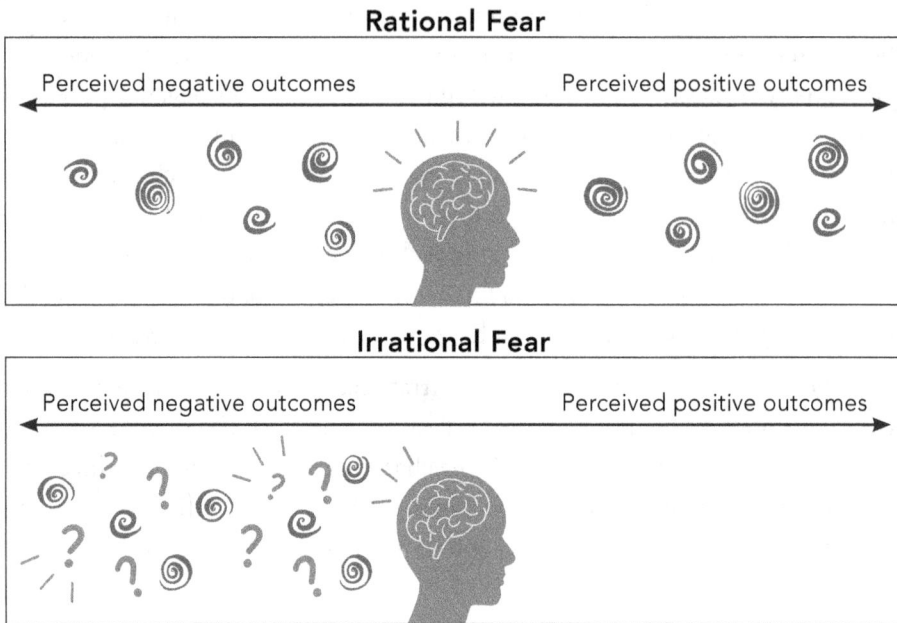

Figure 6.1: Irrational fear tool.

*Visit **go.SolutionTree.com/SEL** for a free reproducible version of this figure.*

- Think of something in your class that might produce irrational fear for students. How much do students think negatively about that thing? How much do students think positively about it?

- If a student has an irrational fear about something at school, how can you (as a teacher) help them reduce their negative thoughts about it? How can you help them reduce their resistance to it?

- Stress and anxiety come from overemphasizing negative potential outcomes over what is causing fear in our minds (for example, we have an administrator coming to evaluate one of our classes, and we only think about what could go wrong). What would happen if you didn't judge the potential outcomes of what is causing the fear? Is it preferable to think about positive outcomes instead? How positive should you be in thinking about outcomes (should potential negative outcomes enter your mind at all)?

Questions to Prompt Class Discussion

These are questions to promote class understanding about the tool. This can be done with small- or large-group discussion or by quietly reflecting in a journal.

- How do you define *fear*? How does your body react when you experience fear? Fear comes when we don't know how something is going to turn out. How often do you experience fear in school? How does it make you feel?

- How is irrational fear different than rational fear? How much of each do you see at your school with other students?

- Think about the last time you had an assessment in school. Use the first tool to think of all the positive, neutral, and negative potential outcomes. In the second tool, you're focused mostly on negative potential outcomes, leading to irrational fear. Before the assessment, which tool best explains your mindset? Did you think something differently than those tools?

- If you have irrational fear about some fear-inducing event (like a public speaking assignment, assessment, or sport competition), how do you feel?

- How might it help or hurt you to have more positive thoughts? If you wanted to think about more positive outcomes, how would you do that?

- Is it better to have positive outcome thoughts about what is causing fear or is it better to not judge the outcome? Explain your answer.

Questions for Student Reflection

After a content-specific lesson that is also an opportunity to assess irrational fears, these questions can assist students in evaluating their thoughts and behavior during the lesson as they pertain to the concept.

- During the challenge, did you feel fear? How do you know? How much did you focus on negative outcomes during the challenge, and how much did you think about positive outcomes?

- Before the challenge, how did you predict it would end? What happened? In school, how often do you

Elementary Teacher Tip

In advance, create a list of things that may create fear. Some examples are getting sick, being late for school, forgetting to bring something important to school such as their lunch, monsters under the bed, snakes falling from the sky, and aliens attacking. Read each fear aloud and have students indicate whether they think it's a "real" fear or a "made-up" fear. You can have them respond in any way you choose: calling out their response, holding up a popsicle stick with a smiley face or a sad face, thumbs up or thumbs down, and so on.

focus too much on negative outcomes such as failing a test or poorly executing a presentation? If you wanted to, how could you change this?

Fear and Excitement

Fear is a necessary and powerful emotion. Evolutionarily speaking, it is meant to give us energy to fight or run away from a threat. However, if students focus too much on potential negative outcomes, it can lead to anxiety. What if students could see fear as a positive, or like a jolt of power they could harness to take on a challenge? Instead of anxiety, fear could be something else. Consider the following scenario in which a high school teacher, Mr. Sinnot, leads a reframing exercise to encourage students to approach stressful or anxiety-inducing situations with a healthier mindset.

"Good morning, students," said high school teacher Mr. Sinnot. "I have a baseball hat here filled with conversation starters. Let me read a few to you:

- *Would you rather be extremely attractive but equally unintelligent or extremely intelligent and equally unattractive?*

- *If you were dating someone who was perfect in every way except that they said the word "like" in every sentence, would you stay with that person or break up?*

"You get to come up here and give a one- to two-minute response in front of the class. I want you to think on your feet and fully explain your response and reasoning. I also want one more thing: I want you to verbally say, 'This is exciting,' before you start speaking.

"I realize that you might be nervous. That's OK. Just realize that, with nervousness and excitement, your body is doing roughly the same things: sweaty palms, increased heart rate, and so on. I want to see if you can use these feelings to shift from nervousness and into excitement. That's why I want you to say, 'This is exciting,' out loud before you start."

Mr. Sinnot raises some interesting questions for his class regarding fear: Is fear a good thing or a bad thing? Can students turn fear into excitement?

For some of our students and, possibly, ourselves, we may lean toward thinking of fear negatively. After all, fear can be very uncomfortable and make us feel uneasy. However, if viewed differently, can fear be productive, giving us energy to perform at our best? If that is the case, courage is the result. How can we accomplish this?

In his book, *Fear Is Fuel*, Patrick Sweeney (2020) offers suggestions. Sweeney (2020) became afraid of airplanes and flying after watching the aftermath of a horrific plane crash on TV as a child. He resisted going on planes for a long time. As an adult, he is now a stunt pilot. He didn't overcome fear; instead, he learned to work with his fear. Sweeney (2020) says this:

> There are only two ways to make decisions: out of fear or out of opportunity. When you make a decision out of fear, it almost always leads to regret. When you make a choice based on opportunity, it will always lead to learning something and getting closer to your goal. When your amygdala—that small gland at the base of your brain—hijacks your body, it wants to make every decision based on simply surviving. The amygdala always wants to fight, flee, or freeze. It will do whatever it thinks gives you the better chance of living to send your gene pool to the next generation. Fear only helps you survive; opportunity makes you thrive. (p. 21)

Sweeney (2020) offers four steps to help make decisions when faced with fear.

1. Recognize fear when it shows up.
2. Create fear-inducing experiences to get comfortable with the emotion.
3. Turn fear into courage.
4. Use the power of fear for peak performance.

Recognize Fear When It Shows Up

First, it's important to recognize when fear shows up. As discussed in the previous section, fear comes to us in situations where we encounter a threat or a perceived threat. To prepare us for that threat, the amygdala causes our pupils to dilate, increases blood flow, and centers our focus (Harvard Health, 2020). When we feel these bodily changes, we can identify that we are experiencing fear. If these bodily changes from fear will help us perform our best in the presence of a threat, can we use them to perform in other situations? For example, a student giving a presentation in front of the class or taking an assessment will likely experience fear. Can they identify the fear response through their body's reaction and welcome it to help them become more aware and succeed?

Create Fear-Inducing Experiences to Get Comfortable

Second, Sweeney (2020) says that we need to become comfortable with the feeling by getting ourselves into situations that produce fear. This is not to say that you should jump into a tiger cage at the zoo. Instead, you can focus on irrational fear inducers that will create the same reactions as a direct threat. However, even irrational fears can lead to unsafe situations. When practicing fear—even irratio-nal fear—please make sure to prioritize safety. As teachers, we need to keep this in mind when assigning challenges for students. It may be important to have them practice experiencing fear, but it's also important that they feel safe. If you have a class environment that supports students while they experience fear, students will benefit from both the challenge and safety net—leading to more risk-tak-ing. Sample rules for a supportive environment include: no student makes fun of another for mistakes, students applaud effort and courage more than results, and other collaborative, respectful measures.

Turn Fear Into Courage

The third step is, perhaps, the most important as you aspire to turn the feeling of fear into excitement to facilitate courage. As per Mr. Sinnot's story, the feelings we get when experiencing fear and the feelings we get when experiencing excite-ment are very similar. Neuroscientist Alex Korb (2014) says the "hypothalamus instructs the body to increase your breathing and heart rate, dilate your pupils, and make your palms sweaty. Surprisingly though, when you feel excitement, the hypothalamus triggers the same physiological reaction." In fact, vocabulary .com (n.d.) offers a word for this feeling: *frisson*. The website says, "A frisson is a thrilling shiver. . . . You're just as likely to feel a frisson whether you're scared or excited; its meaning lies directly between thrill and fear." When the feeling of fear sets in, perhaps the difference between the experience of excitement and the experience of anxiety depends on how we frame it in our mind.

If students experience fear, it seems to be a natural reaction to judge it nega-tively. If there is a threat to them, they might focus on the bad things that could happen. Students worry that they might mess up or make a mistake. Sometimes, this feeling consumes their thoughts and makes it difficult to focus on the task at hand. Fear brings focus; but, fear can be detrimental if students devote that focus to the feeling of fear and what might go wrong instead of the task it supports. If the feeling of fear arrives, students can also view it positively. If students see it for what it's meant for and use it to focus on the task that is producing the fear, that might lead to excitement. How do we and our students do this?

It may be important to get ourselves to rationally think about the likelihood of safety and success. Korb (2014) continues, "We don't like fear per se, we like predictable fear. It gets the limbic system fired up, making us feel more alive, but we don't have to worry about actually dying." If a student doesn't feel safe in a certain situation, fear could easily turn to anxiety. However, if students feel safe, they might take more risks and be excited. If you're on a roller coaster and you feel unsafe (as if you might fall off during the ride), that roller coaster will lead to anxiety. On the other hand, if you feel safe (engineers have designed this well so people don't fall out), the fear has a better chance of turning to excitement.

If the environment of your class is one of support, the student will feel safe and see the likelihood of something bad happening as minimal. With support from their teacher and their classmates, even if they make a mistake, they know that all is going to be OK—they won't be made fun of, and they know it won't ruin their grade. Some students in a supportive class will still feel the body's responses of fear when they, for example, present to their peers. However, the support of the class could lead to more positive thoughts of a positive outcome that could help the student use the fear to become excited and focus on the task. Let's look at the following scenario for an example of a student experiencing what it is like to attend a class where the teacher establishes a supportive environment.

> Bennie loved coming to sixth period. It was the one class of the day where he felt his teacher, Mr. Mintey, supported him and the other students. This might be because Mr. Mintey spent the first two weeks of school making sure that the students really got to know each other. This made the class different than others on Bennie's schedule. In his other classes, students seemed to be competing against each other for grades. In Mr. Mintey's class, the students seemed to collaborate to help each other succeed. Bennie would get nervous in other classes when called on or when giving a presentation, but this class was different. His heart would still race when he was the focus, but he felt more in control. After all, if anything went awry, it would all be OK.

According to Sweeney (2020), imagining positive and safe outcomes can also be done by reframing things in your mind. For an example, he discusses someone going kayaking after flipping upside down in the water the time before. If that person falls prey to destructive self-criticism, they will be thinking negatively about this latest foray on the water: *I flipped before, and I'll probably flip again.* They'll focus on negative outcomes, which will turn the fear that comes with getting back in a kayak to anxiety (lessening focus on the task of kayaking). If, instead, the kayaker says to himself, "I am super tough and awesome for getting back on this kayak again after flipping," that positive thought might just interpret fear as excitement.

Harvard Business School professor and organizational behavioralist Alison Wood Brooks (2014) administers experiments that test reframing the mind in fear-inducing situations, including performing karaoke in front of strangers, giving a speech in front of strangers, and trying to solve challenging mathematics problems.

In alignment with the concept of frisson, Brooks notes, "Anxiety and excitement have divergent effects on performance, but the experience of these two emotions is quite similar. They are both felt in anticipation of events and are characterized by high arousal" (p. 1144). Therefore, she had one group in each study complete a simple reframe, saying "I'm excited" out loud before the task. Other groups either said "I'm anxious" or nothing before their challenge. The group who said "I'm excited" before the task did better (in that they had a higher karaoke accuracy score) than the other groups and rated the experience as more enjoyable.

This reframing of saying one sentence seems like a simple thing, but it could pay dividends for students. By saying "I'm excited," students associate their fear experience with excitement. When that happens, their mind can focus on the challenge instead of what might go wrong. When a student says, "I'm anxious," they may start thinking about potential negative outcomes, focusing on those instead of the task. Anxiety clouds the mind from the challenge while excitement seems to open it to the experience.

Brooks (2014) also had groups say "Try to remain calm" before a task. Brooks notes that, in many higher-stress situations, some will give advice that, to perform well, a person must calm these feelings of fear. In the experiment, those who said "I am calm" had the same heart rate as the other groups. In other words, saying "Try to remain calm" did not calm the people in these fear-inducing situations. It seems that, when a trigger activates the fear response, it is difficult to counteract. Like the "I'm anxious" and the control groups, the "Try to remain calm" group was not as effective and happy as the "I'm excited" group.

It might not work out favorably even if you were able to calm yourself using the "I am calm" statement, especially if you prescribe to the Yerkes-Dodson Law. According to neuroscientist David M. Diamond (2005), a professor at South Florida University, the Yerkes-Dodson Law shows that both animals and people need the correct amount of stress to perform at their peak. Those with no stress or too much stress tend to underperform while those with a moderate amount of stress perform best. In fact, the visual of their law is a true bell curve with poor performance at both ends of the stress level and ideal performance directly in the middle. If minimum stress is zero and maximum stress is ten, ideal performance is a five. In other words, being calm does not help us perform but having the right amount of stress does.

An interesting example of reframing fear comes from Ulmer's (2018) book. She had a confrontation with a hostile waterbuck in Uganda. The animal had been terrorizing the area and attacking people with its long horns. Others warned her about the danger of this waterbuck, but she was still surprised when it appeared roughly fifty feet away. Like all of us would, she had an immediate fear response. Having practiced this many times before, she was able to reframe the situation as excitement. She put her hands to her sides and shuffled to safety while the waterbuck stared her down. When the experience was over, she said, "It was one of the most ecstatic moments of my life" (p. 248). Likely, students won't have to deal with an angry waterbuck in class; however, they will experience stressful situations. It would be nice if they could describe the aftermath of those fears as ecstatic instead of miserable.

Use the Power of Fear for Peak Performance

Sweeney's (2020) fourth step for making decisions through fear is to use the power of fear for peak performance. When he knows he's going to take on a difficult challenge, Sweeney will purposely create fear for himself. He thinks of something that might scare him (like presenting to an arena full of people) until he finds himself experiencing a fear response. Then, he uses that energy to focus on the challenge to realize optimal performance. Sweeney took years to perfect this. We cannot expect our students to master this as Sweeney has, but we can introduce them to the process.

As a teacher, you do want to administer challenges that include stress and fear to help students work with the emotion. A class completely devoid of fear is not exciting. With any given challenge, some students may perceive it as very stressful while others will perceive it as hardly stressful at all. For the students who see it as stressful, you may work to get them to reappraise the fear as excitement, convincing them to use its power to focus on the challenge. For students who perceive the same challenge as not stressful, they might imagine themselves in a situation that does create fear so that they can harness its power to create more excitement. Students may be taking solid steps toward courage when they can identify fear in themselves, learn to practice working with it, and start reframing the experience as a positive.

The Fear and Resistance or Acceptance Tool

Fear is a necessary emotion that we experience when we encounter a threatening situation where we don't know what the outcome will be. Fear should help us focus on that situation, but it doesn't always work that way. If we resist the fear we have and focus too much on what might go wrong instead of the task or challenge at hand, our fear might turn into anxiety that can be detrimental to success. Instead, if we accept the fear as an extra jolt of energy that can assist us in taking on the task or challenge, it might turn into courage, clearing our minds to perform as well as we can. Use the tool in figure 6.2 to springboard into a rich class discussion about fear and excitement.

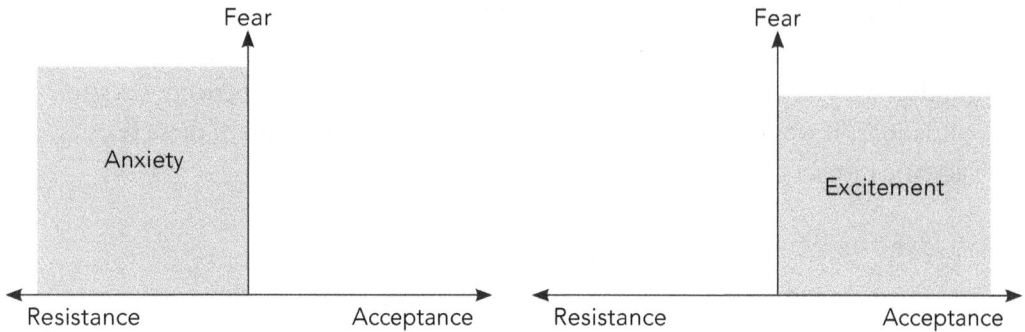

Figure 6.2: Fear and resistance or acceptance tool.

*Visit **go.SolutionTree.com/SEL** for a free reproducible version of this figure.*

After reviewing the tool with the class, your peers, or on your own, please use the following questions to discuss and reflect. See appendix A (page 189) for the complete instructions on using the tools in this book.

Questions for Educators and Their Colleagues

Use the following questions to help you discuss the fear and resistance or acceptance tool with colleagues to gain a more personal and broader understanding.

- How do you describe fear? How might fear be a bad thing? How might fear be a good thing?

- How would you describe how your body reacts when you feel anxiety? How would you describe how your body reacts when you're excited?

- What are some situations at school when you experience fear? What are some situations outside of school?

- What does it mean to resist fear? What does it mean to accept fear? How often do you resist or accept fear?

- The two tools show that, based on your acceptance or resistance of fear, you can feel anxiety or excitement. If this is true, how can someone do that?

- If you were to get on a roller coaster, which tool best describes your reaction and why? If you were to go skydiving, which tool best describes your reaction and why? How can someone get themselves excited for roller coasters and skydiving?

- How often do you give yourself opportunities to experience fear and work on this concept? How often do you give your students opportunities to experience fear and work on this concept?

- Are there any fear-inducing situations that you cannot channel into excitement?

Questions to Prompt Class Discussion

These are questions to promote class understanding about the tool. You can do this with small- or large-group discussion or by quietly reflecting in a journal.

- What is fear? Is fear a good thing or a bad thing? How does your body react when you experience fear? How does your body react when you are anxious? How does your body react when you are excited? How are body reactions similar and how are they different?

- What are some situations at school when you experience fear? What are some situations outside of school?

- What does it mean to resist fear? What does it mean to accept fear? Do you typically resist or accept fear when encountering a fear-inducing situation?

- Which tool would best describe your reaction to riding a roller coaster? Which tool would describe your reaction to someone putting a snake in your arms or a spider on your hand? How could someone be excited for all these situations?

- Think of a time when you presented in front of a large group of people. Did you feel fear? If so, which tool (page 116) would best explain the situation? How did your body react? How did you feel?

- How can you personally turn fear into excitement? How easy or difficult do you think that is? If you can, how would you describe your process to someone else?

- How often do you give yourself a chance to experience fear and work on this concept? Do you look forward to fear-inducing opportunities?

- Are there any fear-inducing situations that you cannot accept and turn to excitement? Please explain.

Questions for Student Reflection

After a content-specific lesson that is also an opportunity to assess fear and resistance or acceptance, these questions can assist students in evaluating their thoughts and behavior during the lesson as they pertain to the concept.

- During the challenge, did you feel fear? How do you know? Did your fear become anxiety or excitement? If you were in control of this, how did you do that?

- When are some other times you've experienced fear? Can you turn that fear into excitement or not? If you can, how do you do that?

- Why might you pursue more challenges that scare you? How could you make those challenges a positive experience?

Elementary Teacher Tip

Start with a quick energizing activity such as running out to the playground, sliding down the slide, and running back. Talk about how that felt (perhaps they felt excited or fearful). Then increase the challenge, such as having students do twenty-five jumping jacks or go down the slide backward or swing as high as they can on the swings. Ask the same questions again and see if you have any more students willing to admit to a feeling of fear.

Summary

Fear is a necessary emotional and biological response to a direct or perceived threat. It serves to focus our minds and prepare our bodies to best deal with the stressful situation. Two types of fear exist: (1) rational fear and (2) irrational fear. Rational fear is a response to a direct and immediate threat. Irrational fear is an exaggerated response to a threat that is not immediate. Students who have irrational fears tend to overemphasize negative outcomes. Students can be aware that many fears at school are irrational. If they can also think of positive outcomes that could come from a stressful situation, it could lead to less anxiety. Courage is a student's ability to productively work with fear. If a student understands fear's role and works with it, they can use it as a benefit to help them focus and become excited about a challenge. Throughout their schooling, students will experience fear regularly when they present, test, and more. Courageous students who can learn to work with fear can realize more success and happiness.

7

Commitment

The difference between involvement and commitment is like ham and eggs. The chicken is involved; the pig is committed.

—Martina Navratilova

In September 2014, I found myself in Joe De Sena's barn in Pittsfield, Vermont, at five o'clock in the morning, getting ready for a workout. Joe is a legend of endurance racing who has finished over fifty events, including running the Iditarod on foot. On the cover of De Sena's (2018) book *The Spartan Way: Eat Better. Train Better. Think Better. Be Better.*, Angela Duckworth endorses him as "a paragon of grit." That's high praise from a researcher who studies what it means to be gritty. I was nervous about what was about to take place, mostly because Joe is a machine; and I am someone who always seems to want to quit. By this point in this book, that may surprise, but it's true. I'm used to getting up early to exercise before school, but it's always a struggle—always. A voice in my head will make excuses to get me out of exercise, begging and pleading me to quit. As I know I have this voice always badgering me to stop anything challenging, how was I going to keep up with Joe who has proven he's capable of superhuman feats?

The workout was challenging. It was fifty reps of everything—burpees, pull-ups, squats, lunges, burpees again—for about an hour. Because of the level of challenge, the voice was working overtime to convince me that quitting was acceptable. It was a physical and mental struggle, but I made it through. When it was all over, Joe invited me to have breakfast with him at his country store less than a mile from the barn. As we were jogging at a more leisurely pace, I had to ask, "Joe, when you're running an ultramarathon, what do you do? When I exercise, I tell myself to quit all the time. Can you just get your brain to go on autopilot? If you do, how do you do it? I want to learn."

"No," he said. "When I'm running an ultra, my brain tells me to quit throughout the entire race. In fact, we're running really slow right now; and my brain is telling me to quit. I'm just telling myself to get to that tree up there, and it shuts off my brain for a while. When my brain tells me to quit again, I just pick another tree" (J. De Sena, personal communication, September 22, 2014).

Joe wasn't a machine. Like me, you, and everyone else, Joe has a voice in his head that will tell him to quit when he's doing something challenging. This includes your students. But it's important to remember that, while your students bring an array of lived experiences to your classroom, they haven't all had the same opportunities to experience success when faced with challenge. Without experiencing the kind of success that comes from process-focused learning, students may need support to understand the level of commitment required to experience that kind of success.

Since my experience with Joe, I've had the luxury to speak with many other endurance athletes who tell me the same thing: one major key to commitment is to find a way to momentarily quiet the voice in your head that wants to protect you but at the cost of reaching your true potential. In this chapter, we'll look at ways commitment and quitting apply to the classroom setting. This chapter includes research and three tools so students can discuss the best way to commit (known as *deliberate practice*), how long they should commit to something, and how to persist (resist quitting).

The Definition of Commitment

Students may be involved in challenges, but commitment takes effort to an entirely different level. Students will have difficulty reaching their full potential if they don't offer full commitment and dedication to the challenge.

To fully commit, a student must put copious thought and effort into the task. In taking on a challenge, the committed student will need to take the time to research and think about how they can best approach the challenge at the start and along the way. After deciding on the best course of action, the committed student needs to be tough enough to follow through with the plan. As you might imagine, these two steps make commitment especially difficult. However, if students can attack challenges with great thought and effort, their chances of success may rise greatly.

After knowing how to attack challenges, the committed student must log many devoted hours into their pursuit—commitment is not something that ends after a few attempts. Instead, months of devotion of both thought and action toward a craft constitute commitment. During this time, a voice in the student's head will scream at them to stop. While many will give in to this voice, others will push through it toward improvement. While improvement follows commitment, it is a long and difficult process. Students will have to determine for themselves how many hours to devote to something and when they should or shouldn't give in to the voice that tries to stymie commitment. When talking with students about commitment, have them think of themselves at, say, forty or fifty years old. At that age when they look back on their academic experience, will they say, "I really wish I would have worked less hard. I really wish I would've not persisted"? Right now, students may not commit as much as they should to learning. However, from their future vantage point, most students will admit that they would want to commit more in school. All students have potential. Committed students close the gap on reaching their potential.

Deliberate Practice

There are methods of measuring time with the intent to produce learning out of it. To use time wisely, students may use *deliberate practice*, which psychologist Anders Ericsson (1993) coined and describes as "effortful activities . . . designed to optimize improvement" (p. 363). Unlike regular practice, which is simply play or going through the motions without thinking about where you're going, deliberate practice connotes that great thought and application goes into self-improvement and betterment. See the following scenario for examples of how commitment can make a difference in a student's life.

Two students are taking a high school weight-training class. They both attend the same number of class sessions, but they both experience the class very differently. The first student doesn't really have a plan or direction for class. He doesn't think about what he needs to do to improve; instead, he spends most of the time sitting on the equipment and chatting with others. When he does lift weights, he only does bench press (because it's the only exercise he's heard of). The second student has a goal of improving her strength and flexibility so she can be a better athlete for the two sports she plays. She researches plans that will help her attain her goals. She asks the teacher to monitor her workouts and provide feedback on what she's doing well and how she can improve. When the class starts, she completely immerses herself in what she is doing and uses the entire period to follow her plan. If both students keep this same trend for the entire school year, the first student will see little to no gains while the second will see major development. The first student may enjoy the chatting and sitting; however, when it comes to improvement, the class is almost entirely a waste of time. It may not always be enjoyable for the second student in class as she puts forth both mental and physical effort, but she can appreciate her improvements and be proud of what she accomplishes.

Those students who sit around without a plan will squander their time while students who come up with a plan to attack their goal and see it through can see gains. The same concept applies in an academic class. It takes the same amount of time in class to try and improve as it does to not try and stagnate. So, they might as well use that time to improve themselves. Some students may disagree, and that's fine. However, if they are aware of both courses of action, they can make an educated decision on which one is the better choice for them in school.

Before jumping into the amount of time needed to commit to something, let's first look at the quality of commitment. Students are in classes for several hours, five days a week, during the school year. By the time they're done with their K–12 education, they have invested a couple thousand hours into learning. However, the quality of those hours makes a huge difference. If students use the time wisely, they increase their opportunity to learn and improve. Again, when students grow into later adulthood, it's a rare person who says to themselves, "Looking back at school, I wish I would've tried less hard; I wish I would've wasted more time."

Deliberate practice helps students use time more wisely, and it helps them increase their skill or knowledge of a subject. Ericsson (1993) insists that experts are not just born with talent; rather, experts need to engage in years of deliberate practice to attain mastery in some area. He identifies a few key components needed for deliberate practice to work: a set goal or direction for what you wish to improve, complete focus on the task, identification of weaknesses to fix, and consistent feedback. In his book *Peak*, Ericsson (Ericsson & Pool, 2017) says:

> Deliberate practice involves well-defined, specific goals and often involves improving some aspect of the target performance; it is not aimed at some vague overall improvement. Once an overall goal has been set, a teacher or coach will develop a plan for making a series of small changes that will add up to the desired larger change. Improving some aspect of the target

performance allows a performer to see that his or her performances have been improved by the training. Deliberate practice is deliberate, that is, it requires a person's full attention and conscious actions. It isn't enough to simply follow a teacher's or coach's directions. The student must concentrate on the specific goal for his or her practice activity so that adjustments can be made to control practice. (p. 99)

This means that deliberate practice is not just involvement or putting in time. If you play tennis with your friend every day at the park, that's not it. You might improve that way, but you might also stagnate or create bad habits. If you want to employ deliberate practice, you will solicit feedback (both self-feedback and feedback from others who are better tennis players), finding what your weaknesses are and focusing on how to improve those weaknesses. In other words, it's taking a deep dive on what you need to do to improve your craft. Then, it's up to you to practice those things over and over until you can master them, making you better at your chosen activity.

Strengths and Weaknesses

In a classroom setting, the same concept applies—to improve, students should think about what they personally need to work on to be successful. However, all students are different. For example, a student with attention-deficit/hyperactivity disorder (ADHD), a gifted and talented education student, or a student on the autism spectrum may have different things to work on than others. To use deliberate practice, they all should think deeply about what they need to personally improve on and then practice those skills. If they do, they can potentially learn more in class.

The standards of deliberate practice do not entail rote practice memorization; rather, they comprise problem-solving and critical thought by students. It does put the onus on individuals to determine their purpose, to focus, and to think about how they can identify areas for growth and strengthen them.

While the student is responsible for identifying areas of improvement and effort, the teacher's role is also critical. Anders Ericsson, Ralf Krampe, and Clemens Tesch-Römer (1993) explain that they "reviewed the evidence concerning the conditions of optimal learning and found that individualized practice with training tasks (selected by a supervising teacher) with a clear performance goal and immediate informative feedback was associated with marked improvement" (p. 351). As teachers, we can see where our students need to improve. Often, students can't see that. Educators can constructively make them aware.

Because we (in most cases) know more about the subjects we teach than our students, and because we are empowered with learning strategies that target specific skills, it's incumbent on us, as teachers, to provide appropriate lessons to assist students in reaching short-term goals that will eventually lead to long-term improvement. For example, an English teacher having students write a research paper for the first time can split the assessment into smaller tasks. First, the teacher can have students write down questions they want answered for the paper. Next, students can research answers to those questions, making sure to write down where the information came from. After, the teacher can have students write both long and short citations for each source. Once students find and cite the relevant research, the teacher can assist the students with writing a solid introduction. After, students will get to work on their individual body paragraphs, conclusion, correct in-text citations, works cited page, and editing. Some students may understand right away, and others may take longer to master each step (each student is different with different needs). This is where your teaching experience is invaluable—you can speed up or slow down based on the class's understanding and you can have students who understand assist their peers.

Along the way, we can provide students with both positive feedback about successes and constructive feedback where students still need to develop their knowledge and skills. (Some teachers forget the importance of positive feedback in this process, focusing fully on areas of growth; students need specific feedback on what they're doing well too.) With deliberate practice, education is a two-way street, involving both educator and student. If this partnership is realized with both parties working together, students are far more likely to learn better and faster.

Deliberate Practice in Classroom Instruction

To further explain the relationship between teacher and student regarding deliberate practice, educational psychologist Benjamin S. Bloom (1985) studied people pursuing improvement in science, the arts, and sports. As he watched people in these areas blossom, he identified three stages in the career of an expert: (1) initiation, (2) development, and (3) perfection. In the *initiation* stage, children are introduced to the activity that they seem to enjoy or show promise in. This stage is not serious or focused, and it looks to include mostly play. When an adult becomes aware of the child's promise, they may move them to the second stage, *development*. In this stage, a teacher or coach leads the child through deliberate practice, focusing on areas of weakness with consistent and meaningful feedback from an expert. In this stage, the student shows initial rapid improvement, which starts to level out over time (as hours of deliberate practice accumulate, weaknesses become fewer and smaller). In the final stage, *perfection*, students commit their lives to that field of study, immersing themselves completely in the activity (which may end up being the student's profession). Here, they should be very good at self-assessing their own weaknesses and finding those who are even more expert to help them along.

As elementary, middle school, and high school teachers, we are likely focused on the development stage. If we allow students to stay in the initiation stage, there's a decent chance they won't improve or learn more. As teachers, we can provide targeted lessons, activities, assessments, and feedback that can help students improve. As time goes on, improvements will level out, but students should be able to raise their level of skill and understanding under our watch. The perfection stage is unlikely to come during students' K–12 learning. Instead, students perfect their skills in college and graduate school with professors or through on-the-job training with experts in their field of interest.

It must be noted that, while deliberate practice (especially working with a demanding instructor) does lead to acquisition of skill and expertise, it isn't always fun. It takes a great deal of effort and focus, and the practitioner must pay particular attention to where they need to improve. Those who use deliberate practice can experience frustration, especially if they don't view mistakes as a pathway to improvement. However, if the student does see improvement, they might enjoy the process and the results.

In a study with nursing students, researchers Jennifer Ross, Elizabeth Bruderle, and Colleen Meakim (2015) had a group receive a training on deliberate practice while another group did not. Afterward, the first group of nursing students put deliberate practice into play in a laboratory session, asking peer mentors to provide consistent feedback so the students could think deeply about the skills they were acquiring. Evaluating these sessions, Ross and colleagues (2015) write, "Overall, the . . . students enjoyed the experience and noted that it was a constructive assignment that helped prepare them for their clinical experience" (p. 53). For the most part (three students reported frustration with the sessions), these students felt that their time spent using deliberate practice held value and made them feel more competent and prepared.

As educators, we can also engage in deliberate practice to improve our pedagogy. In *The Art and Science of Teaching*, Robert J. Marzano (2007) writes that educators can show gains in teaching by using deliberate practice if they have four major components.

1. **A common language of instruction:** Having a common language of instruction helps conversation and aids in comprehending important concepts.

2. **A focus on specific strategies:** Focusing on the strategies that they excel in and those where they falter enables teachers to identify mistakes so they can work on and improve them.

3. **Tracking of teacher progress:** Administration or teacher leaders should observe and evaluate teachers to see what they do well, what they can work on, and how they can improve. While issues with evaluations exist, they could allow a teacher to see an area of weakness that they may have missed through self-evaluation.

4. **Opportunities to observe and discuss expertise:** Teachers need a chance to watch peers teach and talk with other teachers about how to best educate students.

Consider the following scenario, in which an educator, Ms. Burton, embodies some of the four major components of deliberate practice for teachers.

> Ms. Burton wasn't normally a fan of standardized tests, but she wanted to be optimistic about them, focusing on what she could learn from them to improve her teaching practice. When she received a spreadsheet of her test results, she noticed that it showed overall scores but also scores from various sections. As a world history teacher, her students seemed to do very well on the Imperialism, World War I, and World War II sections, but scores for the Cold War section were lacking. This made sense as she loved to teach the previous three units and tended to run out of time at the end of the year, having only a week to teach the Cold War before testing. She looked at her other units to see what she could trim. Additionally, she sought out Mr. Vucerevich, who she knew taught an amazing unit on the Cold War. She knew that she could do both things to improve. She also understood she would have to be tough enough to shorten her earlier units, add to her unit on the Cold War, and seek out Mr. Vucerevich for advice and lesson ideas. She would set up a time to watch his class during her prep. Later, her plan was to work with him to come up with more lessons and get him to watch her teach at least one (offering feedback on what he saw). These three things would take some thinking and effort, but she knew it would help her teach a more well-rounded class.

If teachers or students want to improve, deliberate practice is key. To help with actionable guidance for students (and educators), author Gene Kerns (2020) offers his four Rs to deliberate practice: repetition, resistance, results, and recovery. For deliberate practice to work and for improvement to happen, many repetitions are necessary to learn new skills. Students need the resistance of something difficult to challenge them (deliberate practice is not meant for easy things students already know how to do). Results need to happen so that the teacher can give feedback (both positive and constructive), and recovery is necessary because deliberate practice takes a lot of focus and effort; students need time to recover (Kerns, 2020). As a teacher, if you provide the four Rs, your students have an excellent chance of improving their skills with deliberate practice.

The Tough–Smart Tool

Use the tool in figure 7.1 to serve as a springboard for a rich class discussion about deliberate practice. *Tough means that you don't give up but do persevere through difficulty, effort, and fear. Smart means taking the time to think about what you personally would need to do if you wanted to improve at your activity (make sure to share this definition with students—in this case, all people can be smart if they take the time to think about how they can improve).* If you have both, you are in quadrant 1 using deliberate practice, which is the best way to improve at something.

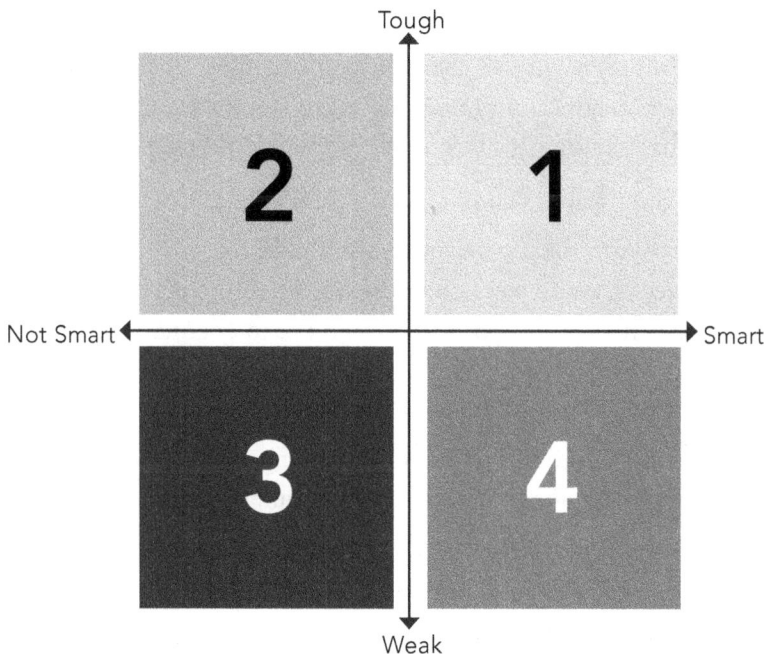

Source: Created by Chris Horpel. Used with permission.

Figure 7.1: Tough–smart tool.

*Visit **go.SolutionTree.com/SEL** for a free reproducible version of this figure.*

After reviewing the tool with the class, your peers, or on your own, please use the following questions to discuss and reflect. See appendix A (page 189) for the complete instructions on using the tools in this book.

Questions for Educators and Their Colleagues

The following questions help you discuss the tough–smart tool with colleagues to gain a more personal and broader understanding.

- If a teacher did the following things, which quadrant do you think they would belong in for that action?
  - The teacher goes to a colleague to get ideas or help on a lesson.
  - The teacher knows that they should walk around the class to give immediate feedback to students, but they sit at their desk instead.
  - The teacher stays up all night correcting papers.
  - The teacher shows up to work without a plan.
- If you were training for a marathon and had six months to prepare, what would you be doing in quadrants 1, 2, 3, and 4 to get ready?
- If people were trying to be better teachers, what would those in quadrant 1, 2, 3, and 4 be doing?
- Where are most teachers on the tool regarding their teaching practice? Why? Which quadrant promotes the most happiness and why? (Please be aware that quadrant 1 takes a lot of thought and effort.)
- What quadrant would you put sleeping and taking breaks in and why?
- Where are you on the tool regarding your teaching practice? If you're in quadrant 1, how do you personally stay there? If you're in one of the other quadrants, what might you do to move to quadrant 1?

Questions to Prompt Class Discussion

These are questions to promote class understanding about the tool. This can be done with small- or large-group discussion or by quietly reflecting in a journal.

- What does smart mean to you? What does tough mean to you? If a student did the following things, which quadrant do you think they would belong in for that action?
  - The student cheated on a test.
  - The student studied all night for a test.

- The teacher gave the student advice on how to improve, and the student didn't listen.

- The student asked a question when she didn't understand.

- The student knew that he should pay attention, but didn't.

- If you were training for a marathon and had six months to prepare, what are all the things you'd be doing in quadrant 1? What would your preparation look like in quadrants 2, 3, and 4?

- If someone wanted to be a better student, what would it look like and what would they be doing in quadrants 1, 2, 3, and 4?

- Regarding school, are most students in quadrant 1, 2, 3, or 4? Why?

- Which quadrant promotes the most happiness and why? (Please be aware that quadrant 1 takes a lot of thought and effort.)

- What quadrant would you put sleep and taking breaks in and why?

- Which quadrant are you in regarding school? If you're in quadrant 1, how would you stay there? If you're in another quadrant, what would you personally need to do to move to quadrant 1? Why would it be worth it or not worth it?

- How can you use the tool (page 127) in other areas in your life beyond school (for example, sports and activities, hobbies, relationships)?

Elementary Teacher Tip

Use tape to create the quadrants on the floor and have students physically go stand in the appropriate quadrant as you're discussing certain events or choices. If you don't have enough space in the classroom, see if you can conduct the lesson outside. Sample events and choices may include the following.

- My parents ask me to clean my room. I put up resistance but eventually do it.

- I stay in during recess to help the teacher clean the classroom.

- I run out to be first on the swings and fall and hurt myself (or someone else).

- During the mathematics quiz, I look on my friend's paper for some of the answers.

- I tell a friend when they hurt my feelings.

- I apologize to a friend when I hurt their feelings.

- I get up early so that I can feed the family pet and have myself ready to go to school on time.

- I pout in the dugout at my baseball game because I didn't get to play the position I wanted.

- I spend time after school on my trampoline working to be able to do a front flip.

Questions for Student Reflection

After a content-specific lesson that is also an opportunity to assess deliberate practice, these questions can assist students in evaluating their thoughts and behavior during the lesson as they pertain to the concept.

- During the challenge, what quadrant were you in? Why? During the challenge, if you were in quadrant 1, how did you do that? If you weren't in quadrant 1, how could you move to get into quadrant 1?

- How did being in the quadrant you were in make you feel during and after the challenge?

Length of Commitment

In his bestselling book *Outliers*, Malcolm Gladwell (2019) famously writes that it takes roughly ten years or ten thousand hours to become world-class at something. Among others, Gladwell (2019) cites the Beatles as an example. Before the band reached international success, it played eight-hour sets at nightclubs in Germany seven nights a week, accumulating hours and perfecting its craft. In another example, Gladwell (2019) writes about learning chess:

> To become a chess grandmaster also seems to take about ten years. (Only the legendary Bobby Fischer got to that elite level in less than that amount of time: It took him nine years.) And what's ten years? Well, it's roughly how long it takes to put in ten thousand hours of hard practice. Ten thousand is the magic number of greatness. (p. 41)

With the book's popularity, the ten-thousand-hour rule went viral. Many pundits attacked Gladwell, saying his rule was oversimplified and that success does not come solely from time spent practicing (Bradley, n.d.). First, some said that natural ability plays a role. If a basketball player who is five feet tall and lacks leaping ability put in ten thousand hours of practice, the player would still have great difficulty making it to the NBA against those who are seven feet with leaping ability and thousands of hours of practice as well. Gladwell (2009) counters on Reddit's forum thread Ask Me Anything:

> There is a lot of confusion about the 10,000 rule that I talk about in *Outliers*. It doesn't apply to sports. And practice isn't a sufficient condition for success. I could play chess for 100 years and I'll never be a grandmaster. The point is simply that natural ability requires a huge investment of time in order to be made manifest. Unfortunately, sometimes complex ideas get oversimplified in translation.

So, Gladwell understands that those without the necessary natural ability could never be at the top of their field; however, even those without natural ability, with thousands of hours of the right kind of practice, could still become great (or, at least, more than proficient). The five-foot basketball player may not make the NBA, but with thousands of hours of deliberate practice, the player would still excel at playing basketball. In fact, Gladwell (2019) notes Ericsson's (1993) study in his book where Ericsson says that "maximation of deliberate practice is neither short-lived nor simple. It extends over a period of at least 10 years" (p. 368). I think that both Ericsson and Gladwell would agree that, to gain expertise in some area, thousands of hours of deliberate practice are necessary.

Regarding students in our classes, teachers will not have enough time to create world-class individuals. Often, we only have a week or two to focus on one unit or skill before we move to another. However, focused deliberate practice remains important. Students who use deliberate practice with the time they have in our class will improve more rapidly than students who don't—even on daily lessons. Students may not have enough time in your classroom to achieve best-in-the-world status, but we can work with them with our time together to get them to achieve much more than they would on their own.

Expertise

In the landmark experiment on expertise, Ericsson, Krampe, and Tesch-Römer (1993) studied musicians, all eighteen years old or younger, at West Berlin Music Academy. At the Academy, all violin students had access to knowledgeable instructors who had the ability to provide consistent feedback. Student violinists were grouped into three categories based on achievement and skill: (1) the elite group, (2) the good group, and (3) the least accomplished group. (Although they were categorized into three groups by ability, all musicians were skilled at playing violin—especially compared to other musicians their age.)

After the experimenters determined the three categories, they asked the students in the three different groups how old they were when they started practicing, how much they practiced, and how they practiced. By the age of eighteen, the top group of the most accomplished violinists, on average, logged over seven thousand hours of deliberate practice, the second most accomplished group averaged five thousand hours of deliberate practice, and the third group averaged three thousand hours of deliberate practice. Deliberate practice was important to be an expert, but the number of hours of this focused practice led to the highest levels of skills. Those students in the seven-thousand-hour group are the best at playing violin. But are they happy?

If students put in hours of deliberate practice, they will become more successful in their chosen area, but will their life be joyful if they're investing so much time and effort to acquire that level of expertise? Before answering, it is important to understand that hours of focused practice are not easy. If we're teaching and getting our students to use deliberate practice, we should challenge them just above their ability levels (it makes no sense to challenge them with things they have already mastered). While they are working on these skills, it will be a struggle—students will make mistakes that may lead to anger and frustration. Author Barbara Blackburn (2018) talks about challenging students while giving an appropriate amount of assistance (not too much) so that they productively struggle. She says:

> Productive struggle is what I call the 'sweet spot' in between scaffolding and support. Rather than immediately helping students at the first sign of trouble, we should allow them to work through struggles independently before we offer assistance. That may sound counterintuitive, since many of us assume that helping students learn means protecting them from negative feelings of frustration. But for students to become independent learners, they must learn to persist in the face of challenge. (Blackburn, 2018)

The sweet spot is where deliberate practice lives. It is also where failure and, potentially, frustration might reside. Deliberate practice is not easy, but no worthwhile challenge is. If we can help students find their sweet spot, the likelihood of deliberate practice and learning increases. To help students productively struggle, Blackburn (2018) suggests a few things:

- Challenge the specific weaknesses of the student or small group rather than overwhelm them.

- Be productive rather than frustrating. For example, if you want to learn to play tennis, you will struggle appropriately playing a slightly superior coach who challenges you rather than playing someone completely out of your league.

- Let students use metacognitive reflections to process their thinking. With metacognitive reflections, students think about how they learn in addition to what they learn.

For the final suggestion, the tools in this book can assist. If students understand the processes and concepts of performance character, they may have a better chance to persevere through deliberate practice.

Beneficial Hardship

Your students can gain mastery through the productive struggle of deliberate practice, but would they be willing to go through this? Mastery is amazing, but it takes a huge amount of time and effort to get to expertise. A few years ago, I had an opportunity to think deeper about this concept of commitment coupled with the beneficial hardship of deliberate practice. When I was exercising during my prep period, I saw Christian, one of my former students, jogging around our school track. He told me that, along with working, he was training for an ultra-marathon. After a meaningful conversation, he asked me what we were currently studying in my sports psychology class. When I told him we were in a unit on commitment, he said that he had a good lesson for the subject and asked if he and another former student, Jason, could share it with my students. We set a time, and I eagerly awaited to see what they were planning.

Christian and Jason arrived at the classroom with eight caramel apples. They introduced themselves to the class then asked for eight volunteers. Each volunteer received an apple, and Christian and Jason let them know that the challenge was to finish their apple before the others. What the eight students found out very quickly after the contest had begun was that not all the caramel apples were apples. Under the caramel wrapping, two were, indeed, apples, while two were persimmons, two were tomatoes, and two were onions.

When some of the volunteers realized that they were eating something other than what they expected, they immediately stopped. Others plodded through. In fact, one student who procured an onion kept right on eating through the contest. Her eyes were watery, and she wasn't necessarily enjoying the experience, but she kept eating.

After six minutes, Christian and Jason stopped the students. Then, they shared the moral to the lesson: If you're going to commit to something, it's not always going to be fun or easy. Additionally, it may not be what you think or go the way you expect it to go. Those who are successful are going to eat the onion (or whatever they are given) even when it's difficult. Those who are successful and happy will be those who find a way to enjoy eating the onion. After their explanation, they led a discussion on whether the difficulty was worth it.

Deliberate practice for thousands of hours may lead to improvement and even world-class expertise; but it will also bring with it effort, hardships, and potential frustration. Not practicing deliberately in school will make life easier for the student in the present, but they will learn very little. Students may choose this option, but many hours of deliberate practice will help students become better.

The Commitment Tool

Experts say that to become world-class in something requires thousands of hours of deliberate practice. This means that you need to focus your full attention to trying new things and improving your weaknesses by getting constructive feedback daily for around a decade. Use the tool in figure 7.2 to serve as a springboard for a rich class discussion about length of commitment. Remember, deliberate practice is not easy and is often frustrating, but it almost ensures improvement if done over a long period of time. Those who don't use deliberate practice tend to stagnate, even if they spend years practicing.

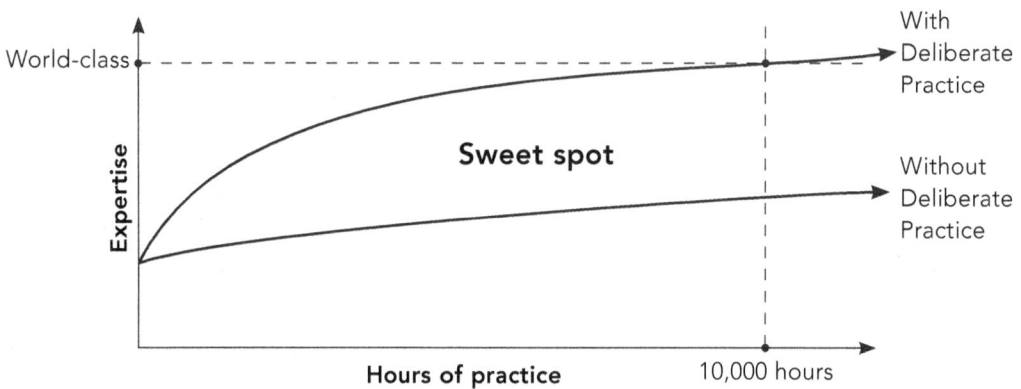

Figure 7.2: Commitment tool.

Visit **go.SolutionTree.com/SEL** *for a free reproducible version of this figure.*

After reviewing the tool with the class, your peers, or on your own, please use the following questions to discuss and reflect. See appendix A (page 189) for the complete instructions on using the tools in this book.

Questions for Educators and Their Colleagues

Use the following questions to help you discuss the commitment tool with colleagues to gain a more personal and broader understanding.

- How do you describe deliberate practice? Explain why the trajectory of deliberate practice is the way it is on the tool.

- According to the tool, explain the trajectory of someone who doesn't use deliberate practice. If you don't use deliberate practice, how much better will you get at something (in other words, might the tool be wrong)?

- How many hours have you put into teaching? Where would you put your trajectory—on the With Deliberate Practice line, on the Without Deliberate Practice line, or somewhere in between?

- How is deliberate practice difficult?

- Deliberate practice is difficult, and teachers also have lives beyond teaching. Saying this, how many hours should a teacher devote to deliberate practice of their pedagogical practice?

- Do you think any teachers at your school are world-class at teaching? How happy do you think they are?

- Teachers don't have enough time to get a student to world-class in a subject. What part of the tool would you be responsible for helping students through? How might it be important to assist students through that stage?

- What is the sweet spot on this tool? Do you think your students are in the sweet spot? How close are they to the With Deliberate Practice line and the Without Deliberate Practice line? How hard should you push your students to the upper line?

Questions to Prompt Class Discussion

These are questions to promote class understanding about the tool. This can be done with small- or large-group discussion or by quietly reflecting in a journal.

- How do you describe deliberate practice? Explain why the trajectory of deliberate practice is the way it is on the tool.

- How many days or years would it take to put in ten thousand hours of deliberate practice? How many hours do you think you need to be world-class in something? (Do you think the tool is wrong?)

- In a class, you don't have enough time to become world-class in something. Where are you on this tool in a yearly class? How important is this part of the tool whether you pursue this area of study later in life?

- How much better do you get without deliberate practice? (Is the tool wrong?) What is the sweet spot? At your school, where are most students on the tool—closer to the With Deliberate Practice or Without Deliberate Practice line?

- Deliberate practice takes a lot of effort. How much deliberate practice should a student put in at school?

- Do you think that being world-class in something can make you happy? How happy can you be on the way to becoming world-class?

- What if you didn't have the ability to be world-class in something (for example, you wanted to play in the NBA, but you're five feet tall); how many hours of deliberate practice should you put into that activity?

Questions for Student Reflection

After a content-specific lesson that is also an opportunity to assess commitment, these questions can assist students in evaluating their thoughts and behavior during the lesson as they pertain to the concept.

- During the challenge, were you deliberately practicing? If you were, explain how you were using deliberate practice. If not, why not?

- If you were using deliberate practice, how happy did you feel? If you weren't, how happy did you feel?

- When working on this challenge, did you stop and say, "This is good enough," or did you continue to think about how to optimize your time? When do you determine that something is good enough?

How to Resist Quitting

How many times a day do you want to quit something? For example, let's say you have a large stack of papers to correct. During the process of completing the pile, does a voice try to get you to stop and do something easier? If you're like me, your classroom gets much cleaner when you have papers to correct. While I'm adding comments and assigning evaluations, I'll start looking around the room for things to rearrange and clean. Because I deem that cleaning windows or reconfiguring desks is easier than the paper-correcting task, I find myself opting to improve the neatness of my surroundings. After all, cleaning is a good use of time, right? The voice is always playing tricks to get you out of doing something difficult in lieu of something easier.

When it comes to commitment, it is important to understand that all of us want to quit when we're doing something challenging or difficult. Our brains seem to be programmed to go toward what is easy and pleasurable. Evolutionarily speaking, the reward of pleasure was necessary to get a prehistoric person to work hard to hunt and gather or seek or build shelter. If they suffered doing these things, they would feel the pleasure of a full belly or a comfortable and dry place to sleep. Things have changed in the 21st century. University of Michigan psychologist Kent C. Berridge and researcher from Oxford University Morten L. Kringelbach (2015) write, "In a sense, pleasure can be thought of as evolution's boldest trick, serving to motivate an individual to pursue rewards necessary for fitness, yet in modern environments of abundance also inducing maladaptive pursuits" (p. 647). Modern amenities mean many teachers and students seek pleasure without working for it. Why wouldn't someone want to feel pleasure without the suffering?

The voice in a student's head will do what it can to steer them away from difficulty and toward rest. Quitting is when students give in to the voice and stop their commitment to a goal. If a student's challenge is writing an essay, they quit when they abandon the assignment and, instead, start doing something easier and more pleasurable than the paper.

To learn to control the voice that tells us to quit, teachers and students should first comprehend when and why they quit. In *Psychology Today*, Alex Lickerman (2011) writes about the thoughts of quitting he has when he's near the end of a long-distance run. He comments that he's fine at managing discomfort for the first leg of the run. Then, he offers:

> Once I'd begun to think about the end of my run, *reaching* the end of my run—and therefore the end of my pain—was all I could think about. The idea that my pain was about to end became so enticing that my ability to withstand it dramatically declined.

In other words, Lickerman (2011) explains something that we all do. If we are engaging in something difficult, our brain is naturally going to tell us to stop doing that thing. If we focus our attention on being done or ending that discomfort, the thought of that fills our head, and we are more likely to quit.

Lickerman (2011) continues:

> When my mind started to visualize the end of the run, it shifted from *managing* the pain my body was feeling to *preparing for it to end.* And in preparing for it to end, its ability to resist the influence of that pain rapidly fell apart.

What he is saying is that, if we focus on the present moment, we can manage our discomfort and keep quitting at bay. However, if we focus on being done, our brain starts to latch onto the thought of ending discomfort, and we quit. To control quitting, we could find a way to focus on the present and the task at hand. Our brains may try to focus on being done several times while doing something challenging, but we can stave off this urge by finding a way to get ourselves back to the present. If we can do this, we can control when we quit. It's not our urge to be done making the decision for us to stop. Rather, it turns into our own choice. We know that we must stop at some point, but we determine when.

While quitting is evident in a difficult physical situation like distance running, the concept also applies in an academic setting. If a middle school student is told to work on a difficult mathematics problem, for example, the battle starts in their head. Their brain starts to focus on pleasure and how great it would be to be done with the task. If they give in to these thoughts, they quit. Instead, if they keep themselves in the present and disregard their thoughts of being done, they will continue to attack and work on the problem. Again, the longer they struggle, the more times their brains will try to focus on being done and ending the discomfort. Students who persevere can find a way to keep moving themselves back to the present through the process.

If students are mindful of why their brains want to quit and how they can personally quell the voice that always wants pleasure, they have a better chance at persisting. The quitting tool will help them understand this and give teachers a common language and a visual with the students so the process can be easily accessed for a conversation. This can be particularly useful when you notice a student in your class who chose pleasure over learning.

Rate of Quitting in Students

To discuss how to help students through this process, senior *Education World* contributor Nicole Gorman (2017) states that it's important for teachers and students to be aware of student quit rates. According to the author, one must analyze how many times students got to a particular problem and simply gave up to understand the quit rate. A teacher could identify assessments with high student quit rates in their classes and use them to teach perseverance, as the following scenario portrays.

> *To test her students' quit rates, fifth-grade teacher Mrs. Gavin creates a series of mathematics questions for her students. Most of the questions are challenging, but one question is more difficult and will require more thought and effort. Mrs. Gavin is curious whether the students will persist or quit on the more challenging question. As she walks around the room, she notices that quite a few students left the question blank or wrote a random answer without even trying. Even when they finish all the other problems, many give up on this one question.*
>
> *Seeing this trend, Mrs. Gavin has a wonderful opportunity for a discussion. For those who abandoned the difficult problem, she tries to learn what it was that made them quit en masse. They reply with the following.*
>
> *"I didn't want to make a mistake."*
>
> *"It just seemed too hard."*
>
> *"It was going to take too much time and effort."*
>
> *Then, she asks the students who did try what they were thinking and how they convinced themselves to stay in the present and attack it. She also questions the students, "Do you feel better when you give up or, at least, try to figure it out?"*

Students have differing responses, but most say that they feel better if they try to attack the problem—even if they don't finish or get it right. We all tend to feel more in control and better afterward if we put up a fight.

How do students overcome their urge to quit? How do they persevere and remain committed? The answer could lie in physiology. Neuroscientist Andrew Huberman (2022), who runs a neurobiology lab at Stanford University, offers that controlling our dopamine output is essential to perseverance. Dopamine, which we talked about in the joyful learning section (page 90 in chapter 5), is one of our body's neurotransmitters that plays an important role in pleasurable feelings and focus. Huberman (2022) says that, when we are doing something difficult for a long period of time, it's essential that we find ways to release dopamine along the way. If we do, it will make us feel good and help us keep our focus throughout a long and difficult journey. While you're struggling or you find your focus straying to being done, Huberman suggests that you find a way to release dopamine, which will make you feel good and keep you focused. It also gets us back to the present. Persevering over a long period is very difficult and draining unless a person can periodically produce dopamine throughout the journey.

Dopamine and Quitting

What does this mean for students? For many, projects and the school year are long and arduous. If students can wisely control their dopamine output, they'll have a very good chance of persisting. Throughout their struggles, students' brains are going to often tell them to quit. If students can release dopamine at this point, their brains will return to focus on the task at hand rather than latching onto the desire to be done and end discomfort.

Students can release dopamine in many ways. Two things that elicit the release of dopamine are smiling (Wiswede, Münte, Krämer, & Rüsseler, 2009) and praise (Murray, 2016). If you sense a student's quit rate for something is high, it may be a good time to get the student to smile or let them know how well they're doing by trying hard. It also may be important for educators to help students recognize and celebrate the small goals they have overcome already on their journey to the larger goal.

If educators can also share with students how quitting happens, students can identify it throughout the day. If students can find their motive from quitting and back to the challenge, they are more empowered to control their commitment level.

The Quitting Tool

To quit or not to quit is mostly a mental battle. Typically, when we are doing something difficult, our brain will tell us to stop. At this point, we all have a choice: we can focus on ending the discomfort and quit, or we can focus on the present and re-engage and persist until our brains tell us to stop again, putting us back where we started. We might think that some people out there are super-human and go on autopilot when they are doing difficult things, but the reality is that all people go through this process—some people are just good at resisting quitting. Use the tool in figure 7.3 to serve as a springboard for a rich class discussion about how to resist quitting.

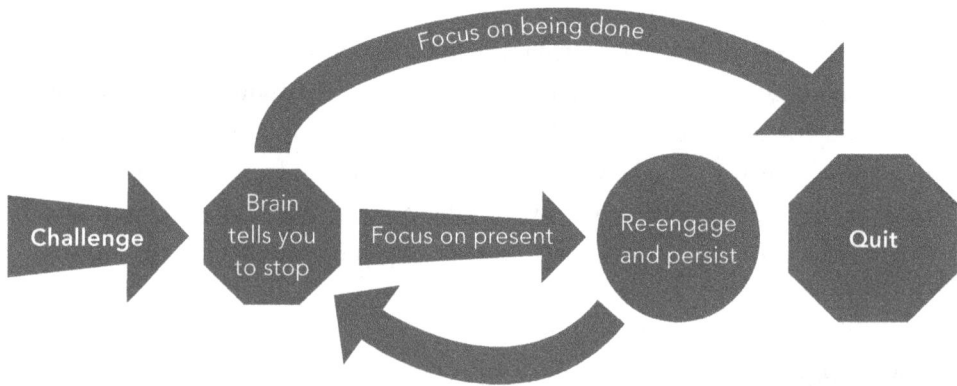

Figure 7.3: Quitting tool.

*Visit **go.SolutionTree.com/SEL** for a free reproducible version of this figure.*

After reviewing the tool with the class, your peers, or on your own, please use the following questions to discuss and reflect. See appendix A (page 189) for the complete instructions on using the tools in this book.

Questions for Educators and Their Colleagues

Use the following questions to help you discuss the quitting tool with colleagues to gain a more personal and broader understanding.

- Give an example of when you have encountered the process that the quitting tool describes.

- How often does your brain tell you to quit when you are doing something difficult or something you may not want to do? How often does this happen for you in a typical day?

- What activities in your job as an educator make you want to quit the most?

- What process or processes do you use to keep yourself from quitting when things get difficult and the voice in your brain tells you to stop? In other words, how do you re-engage and persist (according to the tool)?

- Is there a difference between quitting and stopping? Please explain. How do you know when it's the correct time to quit or stop?

- How does it make you feel when you're in control of when you quit something?

- When do you see your students quit in school? How many times do you think they go through the lower loop before they quit?

Questions to Prompt Class Discussion

These are questions to promote class understanding about the tool. This can be done with small- or large-group discussion or by quietly reflecting in a journal.

- Explain the tool. Give an example of when this happens to you. How often does your brain tell you to quit when you are doing something difficult or something you may not want to do? How often does this happen for you in a typical day?

- Which course in school makes you want to quit the most and why?

- How often do people quit before they've even tried something? Why do people do this? What process do you use to

Elementary Teacher Tip

Teach students a yoga pose and tell them that you are going to ask them to hold the pose until you say "stop." Explain that the goal is to be still and silent and to hold the pose the whole time, even when it is difficult. Start with a short amount of time and repeat the activity several times, having them hold for progressively longer amounts of time. When finished, ask questions such as the following.

- Was this a hard exercise? If so, what made it hard?

- Did you want to quit at any point?

- Did you quit? If not, how did you keep going?

- How do you feel now that it's done?

Then, as a class, help students brainstorm things they could say to themselves during any type of activity or task (not just yoga) to keep going in times that they want to quit. Make a list and post it in the classroom so that when they are feeling challenged at any point during the school day, they can choose something from the list to say to themselves to keep themselves from quitting.

keep yourself from quitting when things get difficult, and your brain tells you to stop?

- We all must quit at some point. How do you know when it's the right time for you to quit or stop?

- When you are in control of when you quit (you don't just give in to the voice that tells you to stop right away), how does it make you feel?

Questions for Student Reflection

After a content-specific lesson that is also an opportunity to assess quitting, these questions can assist students in evaluating their thoughts and behavior during the lesson as they pertain to the concept.

- During the challenge, did you quit or not? How did it make you feel? If you didn't quit during the challenge, did an inner voice try to convince you to stop? If so, how did you deal with that?

- When might be an appropriate time to quit or stop on this challenge?

- Were you in control of when you quit? How do you know?

Summary

A student who is committed to a challenge will, first, think about the best course of action to improve themselves; then, they will be diligent and stick to the plan. To think about how to best take on a challenge, successful students use deliberate practice. Deliberate practice focuses attention on task improvement coupled with consistent expert feedback. Those students who use deliberate practice for an extended period will outperform those who don't. While deliberate practice speeds up improvement, it is taxing, difficult, and potentially frustrating. When students take on challenges (especially with deliberate practice), many will have a voice in their head trying to convince them to quit. Students who are very good at resisting quitting find a way to focus on the present and quiet the voice. If students can persist and continue using deliberate practice, they will see gains and improvement. Students may not like deliberate practice in the throes of it; but it will likely lead to more success, pride, and positive feelings.

8

Grit

Grit is that 'extra something' that separates the most successful people from the rest. It's the passion, perseverance, and stamina that we must channel in order to stick with our dreams until they become a reality.

—Travis Bradberry

My dad gifted me with a love for wrestling. He was a coach, and his passion for the sport was contagious. He also passed down his genetics, meaning that I wasn't destined to be very fast or tall. Thank goodness a sport like wrestling exists where body type and ability aren't as important as drive and persistence. While genetic talent is important, much of performance in wrestling comes from passion, effort, and confidence.

After competing in college, I returned to my alma mater to be an assistant coach. An exceptional recruiting class was coming to the school with several wrestlers around my weight; therefore, the head coach asked if I was interested in mentoring this crop of talent. One of the wrestlers was Matt Gentry, who eventually won an NCAA title at 157 pounds during his junior year (Stanford Athletics, 2016). During Matt's senior year, he was getting some extra work after practice with our freshman 125-pounder Tanner Gardner (an incredible wrestler in his own right who went on to be a three-time All-American). The three of us were the only people left in the room, so I sat against the wall to watch the two spar.

To my amazement, Tanner was destroying Matt, scoring points almost at will. The pair wrestled for about fifteen minutes, and nothing changed—Tanner would put Matt in one precarious position after another with Matt struggling to fight out. Having a freshman crushing our senior returning national champ four weight classes above him didn't compute to me.

As the two finished, the freshman left the room feeling great about himself. Matt walked toward me with, of all things, a smile on his face—which didn't make sense either because he had just gotten shellacked.

"Are you OK?" I asked.

"Yeah. Why?" he said.

"Because he just cleaned your clock. Are you sure you're not sick?" This is how Matt responded (and it also explains to me why he was an NCAA champion and eventual two-time Olympian for Canada):

> In wrestling, I believe there is a finite number of positions that two people can get into. My goal in practice isn't to score points. My goal in practice is to improve. That's why I try to get myself in as many positions as I can so that I can learn how to get out of them. (M. Gentry, personal communication, 2005)

In other words, Matt was purposely putting himself in positions that he rarely got into and wasn't comfortable with yet. His belief was that, if he put himself in these situations more, he would figure out what he would need to do. This, in turn, would expand his comfort zone and make him a more complete wrestler. Matt clearly had a passion for betterment, along with a way to deliberately practice things that he knew he needed to improve. Years of this drive and focused attention led to his many successes. Additionally, I would say that he was happy throughout his four years in college because he focused on process over outcome. Improvement and enjoyment seem to always be related.

I know I was supposed to be the coach and mentor, but I would argue that I was the one who learned more in this coach and athlete relationship. The thing I noticed the most was Matt's grittiness. Teachers can adapt Matt's habit of deliberately entering uncomfortable situations for the sake of efficient learning within the classroom. Grit is a pattern of behavior that students can learn. Students can use grit to help them reach levels of learning if you give them the guidance they need to implement this kind of thinking. This chapter will review the grit cycle, identify the limits of your comfort zone, and apply both to improving performance. This chapter includes three tools to help you and your students better understand grit and how to use it to make both teachers and students better versions of themselves.

The Definition of Grit

The word *grit* had been a vague part of our vernacular for centuries, but public attention to it renewed with Angela Duckworth's (2016a) book *Grit: The Power of Passion and Perseverance*. Duckworth (2016a) shared that it wasn't necessarily natural ability that led to success. Rather, *grit*—which she defines in *Journal of Personality and Social Psychology* as "perseverance and passion for long-term goals" (Duckworth, Peterson, Matthews, & Kelly, 2007, p. 1087)—was the main driving force that made people successful. Through her studies, this played out in groups who were involved in stressful challenges, including West Point cadets, Scripps National Spelling Bee contestants, and new teachers in inner-city schools. Those who succeed in those environments are not necessarily the smartest or most qualified candidates; instead, those who show a great deal of passion and perseverance are the ones who are able to navigate through those experiences most successfully.

With passion for their goal, successful people are motivated to start and stick with a challenge. With perseverance, successful people will continue pursuing a long-term goal, even when they encounter failure, fear, or both. Instead of packing their tent and giving up when things get difficult, the gritty person remains motivated and continues to move forward. As researchers in psychology Álvaro Postigo, Marcelino Cuesta, Rubén Fernandez-Alonso, Eduardo Garcia-Cueto, and José Muñiz (2020) say, "Being gritty is falling seven times but getting up eight" (p. 77). If a person is gifted in some area but doesn't have the drive or the persistence to work through failure, they will not have as much of a chance of being successful as those to whom that same skill comes less naturally who are gritty. If this is true for the groups Duckworth (2016a) studied, shouldn't it be true for students who partake in challenges school and academics provide?

Duckworth's thoughts and studies were a revelation to many, but she did encounter her critics. Author David Denby (2016) counters Duckworth's claims.

In the *New Yorker*, he quotes Jack Shonkoff, the director of Harvard's Center on the Developing Child:

> If you haven't in your early years been growing up in an environment of responsive relationships that has buffered you from excessive stress activation, then if, in tenth-grade math class, you're not showing grit and motivation, it may not be a matter of you just not sucking it up enough. A lot of it has to do with problems of focusing attention, working memory, and cognitive flexibility. And you may not have developed those capacities because of what happened to you early in life.

Shonkoff expresses that grit is not always a choice students can make. Students may have legitimate biological reasons or childhood traumas that make grit unattainable. Additionally, professor and chair of higher education at Azusa Pacific University Laurie A. Schreiner (2017) writes that privilege also plays a major role in student grittiness.

> And therein lies the privilege implicit in grit. Swimming lessons, access to a pool, and the ability to take time off work to attend a child's swim meets is a luxury that is simply unavailable to low-income persons . . . Other aspects of a supportive environment are also laden with social class privilege that many take for granted: being able to purchase soccer or softball uniforms or a musical instrument, having a car to drive a child to games or lessons, even going to a school that still has the budget to offer extracurricular activities, music, and art. There is an ever-widening gap in the US between the rich and poor, and that gap extends to participation in extracurricular activities. (p. 12)

Schreiner argues that, to pursue a passion, students need access to their passion and assistance to help them persevere. Many lower-income schools do not allow students the same passion opportunities as schools with more privilege. Additionally, some families do not have the time to support a student's passion or simply can't afford it. For these reasons (and others), Schreiner believes that certain students don't have the same opportunity to be gritty as others.

While the concept of grit may be out of reach to many students, I contend that grit is an important concept of which students should be aware. I see many students who, due to any number of factors, gave up on a subject or school in general because they feel they don't have anything left to give. That said, while grit may not be the only factor in success, it's certainly a major contributor and how you support your students can influence their ability to reserve grit for their learning. When students can at least be aware of the concept and combine that mindset with the other traits we discuss in this book, they might see that ability alone does not solely determine success—that they do have more to give. Their own motivation and consistent effort do play a huge role in betterment. If students can find capacity to reserve even just a little bit of grit to apply to their learning, they should see improvements as they move closer to their potential.

While gritty students have a good chance at improvement, they also have a good chance at happiness. If students focus on a long-term challenge, they will start to think more about the task at hand and less about ego-driven thoughts. In other words, being gritty and locked in on the present moment without fear of mistakes can take a student out of thinking about comparison to others (which can breed anxiety and depression). If students can be in the present working as hard as they can to improve themselves, they might realize both success and happiness.

The Grit Cycle

Grit is a combination of passion and perseverance. Those two components of grit tend to build on each other—passion leads to more perseverance and perseverance leads to more passion. Sometimes, however, the embodiment of the relationship between passion and perseverance isn't quite as one might imagine when conjuring the word grit. Consider the following scenario in which an educational administrator, Mr. Murchison, considers how best to implement the concept of grit in his school.

After reading Duckworth's (2016a) book, Principal Murchison thought about how he might integrate more grit into his life and the lives of the teachers and students at his school. As he walked around the school to different classrooms, grit was always on his mind—if he wanted the students at his school to be successful, he would need teachers who assisted students in becoming gritty. He just wasn't sure what that looked like.

Mr. Murchison popped into the first classroom where he watched one of Mr. Hess's lessons. It was loud. Mr. Hess had students working on a project where they were involved and excitedly talking with each other. When students made mistakes, Mr. Hess assured them that their mistakes helped the learning process. Walking around the room, Mr. Murchison asked students what they were doing, and they were eager to share their projects, their failures, how this lesson would help them in "real life," and the fact that they had been working on the project for three days.

Leaving Mr. Hess's classroom, Mr. Murchison went to observe Mrs. Smith's classroom. Her classroom was silent. Students were working individually on a series of problems. When they corrected their answers as a class, Mrs. Smith scolded the students for wrong answers, telling them they needed to try harder. At the end of the period, she unloaded an hour's worth of homework on students so they could, as she said, "get tougher and get the answers right for the test." Mr. Murchison left Mrs. Smith's room thinking about which teacher did a better job of promoting grit.

Grit is a tricky concept and word. When some people hear the word *grit*, they may automatically assume it means more and harder work around the clock. After all, isn't grit developed in the arena of pain and suffering? In her book, Duckworth (2016a) says:

> Some believe grit is forged in the crucible of adversity. Others are quick to paraphrase [Friedrich] Nietzsche: "What doesn't kill you makes you stronger." Such invocations conjure an image of scowling mothers and fathers dispensing endless criticism on the sidelines of games that had better be victories or chaining their children to the piano bench or violin stand, or grounding them for the sin of an A–. (p. 200)

Some teachers might look at grit through this lens as well. To teach grit, they think that students must receive more homework. They think mistakes require severe punishment to teach students to work harder. However, this is not Duckworth's (2016a) interpretation. Instead, grit is pursuing a goal with purpose that, through the lengthy process of improvement, will inevitably lead to mistakes and failures that a successful person will work through. Teachers, then, who want to teach grit could work to spark passions and offer difficult challenges without giving students repercussions for inevitable mistakes. While some might look at Mrs. Smith's class above as the difficult and gritty one, Mr. Hess's class is much more likely to produce more passion and perseverance from students.

So, how does a teacher instill grit in their students? To think about this, we might want to look at Duckworth's (2016a) thoughts on how parents can pass grit on to their children. First, she mentions that it may be important for a parent to model grit. As a parent myself, my children may listen to some of what my wife and I *say* to them about passion and perseverance; but they pay attention to almost everything we *do*. It would be hypocritical to tell my sons to be gritty while I lazed around watching television all day. Similarly, it would be difficult to tell students to be gritty if I spent no time on, didn't care about, and didn't take risks with my lessons.

Along with modeling grit, Duckworth (2016a) also writes about authoritative or wise parenting. Parents who are both demanding and supportive at the same time fit within these monikers. Parents may do this in different ways; however, demandingness and support must always be present. If a parent demands, they will nudge their child toward challenges. Support must also be present as the child will surely make mistakes and fail—especially if they are being challenged with what they have yet to become proficient in. When that happens, support serves as the safety net that lets children know that everything will be all right and that they can still succeed through these mishaps. In my case, I was blessed to have motivational parents. Throughout my childhood, my mom and dad challenged me to do things that were difficult and maybe a little scary; but they also coached me through the difficulty and failures. I may not have always liked it at the time; but, looking back, I am extremely grateful for their parenting style.

By being demanding and supportive, teachers can also help students be gritty. Duckworth (2016a) discusses Harvard University economist and scholar Ron Ferguson's study on grit in the classroom:

> He found that teachers who are demanding—whose students say of them, "My teacher accepts nothing less than our best effort," and "Students in this class behave the way my teacher wants them to"—produce measurable year-to-year gains in the academic skills of their students. Teachers who are supportive and respectful—whose students say, "My teacher seems to know if something is bothering me," and "My teachers want us to share our thoughts"—enhance students' happiness, voluntary effort in class, and college aspirations. (p. 236)

By being demanding, motivational, and wise, teachers push students to try hard. By supporting students, teachers can help students through the process of perseverance—even when the challenge takes a great deal of effort, and the students fail. Demanding and supportive teaching practices should elicit more effort from students. This effort will lead to improvement. Improvement can lead to satisfaction and pride, which can spark a passion. Being supportive and demanding is difficult to maintain, but it can yield gritty benefits.

In other words, challenging lessons from a demanding and supportive teacher can lead to something I like to call the *grit cycle*. The grit cycle is based on the two components of grit: passion and perseverance—two components that build off each other. If someone is passionate about something, they tend to work hard at it and persevere. If someone perseveres, they improve and become more passionate. Passion begets perseverance which begets passion which begets perseverance, and so on. If you can find your way in, the two components of grit build on each other, and grit will grow. So, how do you get in?

How the Grit Cycle Works for Educators

Let's look at educators first. One point of entry into the cycle is passion. If you are passionate about teaching, you will put more time into improving your craft. As you put more time into it, you improve. This, in turn, makes you more passionate, which leads to more time spent, and so forth. Passion, therefore, is one way to kickstart the grit cycle.

The other entry point is through perseverance. If we work hard enough at teaching and try new things, we will start to gain some mastery that could ignite our passion. That passion will lead to more time spent that leads to more mastery and thereby to more effort. Again, the grit cycle begins.

Some teachers have an easy time entering the grit cycle. When Mr. Silvernale started as a teacher, he was passionate about helping young people learn and be better versions of themselves. This led him to put more effort into his craft to make this happen. His efforts improved his practices and fed his passion. On the other hand, veteran teacher Ms. Mattingly had lost her passion for teaching several years ago. Then, she found a new practice (let's say from this book) that she started working diligently with to improve her teaching. Adding this new wrinkle to her class elevated her teaching practice and rekindled her passion for teaching. Her passion led to more effort to continue improving. While they didn't enter the cycle in the same way, the two teachers ended up with the same result—enhanced grit.

Both means of entry work well. As an educator, it really doesn't matter how you enter the grit cycle. It's more important to find your way in—especially if you're aware that you've fallen out. If you see yourself as not as gritty as you would like, either you can exhume your purpose and love for teaching, or you can start putting more research and effort into it. Like starting a motorcycle, it might take multiple attempts for a teacher to kickstart their grit. If you keep at it through passion or effort, you will eventually get it running and ready to hum down the road.

If you can do this and enter the grit cycle, you may be happier. We've all seen the educator who has lost their passion and, thus, doesn't put in as much effort as they used to. These educators seem to be bored or burned out, go through the motions, and count the days to retirement. Author and education consultant Anthony Muhammad (2018) calls these exhausted teachers "the survivors." After years of stress, burnout, changing administration, and lack of grit, their only goal is to make it to the end of the day in one piece; this makes them ineffective educators who may fail to inspire their students (Muhammad, 2018). It's drudgery. Then, there are the gritty teachers. They experiment with new lessons and try different things, which makes the school day more exciting. Both teachers spend the same amount of time with students, but one is certainly going to have a more fulfilling day than the other. It does take more effort to be gritty, but which teacher would you rather be? It's much more fun and exhilarating to kickstart and ride a fully functioning motorcycle on a beautiful and exciting adventure than sitting on a defunct one in the parking lot for an entire school year.

While it's important to be in the cycle as educators, we can also think about how we can light a fire within students to tap their inner grittiness (if it isn't already out). For some students, it may be easy if they find their passion early. Gifted student researcher Ellen Winner (2019) describes students who have a deep passion called a *rage to master*:

> Domains in which one most often finds such children are language (speaking in sentences at a very early age), music (playing an instrument), drawing (typically very realistically), mathematics, and chess. These children exhibit what I call a "rage to master," the domain in which they are strong. They spend hours working at developing their craft, and it is often hard for parents to tear the child away in order to eat, go to school, or go to sleep.

These types of students already have a passion, making it our job to provide them with challenges so that they can persevere, gain mastery, and continue to feed their passion. However, these students are rare. Organization Educator Innovator (2013) offers the following:

> Most kids have an interest, but they don't have that driving passion that is going to just make them go wild on their own and build their own learning pathways. Most kids need much more adult scaffolds, supports, institutional invitations, and connections in order to connect the interests that they do have to opportunities and trajectories of learning that will really serve them in their adult life.

In other words, we, as educators, can try to help most students unearth what interests them. If we can help students learn to persevere by giving exciting lessons that challenge them and help them grow, it could spark an interest. As teachers, we understand that not every lesson will spark a passion. However, if students persevere in learning daily, the chance of lighting that fire greatly increases.

How the Grit Cycle Works for Students

When using perseverance to enter the grit cycle, it seems to help if a student's purpose or passion is based on process rather than outcome goals. If students are seeing growth while persevering (focusing on process), it may lead to a passion for that subject area or skill. When students pursue an outcome, they may just work as little as they can to get their expectation, which does not tend to spark emotion. Psychologists Christopher Peterson and Martin E. Seligman (2004) offer this:

> A student with a mastery (or task or learning) orientation, for example, is considered to strive for achievement defined in terms of individual mastery, with his or her progress measured in terms of improvement and effort.

In contrast, a student with a performance (or ability or ego) orientation is considered to strive for achievement with progress measured in terms of performance relative to others or some externally defined standard (e.g., grades). Many researchers suggest that the pursuit of mastery goals is most likely to be associated with a love of learning, because this orientation allows one to maintain a sense of efficacy while learning. (p. 167)

Various studies show that students with purposes and passions that focus on process goals tend to be grittier and have more success. Psychology professor at Sungkyunkwan University Daeun Park along with Alisa Yu, Eli Tsukayama, and Angela Duckworth (2018) study process (mastery) and outcome (performance) goals and their relation to success and grit, concluding:

[We] found that students who perceived their schools as more mastery goal-oriented were grittier and earned higher report card grades. In contrast, students who perceived their schools as more performance goal-oriented were less gritty and earned lower report card grades. In longitudinal analyses, changes in perceived mastery school goal structure predicted changes in grit over the school year, which in turn predicted changes in grades. Changes in perceived performance school goal structure, in contrast, did not reliably predict changes in grit. These findings suggest that school environments that emphasize the value of learning for learning's sake may encourage children to sustain interest in and effort toward long-term goals. (p. 120)

Therefore, if you are attempting to have students enter the grit cycle through perseverance, it may be very important to de-emphasize completion and grades and, rather, emphasize learning. If students put forth effort, set an outcome goal for themselves, and don't reach the desired outcome, passion will most likely diminish or go away entirely. Instead, if students put forth effort with a goal of improvement, their likelihood of achieving that goal is very high. They're more likely to enter the grit cycle, and they may even develop a new passion.

In their own study, researcher Álvaro Postigo from the University of Oviedo in Spain and colleagues (2020) see student grit start to dwindle over time:

As adolescents got older, their levels of academic grit fell, which is in line with findings from previous studies (West et al., 2016). The fall in academic grit in the ages we studied (10–14 years) is outstanding, and it means that determination and pursuit of objectives is much worse in secondary school than in primary school. (p. 81)

Though we cannot truly know why grit falls over time without intensive studies, we can still learn from our students about how to best improve their grit.

Let's start by looking at after-school activities. Studies show that nonacademic activities done outside of class are a breeding ground for grit. School engagement psychologists Jennifer Fredricks, Corinne Alfeld, and Jacquelynne Eccles (2009) mention this in their study of passion among gifted students, writing, "We found that passion was more characteristic of nonacademic activities such as sports and music than academic activities" (p. 26). The authors add that, in school, many of the gifted students they interviewed "were more concerned about demonstrating high ability and showing they were smart, as opposed to being motivated by learning and mastering new skills" (Fredricks et al., 2009, p. 26). Fredricks, Alfeld, and Eccles (2009) further explain this through self-determination theory, the idea that motivation increases when autonomy, competence, and connection are present. The authors write:

> Our findings suggest that voluntary nonacademic activities such as sports and the arts are more likely to be structured in a way to support passion than in traditional academic environments. Self-determination theory may help explain the higher passion in nonacademic activities; individuals' needs for autonomy, competence, and relatedness were more likely to be met in athletics and the arts than in academic domains. Youth in our talent sample were more likely to talk about having opportunities to make choices, receiving public recognition for their ability, and being supported and encouraged by teachers and peers. (p. 26)

Unfortunately, then, something is missing regarding passion in school. If we want to change this and guide students toward purpose and passion, we might want to review at self-determination theory and autonomy, competence, and connection. Especially at the higher grades, I'm not sure that students feel that going to school is their choice. Rather, many see it as something they are forced to do so that they can acquire a result. As they plod through assignment after assignment, they don't feel connected. Instead, as educators, can we foster passion and grit by offering open-ended challenges that allow students to productively struggle to attain mastery, connecting over a bond of shared sacrifice and effort?

Through difficult class challenges, students will falter, and that's where we can coach them through it, sharing ideas and thoughts on how to persevere. In other words, can we work with our classes like sports teams? If we can identify a common goal for the class based on process and mastery, provide them with challenges that will help them improve on their weaknesses, coach them through difficulty, and allow students to help each other reach that goal, we might make our classes something that students look forward to and get excited about. For teachers, this is difficult and takes a lot of effort, but it will be worth it if student grit is the byproduct.

A student may enter your class thinking, "I have absolutely no interest in this subject." Their initial passion for school or what you're teaching is zero, and they plan on the class being a waste of their time. But, if you start to challenge them and they start acquiring improvement and mastery, their passion for the subject will rise. They'll want to put in more effort, which makes them more excited about the subject. Before long, they're in the grit cycle without realizing how they got there. They'll look around and notice that they're on their own working motorcycle and figure, "Well, I'm here, and this is kind of fun. I might as well keep this going and see where this takes me."

The Grit Cycle Tool

Angela Duckworth (2016a) says that grit combines passion and perseverance toward long-term goals. According to her, grit is perhaps the most important factor when it comes to success, especially in working through difficult challenges. If a person is passionate about something, they will want to persevere. If someone perseveres, they will improve, which should elevate their passion. Therefore, passion and perseverance build on each other, creating a cycle of grit. Use the tool in figure 8.1 to serve as a springboard for a rich class discussion about the grit cycle.

Source: Adapted from Duckworth, 2016a.

Figure 8.1: Grit cycle tool.

Visit go.SolutionTree.com/SEL for a free reproducible version of this figure.

After reviewing the tool with the class, your peers, or on your own, please use the following questions to discuss and reflect. See appendix A (page 189) for the complete instructions on using the tools in this book.

Questions for Educators and Their Colleagues

Use the following questions to help you discuss the grit cycle tool with colleagues to gain a more personal and broader understanding.

- Explain the tool. How might perseverance and passion build off each other? Give an example.

- How do you know if you're gritty with something in your life? How much effort are you putting in when you're gritty? How does it make you feel?

- How gritty are you about teaching? How passionate are you about it, and how much do you persevere?

- How happy are those who are in the grit cycle? How happy are those who are not in the grit cycle?

- One of your colleagues is not passionate about teaching, and they don't persevere. How would you suggest that they enter the grit cycle, and would you want them to enter through passion or perseverance?

- How many students do you think are gritty in your class? What do you think is keeping them from being gritty?

- If a student isn't gritty, how would you get them into the grit cycle and would you do it via passion or perseverance? How could you get a student to be passionate about school?

- If you've ever seen a student become gritty throughout a school year, how did they do that?

Questions to Prompt Class Discussion

These are questions to promote class understanding about the tool. This can be done with small- or large-group discussion or by quietly reflecting in a journal.

- What is your definition of *passion*? What is your definition of *perseverance*? Explain the tool. How do passion and perseverance work with each other? How do the two work together to produce grit?

- How many students at your school are gritty about academics? Why? How happy is someone who does not demonstrate grit compared to someone who does?

- How gritty are you in school? How does that make you feel? If you have a friend who is not gritty in school but wants to get into the grit cycle, what advice would you give them? Is it easier to enter the grit cycle through perseverance or passion? Which entry point is more common for students?

Questions for Student Reflection

After a content-specific lesson that is also an opportunity to assess the grit cycle, these questions can assist students in evaluating their thoughts and behavior during the lesson as they pertain to the concept.

- Were you gritty during the challenge? How do you know? How much did you persevere with this challenge? Did your effort make you more passionate about it?

- How passionate were you about this challenge? How could you become more passionate about it?

- Can you be passionate about something without putting effort into it? Explain your answer.

How to Find (and Leave) Your Comfort Zone

To learn how to best develop your grit, you must first learn where you are most comfortable. Only then can you be intentional about leaving your comfort zone to enter the area of productive struggle. Consider the following scenario in which educator Mr. Lewis and his students discuss what it means to step outside of one's comfort zone.

"Wait. What? Can you say that again?" asks a student who has suddenly perked up in the back of the class.

"An interpretive dance," responds Mr. Lewis. "Your group needs to determine the ten most important people or events of the French Revolution. Once you've figured out who and what those are, you're going to choreograph a ten-act dance that represents those ten things. I want you to couple each act with a different song, and each act will have one narrator explaining what is going on. Everyone else will be dancing."

"Hang on," says another student. "What if we can't dance?"

"Not a problem," says Mr. Lewis. "I'm not expecting stag leaps and pirouettes. What I'm looking for is exaggerated actions without

words set to music that represent the ten most important parts of the French Revolution. Like this ..."

Mr. Lewis takes several small steps and pretends to write in the air with a flourish. "Dancing. That was the signing of the Declaration of Rights of Man and Citizen."

Mr. Lewis hears nervous murmurs through the class. "Look," he says, "I know that some of you are hesitant about this. For most of you, this is outside of your comfort zone, where you feel safe and know how to deal with things. What I'm trying to do is escort you a little outside of that area. I don't want you to jump off a cliff here. Instead, what I'm asking is for you to challenge yourself a little bit and venture outside. You can't learn when you're completely comfortable. If you want to grow, you have to get outside your comfort zone."

The term *comfort zone* is one Judith Bardwick (1995) popularized in her book *Danger in the Comfort Zone: From Boardroom to Mailroom—How to Break the Entitlement Habit That's Killing American Business.* There is plenty of debate to be had around the book's discussion of employee compensation and company success, but for our purposes, Bardwick (1995) notes the following of egocentric behavior among employees: "They will resist accountability and flee from evaluations. People naturally gravitate to the setting where they feel most comfortable or secure, and they will fight any change from that" (p. 30). When someone remains in this zone of comfort, they tend to only partake in things that are easy or things they can already do. There is little to no risk of failure or extra effort in this comfort zone, but there is also no improvement. We cannot become better by only doing things that are safe and unchallenging.

Additionally, failures reside where things aren't comfortable. This all occurs because we are entering a realm where we are encountering new tasks and skills. While people in this area of discomfort invite fear and effort, it does provide them an opportunity to improve and learn new things. If we can understand the potential benefits of discomfort and how to gauge how to best venture outside of our comfort zone, we may be more likely to brave effort, fear, and failures to improve ourselves.

We all need grit to take this journey beyond the realm of comfort. Grit not only gives us a reason to go toward discomfort (passion) but also the fortitude to deal with the struggle that lies outside of our comfort zone (perseverance). Without grit, we would all be nestled safely within our comfort zones, resisting improvement.

Many colleges urge students to get out of their comfort zones to have a more fulfilling post-high school experience. For example, the Southern Utah University website (Johnston, 2020) suggests several ways to do this that are relevant even for K–12, including joining in class discussions, getting to know professors and other students, and participating more in clubs and other student groups. These things might take effort and may be a little frightening, but the payoff is learning more, having more fun, and bolstering social groups.

If middle or high school students don't participate in class discussions, talk with their teachers (especially when they don't understand something), or join school activities, their experience won't be as rich. As teachers, it should be our job to escort students out of their comfort zones. In fact, I would argue that nudging our students beyond what is comfortable for them is the main purpose of our profession. However, a balance between too much discomfort and too much comfort is key to ensuring this will help student learning.

If an educator gives a lesson that is too far outside of the students' ability to accomplish, those students will give up—erasing the opportunity to improve and grow grit. As they do this, students will need to persevere. As they see gains and eventually reach the goal, their passion will grow. Challenges just outside the comfort zone, therefore, lead to passion, persistence, and grit. Challenges too far outside of the comfort zone could lead to anxiety, frustration, and a student or class that gives up.

How to Identify Individual Comfort Zones

But students all have different comfort zones. One student might feel completely at ease with a lesson while another might see the same lesson as too far outside of their ability level. If we're giving the same lesson to all the students, how can we work with the varying levels of discomfort?

The answer may lie in another important educational principle, Lev Vygotsky's (1978) *zone of proximal development* (ZPD), which is the gray area between skills one has and skills they do not yet have. Since the ZPD is just beyond what a student can already do on their own, students in their zone need assistance and scaffolding from someone who already understands the skill. Educators, therefore, should be able to help students through the ZPD with assistance and support, guiding them toward mastery. Professor of psychology Victor K. Zaretsky (2021) offers this about Vygotsky's (1978) theory:

> From a theorist's perspective, L.S. Vygotsky's idea is quite simple: within ZPD,
> in collaboration with adults, children can solve problems that they cannot
> solve independently; and tomorrow they will be able to autonomously handle

problems that they solve in collaboration today. Therefore children's capacities get continuously enhanced and progressive development unfolds when the adult creates proper conditions to this end. (p. 41)

While it's important for educators to challenge and nudge students outside of their current abilities, Vygotsky's (1978) theory preaches that the educator should also support students in their ZPD, aiding and scaffolding until students reach mastery on their own. This assistance from the teacher does not include taking over and doing the challenges for the students, but it might include coaching them through the inevitable failures (sharing that they are essential to learning) and leaning toward process over outcome goals.

Because students' comfort zones are all different, the educator must be aware of how much support they need to give to every individual. Some students in a class may be completely comfortable with a lesson, meaning that the educator does not need to provide support. Others who see the lesson in their ZPD may require occasional small nudges and scaffolding. For the students who see a lesson as far exceeding their abilities, the teacher can give them extra attention and scaffolding. As some students in the class become more comfortable with the concept as it is taught in class, you may want to employ them to work with students who aren't quite so comfortable yet to help guide them toward mastery.

As an educator, you're going to have to judge where your students are. Then, the trick is to find and create lessons that escort the majority students into the ZPD (which, admittedly, is hard to do). Even if done well, you may still have students who feel overwhelmed. You may want to look out for those students and try to offer them extra support.

The purpose of students being in their ZPD or discomfort is growth and learning. If a student is in their ZPD (and provided scaffolding) long enough, they should eventually learn to master the skill on their own. In other words, if a student travels into discomfort just beyond their abilities long enough (and with enough support), that skill will become comfortable for them. This expands the comfort zone, creating a new level of comfort with a new level of discomfort just beyond. Given life never stops confronting us with challenges, supporting students to grow their comfort zones can greatly help them in life outside of school as well.

Another benefit of leaving the comfort zone is the stories you will tell. Good stories do not start within the comfort zone. "Once, I was on my couch watching television and eating chips" is not an exciting story. When someone ventures outside their comfort zone, however, tales become more interesting. If students want to make school more exciting and have stories to tell, discomfort is the way to do that (assuming that students aren't going too far beyond their comfort zones and, for example, jumping off a cliff).

When to Stay in the Comfort Zone

While there are benefits to venturing beyond our comfort zones, there are also reasons to stay. The comfort zone allows us time to rejuvenate and a break from difficulty. Walden University's website (2022) says:

> To make the most of the comfort zones in your life, you must learn to balance time in and outside of them. For personal growth, it's necessary to take risks and endure some ego discomfort, however, it's also important to spend time healing and contemplating in the nurturing environs of your comfort zone.

All our time is spent either inside or outside our comfort zone. At times, we are unable to control being in discomfort as life is unpredictable and will force us out. Other times, being in or out of our comfort zone is our choice. If we can control it, we can ask ourselves what amount of time should be spent inside or outside. Too much time inside can lead to stunted growth. Too much time outside could produce anxiety and fatigue. As we are all individuals, we must all determine the ideal balance for ourselves.

In class, students all have different balances as well. As teachers, we do need to escort students out of their comfort zones. Students need to be challenged so that they can learn and grow. We must also be cognizant that students need time in their comfort zones. If a student has too much homework along with extracurriculars and jobs and has little time to recover, anxiety and fatigue might follow closely behind. The key is helping students become aware of this concept so that they can make an informed decision about how much time to spend inside and outside of their comfort zones.

Elementary Teacher Tip

Have all students get in a plank position and, once they are in it, tell them to hold it for ten seconds. Next, tell them they are going to do a thirty-second hold on their plank. Some students will start to say, "That's too hard," or "I can't do that." Do the thirty-second plank. Next, tell them they are going to do a full-minute plank. Keep this going as long as your students can tolerate it, and when they have reached their limit, have them do a thirty-second plank. After having done much harder planks, they will likely do it and respond with comments like, "Oh, yes! So easy!" even though initially after doing the ten-second plank they were sure it would be too hard. This is a great way to open a conversation up around comfort zone and how it changes when we do hard things.

The Comfort Zone Tool

The human brain seems programmed toward what is easy and pleasurable. Making easy and pleasurable choices will keep students in their comfort zone, an area where they feel safe and confident because they're already capable of the skills there. While it may not be what students always want to do, the only way to improve is to feel discomfort. On the path to improvement, they are going to have to do things that are difficult, unfamiliar, scary, and will include failure. However, if a student is gritty enough, they will venture toward discomfort and stay there until they reach mastery. Use the tool in figure 8.2 to springboard into a rich class discussion about comfort zone.

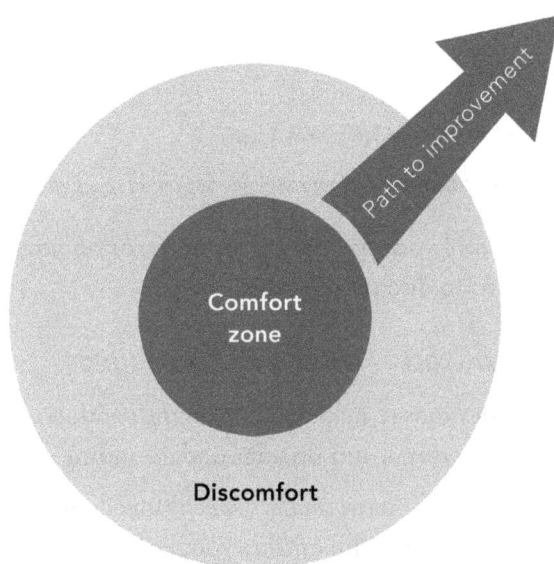

Path to improvement

Comfort zone

Discomfort

Figure 8.2: Comfort zone tool.

*Visit **go.SolutionTree.com/SEL** for a free reproducible version of this figure.*

After reviewing the tool with the class, your peers, or on your own, please use the following questions to discuss and reflect. See appendix A (page 189) for the complete instructions on using the tools in this book.

Figure 8.3 (page 162) is a second helpful tool for facilitating the discussion of the comfort zone in class. Feel free to use both figures in tandem, in succession, or separately.

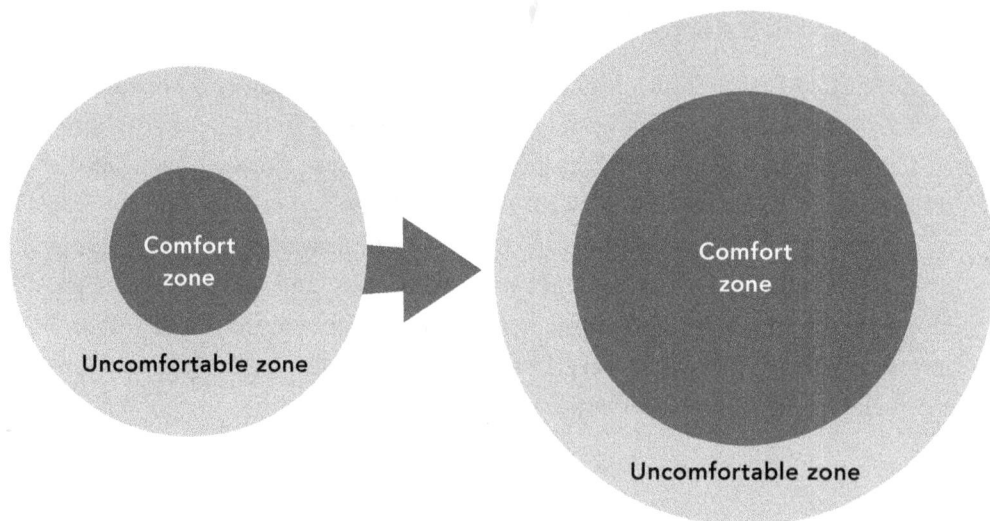

Figure 8.3: New frame of reference tool.

*Visit **go.SolutionTree.com/SEL** for a free reproducible version of this figure.*

After reviewing the tool with the class, your peers, or on your own, please use the following questions to discuss and reflect.

Questions for Educators and Their Colleagues

Use the following questions to help you discuss the comfort zone tool with colleagues to gain a more personal and broader understanding.

- How do you define the term *comfort zone*? How does your comfort zone make you feel? If you venture outside your comfort zone, how does that make you feel in the short term and the long term?

- How might discomfort lead to improvement? How much can you improve if you stay in your comfort zone?

- If a person spent enough time in discomfort, what do you think would happen? How does this relate to figure 8.3?

- If discomfort leads to improvement, how far, as an educator, should you push students outside of their comfort zones?

- Many students will fight to stay inside their comfort zones. How would you convince them to leave their comfort zones? What advice would you give them?

- What percentage of time should students be in or out of their comfort zone in school? What percentage of time should students be in or out of their comfort zone outside of school? Explain.

- How much time do you spend in your comfort zone, and how much time do you spend in discomfort? How much should this change as you become a veteran teacher?

- If someone wants to be happy in the long term, how much time should they spend in and out of their comfort zone?

Questions to Prompt Class Discussion

These are questions to promote class understanding about the tool. This can be done with small- or large-group discussion or by quietly reflecting in a journal.

- How do you define *comfort zone*? How does being in your comfort zone make you feel? How does discomfort lead to improvement?

- If you venture outside of your comfort zone, how does that make you feel in the short and long term?

- If someone stays in their comfort zone their entire life, what would that look like?

- How does getting out of your comfort zone help you improve?

- Do most students at your school fight to get into or get out of their comfort zone? Why?

- If you are advising a friend to get out of their comfort zone, how far into discomfort should they go?

- In school, how much time should you spend out of your comfort zone and how much time should you spend in your comfort zone?

Questions for Student Reflection

After a content-specific lesson that is also an opportunity to assess the comfort zone and new frames of reference, these questions can assist students in evaluating their thoughts and behavior during the lesson as they pertain to the concept.

Elementary Teacher Tip

Give students a physical activity such as jumping jacks, sit-ups, or push-ups and allow them to choose how many they would like to do. Before they start, tell them to then increase the number to challenge themselves more. After the activity, discuss how it felt to push themselves out of their comfort zone.

- During the lesson, how much did you get outside of your comfort zone and why?

- How did you feel before, after, and during this lesson?

- How much time in school should you spend in your comfort zone, and how much time in discomfort? How much time would your teacher say should be spent in your comfort zone?

- How much time do you spend trying to get into your comfort zone at school, and how much time do you spend trying to get out and why? If you wanted to change this, how would you do it?

Grit and Performance

In *Grit*, Duckworth's (2016a) thesis is that grit is the main reason why people succeed. She supports this conclusion by having those entering a long-term, stressful challenge evaluate themselves with her grit scale, which you can find at her website (angeladuckworth.com/grit-scale). The grit scale determines a person's passion and perseverance levels and correlates positively with successful completion of the challenge. In all the groups she has studied taking on challenging circumstances—West Point cadets, Scripps National Spelling Bee participants, teachers starting a school year in rough schools—high grit scale scores correlate to success.

To make students aware of the benefits of grittiness, teachers could lead discussions around the topic in school. This means providing challenges just outside the students' comfort zones to allow students to productively struggle (using inevitable mistakes and failures as a learning tool) and ensuring we empower students to take on these challenges. This means giving them a reason for taking on the challenge (passion) and the tools to persevere in the face of setbacks. Students won't remember the easy challenge you gave them; instead, they will remember with pride those challenges where they worked through difficulty or worked with fear. This, of course, doesn't mean that the challenge needs to be boring and devoid of fun; rather, the challenge could be an open-ended project that allows them to think deeply and be creative. A challenge like this doesn't automatically produce grit, but it does provide the students with the opportunity to be gritty. When teachers make students aware of the concept and coach students on how to be gritty throughout the project, the likelihood of grittiness goes up.

Let's think about why academic grit seems to reduce as students move from elementary to secondary school. Postigo and colleagues (2020) note in their six-year study that student academic performance declined over the six years. They theorize that students may have more challenges in their lives as they get older along with "a decline in non-cognitive variables such as academic grit" (p. 81).

While students in secondary school do have more going on and more to think about (making it harder to persevere), lack of passion could also be a culprit that reduces academic grit as students progress to secondary school. Peter Gray (2018) writes in *Psychology Today*:

> Over the past several decades we've continuously increased the amount of time that children spend at school, and at schoolwork at home, and at school-like activities outside of school. We've turned childhood into a time of resume building. You don't build passions by building a resume, trying to impress other people. You build passions by doing what you love, regardless of what others think.

As they get older, students may start to see school as something that they have to complete as opposed to something that they get to do. They focus too much on resume building or completion and not enough on learning. With outcome goals instead of process goals, their passion may dwindle, lessening their grit.

Some, however, feel the passion component of grit is overrated. Psychological researchers Katherine Muenks, Ji Seung Yang, and Allan Wigfield (2018) don't agree that passion should receive the credit in performance that Duckworth (2016a) gives it. In their study of students, Muenks and colleagues (2018) show that self-efficacy—what you think about yourself and your abilities—trumps passion's role in success:

> The perseverance of effort component of grit was more strongly correlated with self-efficacy, task values, and goal orientations than was consistency of interests. When controlling for motivational variables, perseverance of effort emerged as a significant predictor of end-of-semester grades, but consistency of interests did not. However, self-efficacy was a stronger predictor of grades than either of the grit components. Together, these results suggest that grit is distinct from future-oriented motivation and that perseverance of effort is more strongly associated with motivation and achievement than is consistency of interests for high school students.

In other words, perseverance is important to achieve success. Yet Muenks and colleagues (2018) find that perseverance happens when students have positive self-efficacy and believe they can succeed. In fact, they find that positive student self-efficacy is the main reason why students do well on their marks. So, believing that you can leads to motivation and perseverance, while thinking you cannot leads to giving up.

You might think these findings contradict what Duckworth (2016a) says about the importance of passion in developing grit and achieving success. However, these concepts are not mutually exclusive. The study highlights the importance of self-efficacy in specific tasks; particularly the day-to-day tasks that are inherently part of school lessons are important. Passion is a more big-picture motivator connected to specific interests. Students, for example, may say that they're not passionate about a specific subject. Students who don't enjoy mathematics or language arts may struggle to feel much passion for those lessons, which can be a recipe for motivation to wane. But that doesn't mean students can't believe in their ability to do well in those subjects, and when they know that can be successful, they are more likely to persevere. Further, their broader passions can promote motivation and perseverance across all subjects. For example, if a student's passion is to improve or challenge themselves, this passion can maintain motivation for all classes (even if a student doesn't "like" the subject) and other areas of a student's life. Students with passion to improve and a sense of self-efficacy can challenge themselves and feel motivated across all subjects and lessons.

If grit is important, how can a teacher emphasize and teach grit in their classroom? Author and founder of Growing Leaders Tim Elmore (2014) recommends doing the following, which teachers in Singapore do regularly.

1. Talk about the power of attitude and persistence.

2. Turn the problem into a picture or a puzzle.

3. Start with smaller problems they can solve and put wins under their belts.

4. Share the *why* before the *what*.

5. When possible, place students in communities to work together.

6. Make it a game or competition.

7. Reward hard work and delayed gratification.

Elmore (2014) says that it's important to discuss performance character regularly along with class content, that visuals aid in understanding (like the tools in this book), that explaining the reason why students are doing something is incredibly important, that group work aids in all students learning, that interesting and creative lessons can be very effective in teaching grit, and that rewards should go toward students who put forth effort.

Through the process of writing this manuscript, I wouldn't consider my ability level for organizing a book to be particularly high. Having never written a book before, I had much to learn. Whenever I would feel that my ability was solid as I turned in a new chapter, I was quickly humbled through the editing process. While I had average ability, I would say that my grit level was high throughout. I have a reason for writing this (to help teachers aid students in becoming happier and more successful), and I tend to persevere with challenges. There were times when I felt I wanted to stop and give up, but I found ways to stay committed. None of this means that this book is going to be an amazing piece of literature, but I have seen how my grit greatly helped build my performance level (if I had no grit, I wouldn't even start this process). Grit also improved my ability—through being passionate and persistent with this challenge, my book-writing skills have improved (albeit slightly in my case). As educators, we want students to be aware of this too: Completing difficult challenges is not based solely on ability. It's also not a perfect process—there are mistakes, mishaps, revisions, and much effort along the way. If they can be gritty through all of this, they can accomplish things they never thought they could.

The Performance Tool

Abilities are skills that a student possesses to complete certain tasks or challenges. If a student is gritty with those abilities, they will find a way to pursue and persist when they take on challenges in a given area of expertise. The combined ability and grit are two major factors in performance. Use the tool in figure 8.4 to springboard into a rich class discussion about grit and performance.

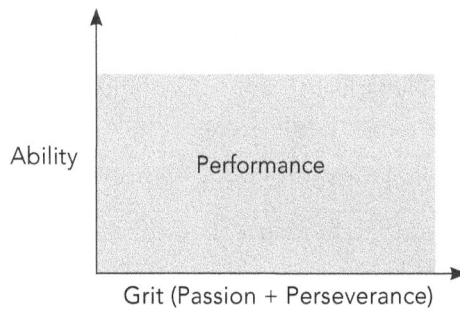

Ability

Performance

Grit (Passion + Perseverance)

Source: Adapted from Duckworth, 2016a.

Figure 8.4: Performance tool.

*Visit **go.SolutionTree.com/SEL** for a free reproducible version of this figure.*

After reviewing the tool with the class, your peers, or on your own, please use the following questions to discuss and reflect. See appendix A (page 189) for the complete instructions on using the tools in this book.

Questions for Educators and Their Colleagues

Use the following questions to help you discuss the performance tool with colleagues to gain a more personal and broader understanding.

- How do you define *ability*? How do you define *grit*? How would you teach a student with low ability and high grit? How would you teach a student with high ability and low grit? Which student do you prefer to teach and why?

- In reaching a performance level, how does ability affect grit? How does grit affect ability?

- What is the best way for a student to raise their performance level? How could you help them as a teacher?

- What does the tool (page 167) look like for someone who is world-class in something? How can someone attain a world-class level?

- How does this tool relate to morals? How much ability do we all have to be selfless? If you'd like to perform well morally, how much of a role does grit play?

Questions to Prompt Class Discussion

- How do you define *ability*? How do you define *grit*? Do you think the effort you put into your work has anything to do with how it turns out?

- Do you think that grit is more important than ability or the other way around?

- Think of someone who is world-class in something. What does their performance tool look like? How much ability is necessary to become world-class? How much grit is necessary to become world-class?

- If you drew this tool for yourself in school, what would it look like?

- In determining your performance, how does ability affect grit? How does grit affect ability?

- Would you rather be a person with high ability and low grit or a person with low ability and high grit? Explain your answer.

- If a student wanted to raise their performance level in something, how would they do that?

- How does this tool relate to morals? How much ability do we all have to be selfless? If you'd like to perform well morally, how much of a role does grit play?

Questions for Student Reflection

After a content-specific lesson that is also an opportunity to assess performance, these questions can assist students in evaluating their thoughts and behavior during the lesson as they pertain to the concept.

- For this challenge, where would you put your ability level? Where would you put your grit level?

- Using figure 8.4 (page 167), how would you rate your performance on this challenge? Why do you think this happened?

- If you were gritty, how did you feel? If you weren't gritty, how did you feel? If you noticed other people being gritty, what were they doing?

Summary

Grit is a combination of passion and perseverance over a long period of time. Psychologists like Duckworth (2016a, 2016b) believe that grit is perhaps the most important factor in improvement and success. Passion and perseverance build off each other. While passion (an emotionally charged purpose) will give a student a reason and motivation to persist, perseverance (positive mindset, courage and commitment working together to keep the student moving forward) toward a goal will lead to improvement, possibly igniting more passion. Teachers can kickstart grit by sparking a passion for students and offering them an opportunity to persevere and feed that passion. Teachers can also encourage students' perseverance so that they improve in an area, leading to an emotional response that starts a passion. Grit will push a person beyond their comfort zone and into an area of discomfort (where learning and improvement happens). Ability also plays an important role in performance. While ability is outside a student's control, the student can determine grit. If a student can learn to be gritty and push beyond their comfort zone, that grit will increase their chances of improvement and success.

Elementary Teacher Tip

After completing a task, ask students to think about how well they did on it and hold up fingers to rate themselves on their effort using the following 1–4 scale. You may want to have them cover their eyes with one hand or put their heads down so they can't see each other's ratings.

1 = I gave little or no effort.

2 = I gave some effort but gave up when I was confronted with a challenge.

3 = I gave my best effort until there was a challenge, and then I gave some effort.

4 = I gave my best effort, even when it was a challenge.

Discuss how the effort they put into a task matters just as much as (or sometimes even more than) their ability. Ability can take you far, but grit is what gets you across the finish line.

9

Flow

Those who flow as life flows know they need no other force.

—Lao Tzu

I was wrestling in the third- and fourth-place match at the Pac-10 wrestling tournament in 1995. I was the first seed but got knocked off in overtime by a competitor from the University of Oregon in the semifinals. Placing third would automatically qualify me for the NCAA tournament, while losing would put my NCAA berth in jeopardy.

I had every reason to be upset and nervous: I had just missed being in the finals by losing to someone I had beaten before; if I lost, my college wrestling career would be over (shattering my opportunity to reach my goals). Plus, my upcoming opponent from Arizona State was another excellent wrestler who I had never faced before. But, for some reason, I wasn't upset or nervous. Instead, I was ecstatic.

I'm not entirely sure why, but my sole focus was on the moment—no other thoughts entered my mind. It could have been that this opponent was roughly my height and build—I rarely went against people who were as short as me. It also could have been the appropriate amount of stress with the NCAA tournament on the line. Whatever it was, it was a challenge that completely matched my ability level. I had to devote all my attention to this moment.

I'm not going to say that the experience was divine, but it did make me feel god-like: wrestling at the time felt effortless, and everything seemed to move in slow motion. Additionally, I didn't care at all about the score. I recall saying, "Wow, that was a great move!" both when I scored on my competitor and he scored on me. I even said out loud, "This is awesome!"

The outcome didn't matter, just the moment; I had become the moment. I felt immense happiness and enthusiasm. There are several names for what I was experiencing—in the zone, optimal performance level, flow state. All I know is this: if I could replicate this feeling repeatedly, I would. It felt that good. And if I could feel like this while achieving something, I want to make sure students can get to this state, too. This chapter will share research on how to help foster flow by understanding how to decide the level of challenge necessary to achieve flow, reviewing the concept of intrinsic and extrinsic motivation, and provide two tools that can help you and your students to think about and, hopefully, practice flow in your classroom.

The Definition of Flow

During World War II, when he was around the age of ten, world-renowned psychologist and the man responsible for recognizing and coining the term *flow* Mihaly Csikszentmihalyi (Oppland, 2016) spent time in an Italian prison camp. During this period, he lost many friends and relatives, including one brother who was killed in action and another who was captured and sent to a Siberian labor camp. He discovered the game chess at this difficult time, calling it "a miraculous way of entering into a different world where all those things didn't matter. For hours I'd just focus within a reality that had clear rules and goals" (as cited in Encyclopedia .com, n.d.). Csikszentmihalyi found that, by putting his full attention toward something challenging, he could find a way to be happy—taking his mind away from life's tragedies and hardships.

This idea of finding happiness even among chaos stuck with Csikszentmihalyi and eventually made it into his life's work. He earned his doctorate in psychology and ran studies to learn more about experiences like his with chess during wartime. In 1990, he wrote *Flow: The Psychology of Optimal Experience* to outline his theory that the amount of time that a person spends focused on and committed to a task outside their comfort zone determines happiness. In other words, Csikszentmihalyi believes that individuals are at their most creative, productive, and joyful when they are in their flow state, where they must dedicate all their attention toward taking on a challenge. He defines *flow* as:

> A state in which people are so involved in an activity that nothing else seems
> to matter; the experience is so enjoyable that people will continue to do it
> even at great cost, for the sheer sake of doing it. (Csikszentmihalyi, 1990, p. 4)

Toddlers, for example, frequently find themselves in flow when learning to walk. Learning to take steps demands their full attention, and they are difficult to distract from the task. Even though they're failing throughout, toddlers also seem to enjoy the experience. When learning to walk, my older son wasn't talking much, but he knew some sign language. Every time he fell in his quest to walk, he would repeatedly sign *more* while smiling and struggling to return to his feet.

Csikszentmihalyi (Oppland, 2016) specifically uses the word *enjoyable* instead of *pleasurable* when discussing flow for a reason. For him, pleasurable things don't take effort, and the positive emotions are reactionary and passive. Sleeping and watching television are examples of things that are pleasurable. Enjoyable things, on the other hand, require effort. Since flow requires effort devoted to a particular challenge, flow is enjoyable (Smith, 2021a). This means that a student watching a movie or listening to a lecture will not experience flow or enjoyment; however, a student working on a project or trying to understand a concept has an opportunity to get into flow and, therefore, realize enjoyment.

Best-selling authors Steven Kotler and Jamie Wheal (2017) in their book *Stealing Fire: How Silicon Valley, the Navy SEALs, and Maverick Scientists Are Revolutionizing the Way We Live and Work* highlight other key components of flow. Kotler and Wheal (2017) use the acronym *STER* to explain how we feel when we are in a state of deep flow.

- **Selfless:** The first letter of the acronym stands for *selflessness*—flow makes our ego evaporate as we become the moment.

- **Timeless:** Flow, they say, is also *timeless*. For people in deep flow, time may become distorted, slowing down or speeding up. If you've ever been so engrossed in a task that everything seems to slow or you are shocked to see that two hours have passed so quickly, that's the timelessness piece of flow.

- **Effortless:** The E in STER stands for *effortlessness*. While flow does take a great deal of effort as you are taking on a challenge, it doesn't feel like it. While in flow, you may not feel discomfort or fatigue—even though you should.

- **Rich:** Finally, flow has the feeling of *richness*. Being fully focused on the moment makes the experience rich and vibrant.

If you've ever been teaching where you're completely immersed into running your lesson, you may be in flow and experiencing STER. You may lose sense of self by becoming the challenging moment and not caring what others think. You may look up and be shocked that the period is almost over even though it felt like you'd been teaching for ten minutes. You may not have felt tired even though you were putting great effort into the implementation of the lesson, and the time spent running the lesson was rich and fulfilling (feeling like your senses were heightened). If you take on a situation like this in flow, chances are that you enjoyed the experience. The same situation without flow and STER might lead to stress and frustration.

Along with enjoyment, those who experience flow tend to learn more. *Psychology Today* staff (n.d.b) says this about flow and its effect on learning:

> It makes sense that people who engage in flow, have feelings of success, pride, and accomplishment—all of which encourage more learning and development. An activity done in flow is pegged as enjoyable or even ecstatic, though the joy isn't at the fore during the task because the person is too busy feeling immersed in the experience.

For example, if a student finds a way into flow while solving challenging mathematics problems, the student will positively reminisce about the experience, wanting to return to flow. This means that they will voluntarily take on more challenging mathematics problems to recoup the feeling flow gives them. Each time they challenge themselves this way, they can reach flow, and they are simultaneously giving themselves an opportunity to learn. As students chase flow, they may not always reach it; but they will put forth effort toward a goal and inevitably improve themselves.

Flow can help students succeed and be happy at the same time; however, I do not have it listed in the same category as integral for performance character as the components in the previous eight chapters. Flow may not be essential, but it is a bonus that comes from a solid foundation of the eight components of performance character. If someone does very well with self-awareness, integrity, purpose, passion, positive mindset, courage, commitment, and grit, they have a great chance at success and happiness, *and* they have a better chance at experiencing flow.

To start, students can begin with a base of *self-awareness* and *integrity*; in this way, they will understand what they are doing without the lens of ego and that they're attacking the challenge honorably (attacking a challenge by cheating completely misses the point of flow). Then, students are going to have to get after the challenge. To do this, students must have a reason (*purpose*) to proceed and, hopefully, emotion is backing that purpose (*passion*). Because challenges are difficult and fraught with obstacles and failures, the student is going to have to persevere and not give up when the road to the goal gets difficult. To persevere, a *positive mindset* and *courage* will assist the student in consistently moving forward among the failures and fear. Along with this, the student must offer *commitment* by putting forth a consistent and lengthy version of the correct kind of effort in the form of deliberate practice. Passion and perseverance work together to form *grit*, which is, perhaps, the most important component of success. As students stay gritty in pursuit of their purpose or passion, their skill and challenge might match perfectly. In these instances, the student may experience *flow*, which could serve as an excellent motivator to continue the process.

Please understand, however, that flow is elusive. It's very difficult to experience deep levels of flow on a frequent basis. Even if you're doing very well with the eight traits of performance character, flow is not a guarantee. Also, flow can be fleeting. You may be in flow for one second and then fall out of flow the following second.

If flow is a hard-to-grasp, fickle outcome, is it worth teaching? My answer is an emphatic "Yes!" If students are aware of the concept and how to potentially get to flow in school, they might have a more positive feeling about academics. Can you imagine a classroom full of students who are trying to be the best they can be in the moment? They would be learning and joyful. To me, that's the dream.

Psychologist from McGill University Lindsay A. Borovay along with Bruce M. Shore, Christina Caccese, Ethan Yang, and Olivia Hua (2018) interviewed fifth to ninth graders to test how they best got to flow in school and how it affected them. The researchers found that inquiry lessons and choice led to more flow state. As to how it affected students, the researchers write, "All preferred challenging over easy work although for different reasons. All highlighted feeling able to succeed and interest in an activity to experience flow" (Borovaye t al., 2018, p. 74). In this study, students who experienced more flow persevered more and felt more positive about challenges. That sounds like an amazing class!

As Csikszentmihalyi (2009) writes, "The best moments in our lives are not the passive, receptive, relaxing times . . . . The best moments usually occur if a person's body or mind is stretched to its limits in a voluntary effort to accomplish something difficult and worthwhile" (p. 3).

Levels of Challenge and Flow

If flow would benefit academic performance and happiness, how can a teacher help students find their way there? How much challenge would usher students into a state where they can completely focus on a task and reach a level of STER (Hint: it may not be the level of effort students want to put into their classwork)? Consider the following scenario in which an educator, Mrs. Kaier, leads a discussion wherein she asks students to gauge their interest in school based on level of challenge.

> *Every day, middle school English teacher Mrs. Kaier writes a question on the board for students to answer in their journal. Some days, the class goes through the exercise and zips by the question. Other days, students turn the question into a full-on debate. With the following question, today would be one of the latter situations: Are you happiest in school when challenges are incredibly simple, very easy, easy, neutral, difficult, very difficult, or nearly impossible? Explain your response.*
>
> *After students had been given time to think and write, Mrs. Kaier opened the question up to the class to garner their responses. Initially, the students who dominated the conversation were the ones vying for "simple" to "easy." One student offered, "Why would I want to try hard when I didn't have to?" Several shouted in agreement.*
>
> *After this initial wave of opinions, some of the deeper thinkers in class started to speak: "I'm not sure that I'm happy when things in school are easy. If the lesson isn't challenging, I'm bored."*
>
> *Another student shared, "I don't want something that's too challenging either. That can get frustrating. I think a challenge in the middle makes more sense. I think I'm happiest when I am being challenged, but not too much."*
>
> *As the conversation went on, many more students took this stance (although saying that you want everything easy may have been the cooler response at the onset).*

The question Mrs. Kaier raised is a good one: Can students find happiness with the appropriate level of challenge? If students prescribe to Csikszentmihalyi's (2009) flow theory, they can influence how happy they are by choosing their challenges wisely.

The Arousal State of Flow

To experience flow, people must venture out of their comfort zones and seek difficult challenges that will match their skill level (a challenge within the comfort zone is too easy). However, the challenges shouldn't be too far outside of the comfort zone (see chapter 8, page 156). If the challenge far outdistances present skill level, this will produce anxiety instead of flow. Csikszentmihalyi (2009) defines this state as *arousal*. The person is focused and aware but not necessarily confident enough with what they're doing to the point where they may be thinking more about failing than the moment. If a person wanted to move from arousal to flow, they would need to raise their skill level. On the other hand, a person who is highly skilled and takes on a challenge that is difficult but doesn't quite match their skill level is in a state of control—they are confident but could do more. To reach a state of flow in the state of control, you would have to push a little further and raise the level of challenge.

Montessori Classrooms and Flow

As educators, is it even possible to manage this balance for our students to get them to flow—especially when most of us have a classroom full of varied skill levels and interests? We might be able to find answers to these questions through Montessori schools. Csikszentmihalyi and University of Utah researcher Kevin Rathunde (2005) find that, compared to their peers in non-Montessori schools, students in Montessori schools experience more "intrinsic motivation, flow experience, and undivided interest . . . while engaged in academic activities at school" (p. 341). Rathunde (2001) offers that this makes sense, as Montessori learning is student-centered, active, and challenging (although not over-challenging) while a teacher scaffolds only when necessary.

Rathunde (2001) adds that, when Maria Montessori developed her method of education, she inherently understood the importance of flow and how to get students there:

> Montessori paid increasing attention to what has become a central tenet in flow theory: the importance of the balance between skills and challenges. Montessori meticulously categorized activities that were appropriately challenging for children at different ages (example: the sensory and motor activities involving the wooden cylinder block), and this resulted in her many pedagogical innovations centered around stage-appropriate activities, sensitive periods, and "prepared" environments. To the extent that activities capture the right balance of skills and challenges, they improve the chances of triggering intense concentration. (p. 24)

In other words, Montessori created situations for children to get into flow. She set up environments that she knew would match the students' interests and skill level. When students start to interact with these challenges, it takes their full focus. If they want to maintain flow as their skills rise, students can increase the challenge. Another bonus of Montessori's method is that they're not on a set class schedule. Perhaps Montessori understood that, once students get zoned in on a challenge, teachers should let them stay in flow.

Most of us are not Montessori teachers, but we can still bring flow to our classrooms. Professor of computer education David J. Shernoff, psychologist Mihaly Csikszentmihalyi, researcher Barbara Shneider, and professor of psychology Elisa S. Shernoff (2003) undertook a longitudinal study of 526 high school students to monitor when they got into flow, concluding the following:

> Participants experienced increased engagement when the perceived challenge of the task and their own skills were high and in balance, the instruction was relevant, and the learning environment was under their control. Participants were also more engaged in individual and group work versus listening to lectures, watching videos, or taking exams. (p. 158)

In this study, Shernoff and colleagues (2003) found many similarities to what leads to flow in Montessori schools. First, flow came from active rather than passive learning. In secondary school, active learning might look like a project, discussion, role play, or a debate. With active learning, students are challenged to seek out and apply concepts and knowledge. It takes effort, but effort leads to flow. Also, students who found flow were in control of their learning. This means that, likely, the teacher explained a challenge to them, then gave them resources and ample time to figure it out.

Therefore, it is possible to facilitate flow in a non-Montessori classroom. The conditions for flow are ideal when teachers give clear directions on a student-focused challenge and provide resources for the students that empower them to work through the challenge, then give students enough time to learn on their own, aiding and scaffolding only when necessary. It does take much effort on the front end to achieve this standard in your classroom, but the benefits are substantial. Students should be more interested in active projects where they construct their own knowledge, potentially leading to flow.

It's important to note, however, that the responsibility of flow does not rest solely on the teacher. If provided with an active, student-focused, open-ended project and time to work on it, students have control over how much they choose to challenge themselves. If they challenge themselves too much, that could prove frustrating. If they don't challenge themselves enough, they'll be bored. It might be a good idea to circulate around the room, noticing when to give a nudge to a student not challenging themselves enough or to tone down or scaffold for a student who is taking on too much. This tinkering takes time and experience, but it could lead to an ideal pairing of challenge and ability.

The Challenge and Ability Tool

To reach flow state, it is imperative that students challenge themselves, as they can't experience flow or enjoyment without effort. However, the challenge should match their abilities so that they are completely focused on the task. Use the tool in figure 9.1 to springboard into a rich class discussion about challenge level and flow.

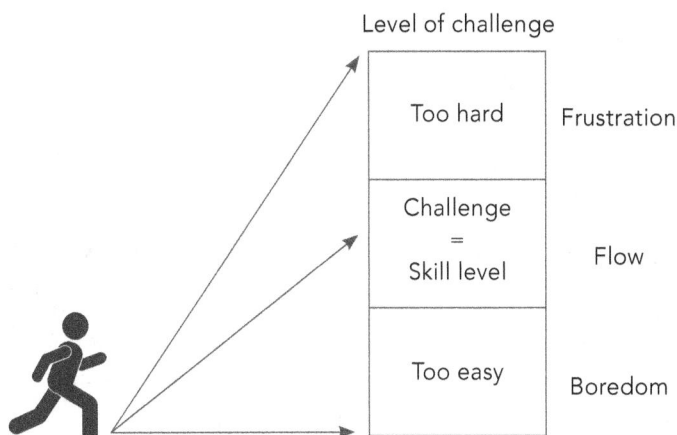

Figure 9.1: Challenge and ability tool.

*Visit **go.SolutionTree.com/SEL** for a free reproducible version of this figure.*

After reviewing the tool with the class, your peers, or on your own, please use the following questions to discuss and reflect. See appendix A (page 189) for the complete instructions on using the tools in this book.

Questions for Educators and Their Colleagues

Use the following questions to help you discuss the challenge and ability tool with colleagues to gain a more personal and broader understanding.

- Think of a time when you've been in flow and feeling STER. How did it feel? How well did your challenge match your skill level?

- In this tool, the person taking the challenge can walk a short distance to *too easy*, try to climb toward *too hard* and slip back, or struggle but have a good chance at traversing the middle line to Challenge = Skill level. For students in your classes, which route do they typically take with school's challenges, and how do you think it makes them feel?

- In teaching, how much do you challenge yourself? How does it make you feel? How might you get yourself closer to flow?

- How can you give students an appropriate level of challenge?

- How big of a role do students play in this process? When you give students an appropriate challenge, how do they respond to it in terms of the tool?

Questions to Prompt Class Discussion

These are questions to promote class understanding about the tool. This can be done with small- or large-group discussion or by quietly reflecting in a journal.

- Think of a time when you were so focused on a challenge that you didn't care about what others thought, you didn't care about outcome, and it felt timeless and effortless. This is called *flow*. How did it feel? How did you get there?

- In this tool, the person taking the challenge can walk a short distance to *too easy*, try to climb toward *too hard* and slip back, or struggle but have a good chance at traversing the middle line to Challenge = Skill level. For challenges in school, how much of a challenge do you try to give yourself? In other words, when you're presented with a challenge, how do you respond to it in terms of the tool?

- How many lessons do you get at school that are too challenging, not challenging enough, or just right? Give an example of an appropriate challenge.

- If you wanted to get to flow in school, how would you do it? How much of students' getting into flow is the teacher's responsibility and how much is it the student's responsibility?

Elementary Teacher Tip

For an initial exposure to flow, students will benefit from a much younger class (say kindergarten or first grade) and some from a much older class (fifth or sixth grade) to demonstrate physical performances (such as shooting a basketball, throwing a baseball, or jumping for distance). Then, older students and younger students will determine an appropriate distance that will challenge the younger students so that it's not too easy or too difficult. This creates an equitable challenge for all and makes a great impression on the younger children.

Questions for Student Reflection

After a content-specific lesson that is also an opportunity to assess challenge and ability, these questions can assist students in evaluating their thoughts and behavior during the lesson as they pertain to the concept.

- How high was the level of challenge on this lesson? How did you respond to that level of challenge?

- Did you get into flow state during this lesson? How do you know? If you wanted to get into flow state more in school, what would you need to do? How can teachers help with this?

Types of Motivation

Students are all unique, but their motivations fall into two very different categories: extrinsic motivation and intrinsic motivation. Students who are extrinsically motivated try hard to get some tangible thing they want while students who are intrinsically motivated try hard to seek the feeling of joy. Both types of motivation can get a student to put forth great effort, but only intrinsic motivation equates to flow. Before we get there, however, let's delve deeper into extrinsic motivation.

Extrinsic motivation is when an individual's behavior is motivated by external rewards, like an incentive, a result, or even a bribe. Many students are extrinsically motivated. They try hard in school for extrinsic reasons (avoiding punishment or securing something they want). Often, extrinsic motivation can get us to work hard at things that we deem unpleasant. Unfortunately, this is how many students seem to view school—as something unpleasant that they feel they need to get through.

Extrinsic Motivation

Extrinsically motivated students follow what they think is the recipe for happiness: If I try hard and get good grades, I'll get into a good college, eventually get a high-paying job, make loads of money, and be happy. Two main problems that they run into with this thinking are the following:

1. They won't be happy until they are in the job necessary to make them money; this means that pre-college schooling is merely an end to a means that can't produce happiness unto itself.

2. They compare themselves to other students who are also vying to get into these top universities, which leads to anxiety (worrying if others are doing better or you're not doing well enough) and depression (thinking that others are getting better grades and, therefore, have a better chance of taking away their eventual happiness).

Educational systems typically place a huge emphasis on grades, which doesn't help. The report card is the marker of success instead of daily learning and improvement. Much as I don't want to overemphasize grades, as a teacher, I still get caught in the trap. Often, I catch myself saying things like, "If you don't do this, you can't pass the class" or "Writing a better introduction paragraph is a great way to turn a B paper into an A."

Intrinsic Motivation

What if, instead of grades, students were intrinsically motivated in school? Intrinsically motivated students try hard because they enjoy the process and the moment. In other words, students are intrinsically motivated when they are in flow.

The benefit of intrinsic motivation is the reason to teach students about flow. If students can grasp the concept and learn to get themselves to flow, their extrinsic motivations—and all the unpleasantness, anxiety, and depression that goes along with them—slowly disappear. Instead, flow replaces those feelings, increasing motivation through process-driven (not to mention joyful) learning. Csikszentmihalyi (2009) writes:

> To overcome the anxieties and depressions of contemporary life, individuals must become independent of the social environment to the degree that they no longer respond exclusively in terms of its rewards and punishments. To achieve such autonomy, a person has to learn to provide rewards to herself. She has to develop the ability to find enjoyment and purpose regardless of external circumstances. (p. 16)

I know any number of students who would question what Csikszentmihalyi (2009) is saying: "That wouldn't work. School and joy don't mix. Other students will get better grades than me if I'm not focusing on grades. Getting good grades should be the motivation, not learning and joy." I get all this. But, if students are unhappy with the current situation of schooling, as teachers, shouldn't we at least try strategies to change such unproductive mindsets?

Critical to flow is for students to approach their work with what Csikszentmihalyi calls an *autotelic personality*, "an individual who generally does things for their own sake, rather than in order to achieve some later external goal" (as cited in Baumann, n.d., p. 117).

Autotelic people are motivated intrinsically. They don't try hard for the sticker, the grade, or to get into what they deem is the best college; instead, autotelic students are motivated by the feeling of enjoyment they receive from being in flow. If you're thinking that autotelic students can't be successful academically and their intrinsic motivation isn't sustainable, I would have to argue. If a student consistently chases (and occasionally finds) flow, they are focused on improving in the moment over and over. If the student continues to improve themselves, the result will be solid grades, good grade-point averages, and so on.

Hosei University professor of intercultural communications Kiyoshi Asakawa (2009) studied 315 Japanese students to find out how many of these students showed autotelic personality traits and how it affected their lives in college. The author writes of the more autotelic students, "They were more likely to report active commitments to college life, search for a future career, and daily activities in general. They also reported more Jujitsu-kan, a Japanese sense of fulfillment, and greater satisfaction with their lives" (Asakawa, 2009, p. 205). This means that the intrinsically motivated students put forth more effort into college, their future, and everything else (which, typically, equates to more success). As a bonus, students were happier.

Flow for Teachers

As educators, if we can get students to experience flow at some point during our class, we may get students hooked on the feeling. Shernoff and Hoogstra (2001) studied students in high school science classes, finding that those who experienced more flow in those classes were much more likely to major in science in college. This indicates that, if we can help students understand the concept of flow and provide appropriate lessons that allow them to actively work on something and appropriately challenge themselves to match their skill level, we can get students into flow and intrinsically motivated about our subject or academics in general. This could get them to both success and satisfaction simultaneously.

As for success and satisfaction for teachers, flow might also be the key. Diana Olčar, Majda Rijavec, and Tajana Ljubin Golub (2019) studied 480 primary school teachers to find "the positive relationship between life goals and life satisfaction is partly due to the increased satisfaction for the need for competence and more frequent flow experience at work" (p. 320). In other words, flow can make us happy too. We can also benefit from the concepts in the previous eight chapters as we find a level of challenge that matches our ability.

During the work on this book, I will admit that flow experiences were sporadic at best. Most of the writing was deliberate practice, where I had to really think hard about what I was doing to improve my research and my organizational writing skills. There were the rare times when I could completely immerse myself in the process, feeling powerful and losing track of time. While a great majority of the time on this passion necessitated me being gritty (finding ways to push past mistakes and my perceived inadequacies to complete chapters), flow did come to me on occasion. While few, those times of flow kept me motivated. In the back of my mind, I knew that I could get myself to that level again, which is always appealing to me. The point is this: flow is not essential when pursuing goals, but even in writing and school, a little flow can go a long, long way.

The Surviving Versus Thriving Tool

In life, students are either thriving or surviving. Those who survive aren't challenging themselves and typically have trouble making progress toward goals. Thrivers, however, are excited to take on challenges and put in effort in their completion, successful or not. Through putting effort into a challenge, either students will be thinking hard about improvement (deliberate practice) or the thinking turns off and they become the moment (flow). Use the tool in figure 9.2 to springboard into rich class discussion about surviving and thriving in school.

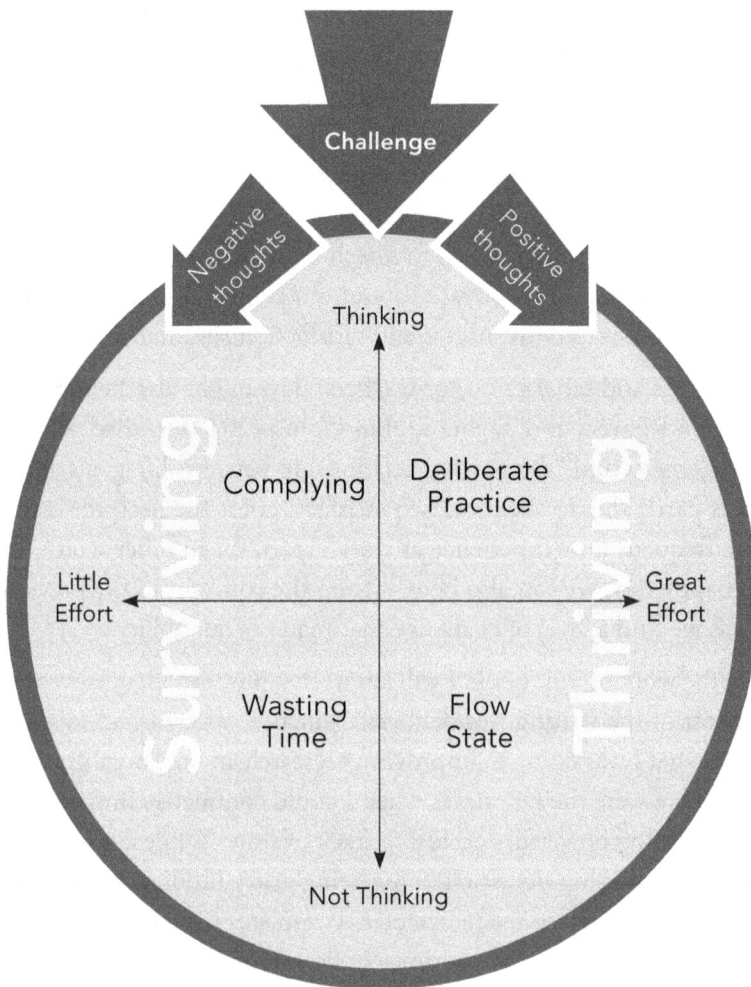

Figure 9.2: Surviving versus thriving tool.

*Visit **go.SolutionTree.com/SEL** for a free reproducible version of this figure.*

After reviewing the tool with the class, your peers, or on your own, please use the following questions to discuss and reflect. See appendix A (page 189) for the complete instructions on using the tools in this book.

Questions for Educators and Their Colleagues

Use the following questions to help you discuss the surviving versus thriving tool with colleagues to gain a more personal and broader understanding.

- According to this tool, what would you say is the difference between surviving and thriving? How does each side make a person feel?

- Have you ever found yourself in flow? How did you get there? How might you replicate that experience? Is saying that flow is "great effort and not thinking" an accurate description? Why or why not?

- When students are taking on challenges in your class, what route do they usually take in terms of the tool? How might you get more of your students to the thriving side of the tool?

Questions to Prompt Class Discussion

These are questions to promote class understanding about the tool. This can be done with small- or large-group discussion or by quietly reflecting in a journal.

- According to the tool, what is the difference between surviving and thriving?

- If you've ever gotten to flow, how did you do that? How could you replicate that experience? Is saying that flow is "a combination of great effort and not thinking" an accurate description? Why or why not?

- With challenges in school, which route do you usually take in terms of the tool? If you wanted to get to the thriving side, how would you do that and how would it make you feel?

Questions for Student Reflection

After a content-specific lesson that is also an opportunity to assess surviving versus thriving, these questions can assist students in evaluating their thoughts and behavior during the lesson as they pertain to the concept.

- For this challenge, explain the route you took in terms of the tool. Where did you end up? How did it feel?

- Think of a time you've gotten yourself to flow state. How accurate is the tool with how you got there?

- How much do you thrive in school? Why?

- How hard or easy is it for you to get to flow state?

Summary

Flow is a state where a student is so focused on the moment that they don't care what others think, the experience is vibrant and rich, time speeds up or slows down, and they feel powerful. Students who are extrinsically motivated focus on tangible results and don't reach flow state. On the other hand, intrinsically motivated students put forth effort because they feel joy through the exertion. These are autotelic students, and their desire to return to the feeling of flow motivates them. Students can reach flow state by taking on a challenge that matches their skill level. Flow is elusive; however, if students discuss and understand this concept and the idea of flow, they may have a better chance of reaching it. If students can get to flow, they will feel amazing as they learn and improve in school. A student in flow is the definition of successful and happy.

Conclusion

At times, students will ask how they can improve in a chosen field—whether it's school, sports, extracurricular activities, or something else. Often, they want a quick answer or one piece of advice that can help them rise above their peers. The process of improvement, however, is complicated and takes much thought and effort. When students are willing to take control of their performance character, they have a very good chance of improving as they take on challenges that will lead them to success.

The eight performance character traits, when developed together, encourage students to be resilient, motivated, and ready for challenges. The process does not come easy or all at once, but it begins with a foundation of self-awareness and integrity. Students must be able to see their actions without self-bias so that they can continue to do what they do well and fix their mistakes. Also, they should be aware of whether they are approaching a challenge with integrity—challenges taken on by cheating may lead to good grades but not learning and improvement.

The next step in a student controlling their performance character is to develop a purpose or passion. A purpose is a student's reason for doing something. It may be wise for a student to see purpose in terms of process instead of outcome—both those with process and outcome goals will work hard, but those with process goals have a better chance of happiness. If a student can connect an emotion to purpose, that combination can lead to a passion. Challenges are inherent in pursuing goals, and challenges elicit emotion. These emotions keep the pursuit of the goal exciting and can drive the student toward more effort and, ultimately, success.

Regarding performance character and attacking challenges, students can also control their perseverance. Three components of perseverance are a positive mindset, courage, and commitment. Those with a positive mindset will be optimistic, grateful, and joyful with a challenge, thinking they can complete it, seeing the good in the challenge, and finding a way to make the challenge entertaining. Fear can also convince a student to stop; they may be too frightened or nervous to attempt a task or continue. If a student can work with fear and learn to be courageous, they will not give up on the challenge. Finally, commitment leads to perseverance. Once a student has a positive mindset and is courageous, they will need to commit to their goal. This takes a great amount of deliberate practice. Deliberate practice is hard work, but the student who chooses to persevere through these hours of focused attention coupled with feedback will see major improvements.

Passion and perseverance together practiced toward a long-term goal demonstrates grit. A gritty student uses passion to become and stay motivated as they persevere without wavering toward their goal. A student who continues to put effort toward learning in school will realize improvement. As they stay gritty through challenges that will lead them closer to their goal, students may find themselves in flow state, a euphoric experience where student egos vanish because their focus is so strong. Flow equates to enjoyment and happiness while the student continues to better themselves. Providing students with challenges that match their ability level and putting them into flow is a worthwhile goal for any teacher.

When teachers understand these concepts and how they personally relate, it can aid in becoming better educators. When teachers share the tools from this book and review the discussion questions in class and students understand these concepts, it leads to student self-awareness that they can be in control of their performance—making them successful and happy throughout the process.

While I do not have quantitative data that these tools are effective, I do have qualitative data. Many teachers who used these tools report back to me that they see more effort from their students. More importantly, students share that, through the tools, they feel that their teacher cares about them. Perhaps giving students a voice to talk about how they can best approach life's challenges leads to this assessment.

Students may not understand these concepts right away, but it's important to know that you're planting seeds. It may take those seeds several years to germinate; you may no longer have contact with your students when they do. Yet even if the lessons you teach only take root later in life, you still are invaluable to your students as they perform better in college, their job, and their relationships. My hope is that you can integrate these tools into your classroom so that you and your students may realize more success and happiness at school and beyond.

APPENDIX A

Tools

These tools have been a staple in my class for a decade. Having a visual and common language allows students to discuss these often deep and ambiguous concepts. I am lucky to share these tools with other educators and coaches to use in their own classrooms.

From my experience and from listening to others using these tools, I find that each teacher will use them a little differently. However, a few general themes arise. To effectively integrate tools into the classroom so that students more fully understand concepts, educators experienced with the tools suggest that teachers should understand the concepts before leading a discussion with students, students should experience the concept (they don't really understand until they do), and students should self-reflect on how they did after the lesson. While you can use these tools however you want, the experience of those successful with the tools follows six steps.

1. **Discuss the tool with a colleague or collaborative team:** Each tool includes general discussion questions to guide a peer discussion; however, I encourage you to generate your own questions for a deeper conversation that is more specific to your circumstances. This should prepare you before you share the tool with your students.

2. **Plan a lesson that includes teaching the performance character concept along with curriculum content:** Teachers often find that they have preexisting lessons or projects that mesh with one or more of the tools. Other educators find joy in choosing a tool first and creating a new lesson or project that couples well with it. This flexibility means

teachers can use them to enhance their class discussion of any academic discipline at any grade level. Mathematics, science, English language arts, physical education, special education, and educators from other subject areas already use these tools successfully.

3. **Lead a short, ten-minute discussion about the tool:** This can be a full-class discussion, small-group discussion, or a simple think-pair-share with the sample questions or new questions that you develop with a colleague or your team. You may find that your students disagree with each other (and perhaps even with you) in how to best answer questions. This is normal, and even good, as conversations with multiple opinions can add to the group's understanding of the concept.

4. **Teach the lesson you planned:** You may want to remind students about the concept before and throughout the lesson. That way, you can be very intentional about students working with the concept.

5. **Have students reflect on how they did with the concept:** It's often the case that students will say one thing in the discussion and do something very different during the lesson or project. So, it's important at the lesson's end for students to have time to reflect. Even if students' behaviors do not match their intentions, they learn something about themselves that they can use to improve. Educators offer this reflection piece in different ways. Some lead a full-class discussion, others facilitate small-group discussions, while others have students write their thoughts and observations in a journal. Typically, the reflection piece is around five minutes, which is long enough to have students think but short enough to retain class time for the subject. Again, you may determine what is best for the situation and your class.

6. **Refer to the tool throughout other challenges in your class when it applies:** All the tools are basically maps of what a student does when dealing with concepts while taking on a challenge. All visuals show what a student will do when they use a concept well or not. With the visuals, you can ask students where they are, where they want to be, and how they can get there.

Reading Recommendations for Students

In this appendix, you'll find recommendations for further reading. Each section corresponds with a chapter in this book and is meant to help cement the lessons learned in each chapter. Feel free to assign these for in-class reading, as a homework assignment, or for bonus credit.

To be intentional about each performance character element, you can pause at moments of the text that highlight these areas of struggle, possibly using a tool or tools from the chapter to emphasize how the character worked through it. For younger elementary students (grades K–2), you can complete this as a read-aloud. For older elementary students (grades 3–5), you can accomplish this as a read-aloud or via independent reading with instructions of when to stop and reflect.

Chapter 1: Self-Awareness

The following books have characters who deal with self-awareness issues when taking on a challenge.

Grades K–3:

- *Confident Ninja* by Mary Nhin (2020)
- *Humble Ninja* by Mary Nhin (2021)
- *Ish, The Dot, Sky Color* (Creatrilogy Series) by Peter H. Reynolds (2012)

Grades 4–8:

- *Wolfpack* (Young Readers Edition) by Abby Wambach (2019)

Grades 9–12:

- *Every Body Looking* by Candice Iloh (2021)
- *The Catcher in the Rye* by J. D. Salinger (1951)
- *The Secret Life of Bees* by Sue Monk Kidd (2003)

Chapter 2: Integrity

The following books have characters who deal with integrity issues when taking on a challenge.

Grades K–3:

- *If Everybody Did* by Jo Ann Stover (1990)
- *Lying Up a Storm* by Julia Cook (2021)
- *The Empty Pot* by Demi (1990)

Grades 4–8:

- *Holes* by Louis Sachar (2002)
- *Samurai Rising* by Pamela S. Turner (2018)

Grades 9–12:

- *Redemption at Hacksaw Ridge* by Booton Herndon (2016)
- *To Kill a Mockingbird* by Harper Lee (1960)

Chapter 3: Purpose

The following books have characters who deal with purpose issues when taking on a challenge.

Grades K–3:

- *Bounce Back Betty* by Cindy Whiteside and Katya Zayakina (2019)
- *I Can't Do That, Yet* by Esther Pia Cordova and Maima W. Adiputri (2017)
- *The Seed of Compassion* by His Holiness the Dalai Lama and Bao Luu (2021)

Grades 4–8:

- *The Harry Potter Series* by J.K. Rowling (1997–2007)

Grades 9–12:

- *A Prayer for Owen Meany* by John Irving (2014)
- *Man's Search for Meaning* by Viktor E. Frankl (2006)
- *The Alchemist* by Paulo Coelho (2002)

Chapter 4: Passion

The following books have characters who deal with passion issues when taking on a challenge.

Grades K–3:

- *My Body Sends a Signal* by Natalia Maguire and Anastasia Zababashkina (2020)
- *Mae Jemison* by Mary Nhin (2020)

Grades 4–8:

- *Where the Red Fern Grows* by Wilson Rawls (1961)

Grades 9–12:

- *The Great Gatsby* by F. Scott Fitzgerald (1925)

Chapter 5: Positive Mindset

The following books have characters who deal with positive mindset issues when taking on a challenge.

Grades K–3:

- *Someday a Bird Will Poop on You* by Sue Salvi and Megan Kellie (2018)
- *The Hugging Tree* by Jill Neimark and Nicole Wong (2016)
- *Serena Williams* by Mary Nhin (2021)

Grades 4–8:

- *Everything Is Going to Be OK* by Bruce Eric Kaplan (2014)

Grades 9–12:

- *Born a Crime* by Trevor Noah (2020)
- *Crying Laughing* by Lance Rubin (2021)

Chapter 6: Courage

The following books have characters who deal with courage issues when taking on a challenge.

Grades K–3:

- *After the Fall* by Dan Santat (2017)
- *You Can Do It, Bert!* by Ole Könnecke (2015)
- *Stacey's Extraordinary Words* by Stacey Abrams (2021)

Grades 4–8:

- *A Storm Too Soon* (Young Readers Edition) by Michael J. Tougias (2016)
- *Mrs. Frisby and the Rats of NIMH* by Robert C. O'Brien (1994)
- *A Season of Daring Greatly* by Ellen Emerson White (2017)

Grades 9–12:

- *The Fellowship of the Ring* by J. R. R. Tolkien (1954)
- *The Two Towers* by J. R. R. Tolkien (1954)
- *The Return of the King* by J. R. R. Tolkien (1955)
- *I Am Malala* by Malala Yousafzai (2013)
- *The Laramie Project* by Moises Kaufman (2016)

Chapter 7: Commitment

The following books have characters who deal with commitment issues when taking on a challenge.

Grades K–3:

- *A Thousand No's* by DJ Corchin and Dan Dougherty (2020)
- *Bruce Lee* by Mary Nhin (2020)
- *Elbow Grease* by John Cena (2018)
- *She Persisted* by Chelsea Clinton and Alexandra Boiger (2022)

Grades 4–8:

- *Esperanza Rising* by Pam Muñoz Ryan (2000)
- *Hatchet* by Gary Paulsen (1986)

Grades 9–12:

- *Always Running* by Luis J. Rodriguez (2020)
- *Angela's Ashes* by Frank McCourt (1996)

Chapter 8: Grit

The following books have characters who deal with grit issues when taking on a challenge.

Grades K–3:

- *Amelia Earhart* by Mary Nhin (2020)
- *Gritty Ninja* by Mary Nhin and Jelena Stupar (2020)
- *Way of the Warrior Kid* by Jocko Willink (2018)

Grades 4–8:

- *Rising Water: The Story of the Thai Cave Rescue* by Marc Aronson (2020)
- *The Impossible First* (The Young Adult Adaptation) by Colin O'Brady (2020)

Grades 9–12:

- *If This Is a Man* by Primo Levi (1947)
- *Night* by Elie Wiesel (1960)
- *Unbroken* by Laura Hillenbrand (2011)
- *The Power of One* by Bryce Courtenay (1989)
- *Their Eyes Were Watching God* by Zora Neale Hurston (2014)

Chapter 9: Flow

Note that because flow is a complex concept, there are very few books for children and adolescents that discuss it directly.

Grades K–3:

- *Flow Discovery Journal: Daily Questions to Spark Your Beginner's Mind* by Carmen Viktoria Gamper (2021)

Grades 9–12:

- *Way of the Peaceful Warrior* by Dan Millman (2010)

References

Abeles, V. (2016, January 2). Is the drive for success making our children sick? *The New York Times.* Accessed at nytimes.com/2016/01/03/opinion/sunday/is-the-drive-for-success -making-our-children-sick.html on June 27, 2022.

Abrams, S. (2021). *Stacey's extraordinary words.* New York: Balzer + Bray.

Achor, S. (2018). *The happiness advantage: How a positive brain fuels success in work and life.* New York: Currency.

American Psychological Association. (n.d.). *Sport psychology.* Accessed at www.apa.org/ed /graduate/specialize/sports on August 28, 2022.

Anderman, E. M., Griesinger, T., & Westerfield, G. (1998). Motivation and cheating during early adolescence. *Journal of Educational Psychology, 90*(1), 84–93. doi.org/10.1037/0022 -0663.90.1.84

Anggoro, S., Sopandi, W., & Sholehuddin, M. (2017). Influence of joyful learning on elementary school students' attitudes toward science. *Journal of Physics: Conference Series, 812,* 012001. doi.org/10.1088/1742-6596/812/1/012001.

Ariawan, V. A. N., & Pratiwi, I. M. (2017). Joyful learning strategy using game method of treasure clue to improve reading comprehension skill. *Jurnal Prima Edukasia, 5*(2), 203–210. doi.org/10.21831/jpe.v5i2.11601

Aronson, M. (2020). *Rising water: The story of the Thai cave rescue.* New York: Atheneum Children's Books.

Asakawa, K. (2009). Flow experience, culture, and well-being: How do autotelic Japanese college students feel, behave, and think in their daily lives? *Journal of Happiness Studies, 11*(2), 205–223. doi.org/10.1007/s10902-008-9132-3

Avildsen, J. G. (Director). (1976). *Rocky* [Motion picture]. United States: United Artists.

Barber, N. (2014, October 2). *Focus on the process and results will follow* [Blog post]. Accessed at edutopia.org/blog/focus-process-results-will-follow-nathan-barber on June 27, 2022.

Bardwick, J. M. (1995). *Danger in the comfort zone: From boardroom to mailroom—How to break the entitlement habit that's killing American business.* New York: Amacom.

Baumann, N. (n.d.). *Chapter 9: Autotelic personality.* Accessed at www.uni-trier.de/fileadmin/fb1/prof/PSY/PGA/bilder/Baumann_Flow_Chapter_9_final.pdf?source=post_page on June 27, 2022.

Belli, B. (2020, January 30). *National survey: Students' feelings about high school are mostly negative.* Accessed at news.yale.edu/2020/01/30/national-survey-students-feelings-about-high-school-are-mostly-negative on June 27, 2022.

Bernabé-Valero, G., Blasco-Magraner, J. S., & Moret-Tatay, C. (2019). Testing motivational theories in music education: The role of effort and gratitude. *Frontiers in Behavioral Neuroscience, 13.* doi.org/10.3389/fnbeh.2019.00172

Berridge, K. C., & Kringelbach, M. L. (2015). Pleasure systems in the brain. *Neuron, 86*(3), 646–664. doi.org/10.1016/j.neuron.2015.02.018

Blackburn, B. (2018, December 13). *Productive struggle is a learner's sweet spot.* Accessed at www.ascd.org/el/articles/productive-struggle-is-a-learners-sweet-spot on September 18, 2022.

Blackwell, L. S., Trzesniewski, K. H., & Dweck, C. S. (2007). Implicit theories of intelligence predict achievement across an adolescent transition: A longitudinal study and an intervention. *Child Development, 78*(1), 246–263. doi.org/10.1111/j.1467-8624.2007.00995

Bloom, B. S. (Ed.). (1985). *Developing talent in young people.* New York: Ballantine Books.

Borovay, L. A., Shore, B. M., Caccese, C., Yang, E., & Hua, O. L. (2018). Flow, achievement level, and inquiry-based learning. *Journal of Advanced Academics, 30*(1), 74–106. doi.org/10.1177/1932202x18809659

Bradberry, T. (2015, November 13). 11 signs you have the grit needed to succeed. *Entrepreneur.* Accessed at www.entrepreneur.com/living/11-signs-you-have-the-grit-needed-to-succeed/252634#! on September 20, 2022.

Bradley, D. (n.d.). *Why Gladwell's 10,000-hour rule is wrong.* Accessed at www.bbc.com/future/article/20121114-gladwells-10000-hour-rule-myth on September 18, 2022.

Brinke, L.T., Lee, J. J., & Carney, D. R. (2015). The physiology of (dis)honesty: Does it impact health? *Current Opinion in Psychology, 6,* 177–182. Accessed at sciencedirect.com/science/article/pii/S2352250X15001980?via%3Dihub on June 27, 2022.

Brooks, A. W. (2014). Get excited: Reappraising pre-performance anxiety as excitement. *Journal of Experimental Psychology: General, 143*(3), 1144–1158. doi.org/10.1037/a0035325

Brown, B. (2015). *Daring greatly: How the courage to be vulnerable transforms the way we live, love, parent, and lead.* New York: Avery.

Cable News Network. (n.d.). *Mandela in his own words.* CNN. Accessed at edition.cnn.com/2008/WORLD/africa/06/24/mandela.quotes on September 17, 2022.

Canfield, J. (2007). *The success principles: How to get from where you are to where you want to be.* New York: HarperCollins.

Cannon, W. B. (1915). *Bodily changes in pain, hunger, fear and rage: An account of recent researches into the function of emotional excitement.* New York: D. Appleton & Company.

Cena, J. (2018). *Elbow grease.* Penguin Random House.

Chen, Q., Gao, W., Chen, B.-B., Kong, Y., Lu, L., & Yang, S. (2021). Ego-resiliency and perceived social support in late childhood: A latent growth modeling approach. *International Journal of Environmental Research and Public Health, 18*(6), 2978. doi.org/10.3390/ijerph 18062978

Cherry, K. (2020, November 19). *How does the James-Lange theory account for emotions?* Accessed at www.verywellmind.com/what-is-the-james-lange-theory-of-emotion-2795305 on August 26, 2022.

Clinton, C., & Boiger, A. (2022). *She persisted: 13 American women who changed the world.* New York: Philomel Books.

Coelho, P. (2002). *The alchemist.* HarperCollins.

Cook, J., & Hyde, M. H. (2021). *Lying up a storm.* Chattanooga, TN: National Center for Youth Issues.

Corchin, D. J., & Dougherty, D. (2020). *A thousand no's.* Naperville, IL: Sourcebooks Explore.

Cordova, E. P., & Adiputri, M. W. (2017). *I can't do that, yet: Growth mindset.* Power of Yet.

Courage. (n.d.). In *APA dictionary of psychology.* Accessed at https://dictionary.apa.org /courage on June 27, 2022.

Courtenay, B. (1989). *The power of one.* Portsmouth, NH: Heinemann.

Cristol, H. (2021). *What is dopamine?* Accessed at www.webmd.com/mental-health/what-is-dopamine on June 27, 2022.

Csikszentmihalyi, M. (1990). *Flow: The psychology of optimal experience.* New York: HarperCollins.

Csikszentmihalyi, M., Montijo, M. N., & Mouton, A. R. (2018). *Flow theory: Optimizing elite performance in the creative realm.* In S. I. Pfeiffer, E. Shaunessy-Dedrick, & M. Foley-Nicpon (Eds.), *APA handbook of giftedness and talent* (pp. 215–229). Washington, DC: American Psychological Association. doi.org/10.1037/0000038-014

Csikszentmihalyi, M., & Rathunde, K. (2005). Middle school students' motivation and quality of experience: A comparison of Montessori and traditional school environments. *American Journal of Education, 111*(3), 341–371.

Dalai Lama, & Luu, B. (2021). *The seed of compassion: Lessons from the life and teachings of his holiness the Dalai Lama.* London: Puffin.

Davidson, M., Lickona, T., & Khmelkov, V. (2008). Smart and good schools: A new paradigm for high school character education. In L. Nucci & D. Narvaez (Eds.), *Handbook of moral and character education* (pp. 386–406). New York: Routledge.

DeBacker, T. K., Heddy, B. C., Kershen, J. L., Crowson, H. M., Looney, K., & Goldman, J. A. (2018). Effects of a one-shot growth mindset intervention on beliefs about intelligence and achievement goals. *Educational Psychology, 38*(6), 711–733. doi.org/10.1080/01443410 .2018.1426833

Deci, E. L., & Ryan, R. M. (2014). *Intrinsic motivation and self-determination in human behavior.* Berlin: Springer Science+Business Media.

Demi. (1990). *The empty pot.* New York: Scholastic.

Denby, D. (2016, June 21). The limits of "grit." *The New Yorker*. Accessed at newyorker.com/culture/culture-desk/the-limits-of-grit on June 27, 2022.

de Saint-Exupéry, A. (2020). *The little prince* (M. Morpurgo, Trans.). New York: Penguin Random House. (Original work published 1943)

De Sena, J. (2018). *The spartan way: Eat better. Train better. Think better. Be better.* New York: St. Martin's Griffin.

Diamond, D. M. (2005). Cognitive, endocrine and mechanistic perspectives on nonlinear relationships between arousal and brain function. *Nonlinearity in Biology, Toxicology, Medicine, 3*(1), 1–7. Accessed at ncbi.nlm.nih.gov/pmc/articles/PMC2657838/#b50-nbtm-3-1-0001 on June 27, 2022.

Duckworth, A. (2016a). *Grit: The power of passion and perseverance.* New York: Scribner.

Duckworth, A. (2016b, May 3). Why millennials struggle for success. *CNN*. Accessed at cnn.com/2016/05/03/opinions/grit-is-a-gift-of-age-duckworth/index.html on June 27, 2022.

Duckworth, A. L., Peterson, C., Matthews, M. D., & Kelly, D. R. (2007). Grit: Perseverance and passion for long-term goals. *Journal of Personality and Social Psychology, 92*(6), 1087–1101. doi.org/10.1037/0022-3514.92.6.1087

Dweck, C. S. (2016). *Mindset: The new psychology of success* (Updated ed.). New York: Random House.

Educator Innovator. (2013, July 9). *What does "interest-driven" look like?* [Video file]. Accessed at educatorinnovator.org/webinars/what-does-interest-driven-look-like on June 28, 2022.

ego. (n.d.). In *APA dictionary of psychology*. Accessed at dictionary.apa.org/ego on June 27, 2022.

Ellison, D. W., & Woods, A. M. (2016). Deliberate practice as a tool for effective teaching in physical education. *Journal of Physical Education, Recreation & Dance, 87*(2), 15–19. Doi.org/10.1080/07303084.2015.1119075

Elmore, T. (2014, May 1). *Seven ideas to build perseverance in students (Part two)* [Blog post]. Accessed at growingleaders.com/blog/seven-ideas-build-perseverance-students-part-two on June 27, 2022.

Encyclopedia.com. (n.d.). *Csikszentmihalyi, Mihaly.* Accessed at encyclopedia.com/history/encyclopedias-almanacs-transcripts-and-maps/csikszentmihalyi-mihaly on June 27, 2022.

Ericsson, K. A. (2016). Summing up hours of any type of practice versus identifying optimal practice activities: Commentary on Macnamara, Moreau, & Hambrick (2016). *Perspectives on Psychological Science, 11*(3), 351–354. Doi.org/10.1177/1745691616635600

Ericsson, K. A., Krampe, R. T., & Tesch-Römer, C. (1993). The role of deliberate practice in the acquisition of expert performance. *Psychological Review, 100*(3), 363–406. doi.org/10.1037/0033-295x.100.3.363

Ericsson, A., & Pool, R. (2017). *Peak: How all of us can achieve extraordinary things* (International ed.). New York: Vintage Books.

Facts and statistics. (n.d.). Albany, NY: International Center for Academic Integrity. Accessed at academicintegrity.org/resources/facts-and-statistics on June 27, 2022.

FAQ. (n.d.). Angela Duckworth. Accessed at angeladuckworth.com/qa on June 27, 2022.

Farkas, D., & Orosz, G. (2015). Ego-resiliency reloaded: A three-component model of general resiliency. *PLOS ONE, 10*(3). doi.org/10.1371/journal.pone.0120883

fear. (n.d.). In *Merriam-Webster's online dictionary*. Accessed at merriam-webster.com/dictionary/fear on June 28, 2022.

Fear of failure. (n.d.). In *APA dictionary of psychology*. Accessed at dictionary.apa.org/fear-of-failure on June 27, 2022.

Ferriss, T. (2017, July 14). *Why you should define your fears instead of your goals* [Video file]. TED Conferences. Accessed at ted.com/talks/tim_ferriss_why_you_should_define_your_fears_instead_of_your_goals on June 28, 2022.

Filippello, P., Harrington, N., Costa, S., Buzzai, C., & Sorrenti, L. (2018). Perceived parental psychological control and school learned helplessness: The role of frustration intolerance as a mediator factor. *School Psychology International, 39*(4), 360–377. doi.org/10.1177/014303 4318775140

Fitzgerald, F. S. (1925). *The great Gatsby*. New York: Scribner's Sons.

Frankl, V. E. (2006). *Man's search for meaning*. Boston: Beacon Press.

Fredricks, J. A., Alfeld, C., & Eccles, J. (2009). Developing and fostering passion in academic and nonacademic domains. *Gifted Child Quarterly, 54*(1), 18–30. doi.org/10.1177/0016986 209352683

Freud, S. (1962). *The ego and the id*. New York: Norton.

Fromuth, M. E., Bass, J. E., Kelly, D. B., Davis, T. L., & Chan, K. L. (2017). Academic entitlement: Its relationship with academic behaviors and attitudes. *Social Psychology of Education, 22*(5), 1153–1167. doi.org/10.1007/s11218-019-09517-2

Gallagher, M. W., Marques, S. C., & Lopez, S. J. (2016). Hope and the academic trajectory of college students. *Journal of Happiness Studies, 18*(2), 341–352. doi.org/10.1007/s10902 -016-9727-z

Gamper, C. V. (2021). *Flow discovery journal: Daily questions to spark your beginner's mind*. San Francisco: New Learning Culture.

Gardner, H. (2018, October 26). *"A rage to master": A blog on gifted children by Dr. Ellen Winner* [Blog post]. Accessed at multipleintelligencesoasis.org/blog/2019/3/14/a-rage-to-master-a -blog-on-gifted-children-by-dr-ellen-winner on June 28, 2022.

Gladwell, M. [MalcolmGladwell]. (2009, May 27). *Hi, I'm Malcolm Gladwell, author of The Tipping Point, Blink, Outliers and—most recently—David and Goliath: Underdogs, Misfits and the Art of Battling Giants. Ask me anything!* [Online forum post]. Accessed at reddit.com/r/I AmA/comments/2740ct/hi_im_malcolm_gladwell_author_of_the_tipping/chx6ku3 on June 28, 2022.

Gladwell, M. (2019). *Outliers: The story of success*. New York: Little, Brown.

Goggins, D. (2018). *Can't hurt me: Master your mind and defy the odds*. Carson City, NV: Lioncrest.

The golden rule. (2014, February 25). Radiolab. Accessed at wnycstudios.org/podcasts/radiolab /segments/golden-rule on June 27, 2022.

Gorman, N. (2017). On the front line of teaching "grit": The battle to stop students from quitting. *Education World*. Accessed at bit.ly/3BPLK5U on June 27, 2022.

Gray, P. (2018). How schools thwart passions. *Psychology Today*. Accessed at www.psychology today.com/us/blog/freedom-learn/201811/how-schools-thwart-passions September 23, 2022.

Greenberg, M. (2012, August 23). *The six attributes of courage* [Blog post]. Accessed at psychologytoday.com/us/blog/the-mindful-self-express/201208/the-six-attributes-courage on June 28, 2022.

Greenberger, E., Lessard, J., Chen, C., & Farruggia, S. P. (2008). Self-entitled college students: Contributions of personality, parenting, and motivational factors. *Journal of Youth and Adolescence, 37*(10), 1193–1204. doi.org/10.1007/s10964-008-9284-9

Grit Scale. (n.d.). Angela Duckworth. Accessed at angeladuckworth.com/grit-scale on June 27, 2022.

Gross, J. J., & John, O. P. (2003). Individual differences in two emotion regulation processes: Implications for affect, relationships, and well-being. *Journal of Personality and Social Psychology, 85*(2), 348–362. doi.org/10.1037/0022-3514.85.2.348

Gross-Loh, C. (2021, August 2). Don't let praise become a consolation prize. *The Atlantic*. Accessed at www.theatlantic.com/education/archive/2016/12/how-praise-became-a-consolation-prize/510845/ on September 11, 2022.

Grubbs, J. B., & Exline, J. J. (2016). Trait entitlement: A cognitive-personality source of vulnerability to psychological distress. *Psychological Bulletin, 142*(11), 1204–1226. doi.org/10.1037/bul0000063

Guiang-Myers, G. (2019, March 19). Tips for teaching realistic optimism. *Edutopia*. Accessed at www.edutopia.org/article/tips-teaching-realistic-optimism on September 13, 2022.

Handford, M. (2012). *Where's Waldo? Deluxe edition.* Somerville, MA: Candlewick Press.

Hardy, B. (2022, May 17). *This one question will make every decision in your life easier.* Medium. Accessed at medium.com/@benjaminhardy/this-1-powerful-strategy-made-the-british-rowing-team-to-go-from-average-to-winning-olympic-gold-b859b7f6cda1 on September 7, 2022.

Harvard Health. (2020, July 6). *Understanding the stress response.* Accessed at www.health.harvard.edu/staying-healthy/understanding-the-stress-response on September 18, 2022.

Hensley, L. (2013). To cheat or not to cheat: A review with implications for practice. *The Community College Enterprise, 19*, 22–34. Accessed at semanticscholar.org/paper/To-Cheat-or-Not-to-Cheat%3A-A-Review-with-for-Hensley/c37ced3cc950e0e8cd5206ccfed59eeb21887e4c on June 28, 2022.

Herndon, B. (2016). *Redemption at Hacksaw Ridge: The official authorized story of Desmond Doss.* Coldwater, MI: Remnant Publications.

Heshmat, S. (n.d.). *Anxiety vs. fear: What is the difference?* [Blog post]. Accessed at psychologytoday.com/us/blog/science-choice/201812/anxiety-vs-fear on June 28, 2022.

Hillenbrand, L. (2011). *Unbroken.* London: Fourth Estate.

Hoose, N. A.-V. (n.d.). *Educational Psychology.* Accessed at edpsych.pressbooks.sunycreate.cloud on September 25, 2022.

Hopper, E. (2019, June 26). *What is the Schachter-Singer theory of emotion?* Accessed at www.thoughtco.com/schachter-singer-theory-4691140 on August 26, 2022.

Horowitz, J. M., & Graf, N. (2019, February 20). *Most U.S. teens see anxiety and depression as a major problem among their peers.* Washington, DC: Pew Research Center. Accessed at pewresearch.org/social-trends/2019/02/20/most-u-s-teens-see-anxiety-and-depression-as-a -major-problem-among-their-peers on June 28, 2022.

Hoy, W. K., Tarter, C. J., & Hoy, A. W. (2006). Academic optimism of schools: A force for student achievement. *American Educational Research Journal, 43*(3), 425–446.

Huberman, A. (Host). (2022). Sleep toolkit: Tools for optimizing sleep & sleep-wake timing. (No. 84) [Audio podcast episode]. Accessed at bit.ly/3YFfTi0 on August 22, 2022.

Hurston, Z. N. (2014). *Their eyes were watching god.* Charlotte, NC: SPARK Publisher.

Iloh, C. (2021). *Everybody looking.* New York: Dutton Books for Young Readers.

integrity. (n.d.). In *Merriam-Webster's online dictionary.* Accessed at merriam-webster.com /dictionary/integrity on June 28, 2022.

Irving, J. (2014). *A prayer for Owen Meany.* New York: William Morrow.

Johnston, M. (2020, October 28). *Online student's guide to stepping out of your comfort zone* [Blog post]. Accessed at suu.edu/blog/2020/10/online-student-comfort-zone.html on June 28, 2022.

John Templeton Foundation. (2018). The psychology of purpose. Accessed at www.templeton.org /wp-content/uploads/2020/02/Psychology-of-Purpose.pdf on September 5, 2022.

joy. (n.d.). In *APA dictionary of psychology.* Accessed at dictionary.apa.org/joy on June 27, 2022.

Joyful Learning Network. (n.d.). *Joyful learning.* Accessed at joyfullearningnetwork.com/what-is -joyful-learning.html on June 28, 2022.

Kaplan, B. E. (2014). *Everything is going to be okay.* New York: Simon & Schuster.

Kaufman, M. (2016). *The Laramie Project.* Brantford, ON: W. Ross MacDonald School Resource Services Library.

Kerns, G. (2020, July 17). *The 4 R's of deliberate practice.* Renaissance. Accessed at www.renaissance.com/2016/09/29/the-meaning-of-deliberate-practice September 18, 2022.

Kidd, S. (2003). *The secret life of bees.* New York: Penguin.

Könnecke, O., & Chidgey, C. (2015). *You can do it, Bert!* Wellington, New Zealand: Gecko Press.

Korb, A. (2014, October 31). *Predictable fear: Why the brain likes haunted houses* [Blog post]. Accessed at psychologytoday.com/us/blog/prefrontal-nudity/201410/predictable-fear on June 28, 2022.

Kotler, S., & Wheal, J. (2017). *Stealing fire: How Silicon Valley, the Navy SEALS, and maverick scientists are revolutionizing the way we live and work.* New York: Dey St.

Krueger, J., & Mueller, R. A. (2002). Unskilled, unaware, or both? The better-than-average heuristic and statistical regression predict errors in estimates of own performance. *Journal of Personality and Social Psychology, 82*(2), 180–188.

Kruger, J., & Dunning, D. (1999). Unskilled and unaware of it: How difficulties in recognizing one's own incompetence lead to inflated self-assessments. *Journal of Personality and Social Psychology, 77*(6), 1121–1134. doi.org/10.1037/0022-3514.77.6.1121

Lee, H. (1960). *To kill a mockingbird*. Philadelphia: Lippincott.

Lee, H. Y., Jamieson, J. P., Miu, A. S., Josephs, R. A., & Yeager, D. S. (2018). An entity theory of intelligence predicts higher cortisol levels when high school grades are declining. *Child Development, 90*(6), e849–e867. Accessed at labs.la.utexas.edu/josephs/files/2018/07/Lee_et_al-2018-Child_Development.pdf on June 28, 2022.

Lemke, D., Marx, J., & Dundes, L. (2017). Challenging notions of academic entitlement and its rise among liberal arts college students. *Behavioral Sciences, 7*(4), 81. doi.org/10.3390/bs7040081

Levi, P. (1947). *If this is a man*. Miami, FL: Orion Press.

Lewis, C., Della Williams, B., Sohn, M., & Chin Loy, T. (2017). The myth of entitlement: Students' perceptions of the relationship between grading practices and learning at an Elite University. *The Qualitative Report*. doi.org/10.46743/2160-3715/2017.2906

Lewis, M. (Host). (2019, April 2). Ref, you suck! [Audio podcast episode]. In *Against the rules*. Accessed at www.pushkin.fm/podcasts/against-the-rules/ref-you-suck on October 31, 2022.

Lickerman, A. (2011, January 9). *Why we quit: Why quitting has more to do with attention than anything else* [Blog post]. Accessed at psychologytoday.com/us/blog/happiness-in-world/201101/why-we-quit on June 28, 2022.

Lippmann, S., Bulanda, R. E., & Wagenaar, T. C. (2009). Student entitlement: Issues and strategies for confronting entitlement in the classroom and beyond. *College Teaching, 57*(4), 197–204. doi.org/10.1080/87567550903218596

MacCoun, R. J., & Kerr, N. L. (1988). Asymmetric influence in mock jury deliberation: Jurors' bias for leniency. *Journal of Personality and Social Psychology, 54*(1), 21–33. doi.org/10.1037/0022-3514.54.1.21

Machiavelli, N. (2020). *The prince* (W. K. Marriott, Trans.). New York: Vintage Classics.

Magnus, J. R., & Peresetsky, A. A. (2022). A statistical explanation of the Dunning–Kruger effect. *Frontiers in Psychology, 13*. doi.org/10.3389/fpsyg.2022.840180

Maguire, N., & Zababashkina, A. (2020). *My body sends a signal: Helping kids recognize emotions and express feelings*. Hamburg, Germany: Maguire Books.

Maier, S. F., & Seligman, M. E. (1976). Learned helplessness: Theory and evidence. *Journal of Experimental Psychology: General, 105*(1), 3–46. doi.org/10.1037/0096-3445.105.1.3

Manson, M. (n.d.). *The three levels of self-awareness*. Accessed at markmanson.net/self-awareness on June 28, 2022.

Markman, A. B. (2014). *Smart change: Five tools to create new and sustainable habits in yourself and others*. New York: Perigee.

Marques, J., & Dhiman, S. (2017). *Leadership today: Practices for personal and professional performance*. Cham, Switzerland: Springer International.

Marshall, D. (2012). *Swimming kids are smarter*. Griffith News. Accessed at news.griffith.edu.au/2012/11/15/swimming-kids-are-smarter on November 8, 2022.

Marzano, R. J. (2007). *The art and science of teaching: A comprehensive framework for effective instruction*. Alexandria, VA: Association for Supervision and Curriculum Development.

McCabe, D. L., Butterfield, K. D., & Treviño, L. K. (2017). *Cheating in college: Why students do it and what educators can do about it*. Baltimore: The Johns Hopkins University Press.

McCourt, F. (1996). *Angela's ashes*. New York: Simon & Schuster.

Merriam-Webster. (n.d.). Fear definition and meaning. Accessed at www.merriam-webster.com/dictionary/fear on August 22, 2022.

Mihaly Csikszentmihalyi—In the flow. (2000, September 1). Claremont, CA: Claremont Graduate University. Accessed at www.cgu.edu/news/2000/09/mihaly-csikszentmihalyi-flow on September 24, 2022.

Miller, K. D. (2019, March 23). *Flow theory in psychology: Thirteen key findings and examples*. Accessed at positivepsychology.com/theory-psychology-flow on June 28, 2022.

Millman, D. (1999). *Mental talent: Improve your mental harmony*. Accessed at www.grandtimes.com/mental.html on June 28, 2022.

Millman, D. (2010). *Way of the peaceful warrior*. New York: Peaceful Warrior ePublishing.

Monticello. (n.d.). *Nothing can stop the man with the right mental attitude . . . (spurious quotation)*. Accessed at www.monticello.org/research-education/thomas-jefferson-encyclopedia/nothing-can-stop-man-right-mental-attitude-spurious-quotation on September 13, 2022.

Muenks, K., Yang, J. S., & Wigfield, A. (2018). Associations between grit, motivation, and achievement in high school students. *Motivation Science, 4*(2), 158–176. doi.org/10.1037/mot0000076

Muhammad, A. (2018). *Transforming school culture: How to overcome staff division (second edition)*. Bloomington, IN: Solution Tree Press.

Muñoz Ryan, P. (2000). *Esperanza rising*. New York: Scholastic.

Murray, M. (2016, February 1). *Dare to praise*. Accessed at thewholeu.uw.edu/2016/02/01/dare-to-praise/ September 18, 2022.

Murphy, S. (2018, October 17). Teaching students to fail forward is vital to innovating higher education. *The Globe and Mail*. Accessed at proquest.com/newspapers/teaching-students-fail-forward-is-vital/docview/2120565600/se-2?accountid=164834 on June 28, 2022.

Neimark, J., & Wong, N. (2016). *The hugging tree: A story about resilience*. Washington, DC: American Psychological Association.

Newman, T. (2018, October 21). Dissecting terror: How does fear work? *Medical News Today*. Accessed at medicalnewstoday.com/articles/323492 on June 28, 2022.

Nhin, M. (2020). *Amelia Earhart*. Edmond, OK: Grow Grit Press.

Nhin, M., & Stupar, J. (2020). *Confident ninja*. Edmond, OK: Grow Grit Press.

Nhin, M., & Stupar, J. (2020). *Gritty ninja*. Edmond, OK: Grow Grit Press.

Nhin, M., & Stupar, J. (2021). *Humble ninja*. Edmond, OK: Grow Grit Press.

Nhin, M., & Zolotova, Y. (2020). *Bruce Lee*. Edmond, OK: Grow Grit Press.

Nhin, M., & Zolotova, Y. (2020). *Mae Jemison*. Edmond, OK: Grow Grit Press.

Nhin, M., & Zolotova, Y. (2021). *Serena Williams*. Edmond, OK: Grow Grit Press.

Nickerson, C. (2021, July 21). *Cannon-Bard theory of emotion*. Accessed at www.simply psychology.org/what-is-the-cannon-bard-theory.html on August 26, 2022.

Noah, T. (2020). *It's Trevor Noah: Born a crime: Stories from a South African childhood*. Toronto: Yearling.

Nonis, S., & Swift, C. O. (2010). An examination of the relationship between academic dishonesty and workplace dishonesty: A multicampus investigation. *Journal of Education for Business*, *77*(2), 69–77. doi.org/10.1080/08832320109599052

NPR. (2012, September 5). *Transcript: Michelle Obama's convention speech*. Accessed at www. npr.org/2012/09/04/160578836/transcript-michelle-obamas-convention -speech September 4, 2022.

O'Brady, C. (2020). *The impossible first* (The Young Adult Adaptation). New York: Simon Schuster Books for Young Readers.

O'Brien, R. C., & Todd, J. (1994). *Mrs. Frisby and the rats of NIMH*. London: Puffin.

Olčar, D., Rijavec, M., & Golub, T. L. (2019). Primary school teachers' life satisfaction: The role of life goals, basic psychological needs and flow at work. *Current Psychology*, *38*(2), 320–329. doi.org/10.1007/s12144-017-9611-y

Oppland, M. (2016, December 16). *Eight ways to create flow according to Mihaly Csikszentmihalyi*. Accessed at positivepsychology.com/mihaly-csikszentmihalyi-father-of-flow on June 27, 2022.

Park, D., Yu, A., Baelen, R. N., Tsukayama, E., & Duckworth, A. L. (2018). Fostering grit: Perceived school goal-structure predicts growth in grit and grades. *Contemporary Educational Psychology*, *55*, 120–128. doi.org/10.1016/j.cedpsych.2018.09.007

passion. (n.d.a). In *Merriam-Webster's online dictionary*. Accessed at merriam-webster.com /dictionary/passion on June 28, 2022.

passion. (n.d.b). In *Online etymology dictionary*. Accessed at etymonline.com/word/passion on June 28, 2022.

Paulsen, G. (1986). *Hatchet*. New York: Macmillan.

Postigo, Á., Cuesta, M., Fernández-Alonso, R., García-Cueto, E., & Muñiz, J. (2020). Temporal stability of grit and school performance in adolescents: A longitudinal perspective. *Psicología Educativa*, *27*(1), 77–84. doi.org/10.5093/psed2021a4

Psychology Today staff. (n.d.a). *Fear*. Accessed at psychologytoday.com/us/basics/fear on June 28, 2022.

Psychology Today staff. (n.d.b). *Flow*. Accessed at psychologytoday.com/us/basics/flow on June 27, 2022.

Psychology Today staff. (n.d.c). *Positive psychology*. Accessed at psychologytoday.com/us/basics /positive-psychology on June 28, 2022.

Psychology Today staff. (n.d.d). *Catastrophizing*. Accessed at www.psychologytoday.com/us /basics/catastrophizing on September 17, 2022.

Pursuit of Happiness. (n.d.). *Martin Seligman*. Accessed at pursuit-of-happiness.org/history-of -happiness/martin-seligman-psychology on June 28, 2022.

Ratey, J. J. (2008). *Spark: The revolutionary new science of exercise and the brain*. New York: Little, Brown.

Rathunde, K. (2001). Montessori education and optimal experience: A framework for new research. *The NAMTA Journal, 26*(1), 11–43.

Rawls, W. (1961). *Where the red fern grows*. New York: Doubleday.

The real health benefits of smiling and laughing. (n.d.). Accessed at www.sclhealth.org/blog /2019/06/the-real-health-benefits-of-smiling-and-laughing on September 18, 2022.

Renninger, K. A., Sansone, C., & Smith, J. L. (2004). Love of learning. In C. Peterson & M. E. P. Seligman (Eds.), *Character strengths and virtues: A handbook and classification* (pp. 161–179). Oxford, England: Oxford University Press.

Reynolds, P. H. (2012). *Creatrilogy*. New York: Candlewick.

Richards, J. (2016). *Missing pieces: 52 vital lessons our kids should be learning at school (but aren't)*. Tempe, AZ: jaimerichards.org.

Richter, C. P. (1957). On the phenomenon of sudden death in animals and man. *Psychosomatic Medicine, 19*(3), 191–198. doi.org/10.1097/00006842-195705000-00004

Riggins, C. G. (2006). Assessing students to erase failure. *Education Digest: Essential Readings Condensed for Quick Review, 71*(9), 34–35.

Robbins, T. (n.d.). *How to benefit from positive thinking*. Accessed at tonyrobbins.com/positive -thinking on June 28, 2022.

Rodriguez, L. J. (2020). *Always running: La vida loca, gang days in L.A.* New York: Atria Paperback.

Roese, N. J., & Summerville, A. (2005). What we regret most . . . and why. *Personality and Social Psychology Bulletin, 31*(9), 1273–1285. doi.org/10.1177/0146167205274693

Roschelle, J., & Burke, Q. (2019). Commentary on interest-driven creator theory: A US perspective on fostering interest, creativity, and habit in school. *Research and Practice in Technology Enhanced Learning, 14*(13). doi.org/10.1186/s41039-019-0107-2

Ross, J. G., Bruderle, E., & Meakim, C. (2015). Integration of deliberate practice and peer mentoring to enhance students' mastery and retention of essential skills. *Journal of Nursing Education, 54*(3). doi.org/10.3928/01484834-20150218-20

Rowling, J.K. (1997–2007). *The harry potter series* (Vols. 1–7). New York: Bloomsbury.

Rubin, L. (2021). *Crying laughing*. New York: Random House Children's Books.

Rujoiu, O., & Rujoiu, V. (2014). Academic dishonesty and workplace dishonesty. An overview. *Proceedings of the International Management Conference, Faculty of Management, Academy of Economic Studies, Bucharest, Romania, 8*(1), pp. 928–938.

Sachar, L. (2002). *Holes*. New York: Dell Laurel-Leaf Books.

Salinger, J. D. (1951). *The catcher in the rye*. Boston: Little, Brown.

Salvi, S., & Kellie, M. (2018). *Someday a bird will poop on you: A life lesson*. Boston: Little, Brown.

Santat, D. (2017). *After the fall: How humpty dumpty got back up again.* Roaring Brook Press.

Schaffner, A. K. (2020, November 16). *Perseverance in psychology: Four activities to improve perseverance.* Accessed at positivepsychology.com/perseverance on June 28, 2022.

Schreiner, L. A. (2017). The privilege of grit. *About Campus: Enriching the Student Learning Experience, 22*(5), 11–20. doi.org/10.1002/abc.21303

ScienceDaily. (2015, February 14). *Exploring the teenage brain, and its drive for immediate reward.* Accessed at www.sciencedaily.com/releases/2015/02/150214184523.htm on September 4, 2022.

Seifert, K., & Sutton, R. (2021, February 21). *6.8: Expectancy X value-effects on students' motivation.* Accessed at socialsci.libretexts.org/Bookshelves/Education_and_Professional_Development /Book%3A_Educational_Psychology_(Seifert_and_Sutton)/06%3A_Student_Motivation /6.08%3A_Expectancy_X_Value-_Effects_on_Students'_Motivation on September 8, 2022.

Seligman, M. E. (2018). *Learned optimism: How to change your mind and your life* [Kindle version]. Boston: Nicholas Brealey. Accessed at Amazon.com.

Sherman, J. E. (2014). Fragidity: The fragile rigidity of the brittle ego. *Psychology Today.* Accessed at www.psychologytoday.com/us/blog/ambigamy/201403/fragidity-the -fragile-rigidity-the-brittle-ego on September 3, 2022.

Shernoff, D. J., Csikszentmihalyi, M., Shneider, B., & Shernoff, E. S. (2003). Student engagement in high school classrooms from the perspective of flow theory. *School Psychology Quarterly, 18*(2), 158–176. Doi.org/10.1521/scpq.18.2.158.21860

Shernoff, D. J., & Hoogstra, L. (2001). Continuing motivation beyond the high school classroom. *New Directions for Child and Adolescent Development, 2001*(93), 73–88. doi.org/10.1002/cd.26

Shih, S.-S. (2011). Perfectionism, implicit theories of intelligence, and Taiwanese eighth-grade students' academic engagement. *The Journal of Educational Research, 104*(2), 131–142. doi.org/10.1080/00220670903570368

Sinek, S. (2016, December 30). *The millennial question* [Video file]. Accessed at www.youtube .com/watch?v=vudaAYx2IcE on June 28, 2022.

Sinek, S. (2019). *Start with why: How great leaders inspire everyone to take action.* London: Portfolio Penguin.

Smith, A. (2021a, June 17). *"Pleasure" vs "enjoyment."* Accessed at coachingleaders.co.uk /pleasure-vs-enjoyment on September 24, 2022.

Smith, E. E. (2021b). *Hope is the antidote to helplessness. here's how to cultivate it: Psyche ideas.* Psyche. Accessed at psyche.co/ideas/hope-is-the-antidote-to-helplessness-heres-how-to -cultivate-it on November 8, 2022.

Sorvo, R., Koponen, T., Viholainen, H., Aro, T., Räikkönen, E., Peura, P., et al. (2017). Math anxiety and its relationship with basic arithmetic skills among primary school children. *British Journal of Educational Psychology, 87*(3), 309–327. doi.org/10.1111/bjep.12151

Spartan Up. (2020, May 26). *Scientifically proven better sleep and less stress Andrew Huberman, PhD + Joe De Sena* [Video file]. Accessed at youtube.com/watch?v=1ystN_hz5l0 on June 28, 2022.

Stanford Athletics. (2016). *Matt Gentry posts two wins at NCAA Championships*. Stanford, CA: Stanford University Athletics. Accessed at gostanford.com/news/2003/3/20/208157156.aspx on August 23, 2022.

Stanford Digital Education. (n.d.). *The Stanford Resilience Project (archive)* [Video files]. Accessed at youtube.com/playlist?list=PLEnKK2QoIn5OiJXmv-SBY4dxv4i4T4mGd on June 28, 2022.

Starecheski, L. (2015, March 2). *Take the ACE quiz—and learn what it does and doesn't mean*. Accessed at npr.org/sections/health-shots/2015/03/02/387007941/take-the-ace-quiz-and -learn-what-it-does-and-doesnt-mean on June 28, 2022.

Stets, J. E., & Trettevik, R. (2016). Happiness and identities. *Social Science Research*, *58*, 1–13. doi.org/10.1016/j.ssresearch.2016.04.011

St-Louis, A. C., Rapaport, M., Poirier, L. C., Vallerand, R. J., & Dandeneau, S. (2021). On emotion regulation strategies and well-being: The role of passion. *Journal of Happiness Studies*, *22*(4), 1791–1818. doi.org/10.1007/s10902-020-00296-8

Stover, J. (1990). *If everybody did*. Greenville, SC: JourneyForth.

Sweeney, P. (2020). *Fear is fuel: The power to help*. Washington, DC: Rowman & Littlefield.

Swift, J. (2021, August 27). *The benefits of having a sense of purpose*. Ithaca, NY: Cornell Research. Accessed at research.cornell.edu/news-features/benefits-having-sense-purpose on September 5, 2022.

TEDxTalks. (2015, May 20). *What is the best business education? Run a marathon. Andrew Johnston TEDxYouth@MileHigh*. YouTube. Accessed at www.youtube.com/watch?v=oW91ATcgXVc on September 6, 2022.

Tenney, E. R., Logg, J. M., & Moore, D. A. (2015). (Too) optimistic about optimism: The belief that optimism improves performance. *Journal of Personality and Social Psychology*, *108*(3), 377–399. doi.org/10.1037/pspa0000018

Tolkien, J. R. R. (1954). *The fellowship of the ring*. Crows Nest, New South Wales, UK: Allen & Unwin.

Tolkien, J. R. R. (1954). *The two towers*. Crows Nest, New South Wales, UK: Allen & Unwin.

Tolkien, J. R. R. (1955). *The return of the king*. Crows Nest, New South Wales, UK: Allen & Unwin.

Tolle, E. (2016). *A new earth: Awakening to your life's purpose* (10th anniv. ed.). New York: Penguin Books.

Tougias, M. (2016). *A storm too soon* (Young readers ed.)*: A remarkable true survival story in 80-foot waves*. New York: Henry Holt.

Turner, P. S., & Hinds, G. (2018). *Samurai rising: The epic life of Minamoto Yoshitsune*. Watertown, MA: Charlesbridge.

Udvari-Solner, A. (2012). Joyful learning. In N. M. Seel (Ed.), *Encyclopedia of the sciences of learning*. Boston: Springer.

Ulmer, K. (2018). *The art of fear: Why conquering fear won't work and what to do instead*. New York: Harper Wave.

Ursula Burns [Profile]. (n.d.). Forbes. Accessed at forbes.com/profile/ursula-burns/?sh=3397827440a0 on June 27, 2022.

Usher, S. (2017). *Letters of note, vol. 1.* Toronto, Ontario, Canada: McClelland & Stewart.

Vallerand, R. J. (2012). The role of passion in sustainable psychological well-being. *Psychology of Well-Being: Theory, Research and Practice, 2*(1). Accessed at psywb.springeropen.com/track/pdf/10.1186/2211-1522-2-1.pdf on June 28, 2022.

Vallerand, R. J. (2015). The dualistic model of passion. In *The psychology of passion: A dualistic model* (pp. 43–68). doi.org/10.1093/acprof:oso/9780199777600.003.0003

Veenstra, K. (2021, Spring). *The effects of standards-based grading and strategies for implementation: A review of literature* [Master's thesis, Northwestern College]. NWCommons. nwcommons.nwciowa.edu/education_masters/309

Vocabulary.com. (n.d.). *Frisson–definition, meaning, & synonyms.* Accessed at www.vocabulary.com/dictionary/frisson on August 4, 2022.

Vygotsky, L. S., Cole, M., Stein, S., & Sekula, A. (1978). *Mind in society: The development of Higher Psychological Processes.* Cambridge, MA: Harvard University Press.

Wagner, T., & Dintersmith, T. (2015). *Most likely to succeed: Preparing our kids for the innovation era.* New York: Scribner.

Walden, A. (2019, April 8). *Rational vs. irrational fear: Differences and effects of both fears.* Accessed at healthresearchpolicy.org/rational-vs-irrational-fear on June 28, 2022.

Walden University. (2022, May 24). *The-pros-and-cons-of-comfort-zones.* Accessed at www.waldenu.edu/programs/psychology/resource/the-pros-and-cons-of-comfort-zones on September 21, 2022.

Wambach, A. (2019). *Wolfpack: How to come together, unleash our power, and change the game.* New York: Celadon Books.

Watts, A. (2014). Why do we develop certain irrational phobias? *Scientific American.* Accessed at www.scientificamerican.com/article/why-do-we-develop-certain-irrationa/ on November 8, 2022.

West, M., & Gepp, K. (n.d.). *Fight, flight, or freeze response: Signs, causes, and recovery.* Accessed at www.medicalnewstoday.com/articles/fight-flight-or-freeze-response#freeze on September 17, 2022.

West, M. R., Kraft, M. A., Finn, A. S., Martin, R. E., Duckworth, A. L., Gabrieli, C. F., et al. (2016). Promise and paradox measuring students' non-cognitive skills and the impact of schooling. *Educational Evaluation and Policy Analysis, 38,* 148–170.

White, E. E. (2017). *A season of daring greatly.* New York: Greenwillow Books.

Whiteside, C., & Zayakina, K. (2019). *Bounce back betty.* Southlake, TX: Three Frogs Press.

Wiesel, E. (1960). *Night.* New York: Hill & Wang.

Wigfield, A., & Eccles, J. S. (2000). Expectancy-value theory of achievement motivation. *Contemporary Educational Psychology, 25*(1), 68–81. doi.org/10.1006/ceps.1999.1015

Willingham, D. T. (2017). When practice does make perfect: What everyone can learn from top performers. *Education Next, 17*(1), 80–81. Accessed at educationnext.org/when-practice-does-make-perfect-peak-ericsson-pool-book-review on June 28, 2022.

Willink, J., & Bozak, J. (2018). *Way of the warrior kid: From wimpy to warrior the navy seal way.* New York: Square Fish, Feiwel and Friends.

Willis, J. (2007). The neuroscience of joyful education. *Educational Leadership, 64*(9). Accessed at ascd.org/el/articles/the-neuroscience-of-joyful-education on June 28, 2022.

Winner, E. (2019, March 14). *"A rage to master": A blog on gifted children by Dr. Ellen Winner* [Blog post]. Accessed at www.multipleintelligencesoasis.org/blog/2019/3/14/a-rage-to -master-a-blog-on-gifted-children-by-dr-ellen-winner on August 22, 2022.

Wiswede, D., Münte, T. F., Krämer, U. M., & Rüsseler, J. (2009). Embodied emotion modulates neural signature of performance monitoring. *PLoS One, 4*(6): e5754.

Yousafzai, M. (2013). *I am Malala: The girl who stood up for education and was shot by the Taliban.* London: Weidenfeld & Nicolson.

YouTube. (n.d.). *The Stanford Resilience Project (Archive)* [Video file]. Accessed at youtube.com /playlist?list=PLEnKK2QoIn5OiJXmv-SBY4dxv4i4T4mGd on August 23, 2022.

Zaretsky, V. K. (2021). One more time on the zone of proximal development. *Cultural-Historical Psychology, 17*(2), 37–49. doi.org/10.17759/chp.2021170204

Zeeb, H., Ostertag, J., & Renkl, A. (2020). Toward a growth mindset culture in the classroom: Implementation of a lesson-integrated mindset training. *Education Research International, 2020*, 1–13. doi.org/10.1155/2020/8067619

Index

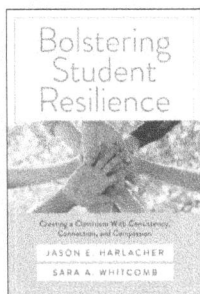

Bolstering Student Resilience
Jason E. Harlacher and Sara A. Whitcomb
Move beyond the buzzwords surrounding social-emotional learning and focus on three fundamentals for successfully supporting your students. This book illuminates the why behind the work and offers proven strategies for building positive, supportive classrooms.
BKL063

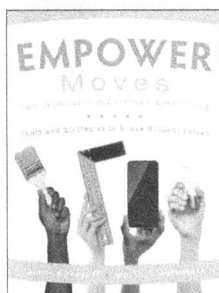

EMPOWER Moves for Social-Emotional Learning
Lauren Porosoff and Jonathan Weinstein
EMPOWER students to discover the values they want to live by. You will learn 28 activities, as well as extensions and variations for each, that will engage students and help them make school a source of meaning, vitality, and community in their lives.
BKG095

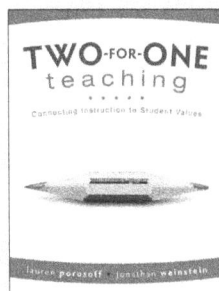

Two-for-One Teaching
Lauren Porosoff and Jonathan Weinstein
Embed student-centered, equity-driven social-emotional learning into every stage of an academic unit. *Two-for-One Teaching* offers 30 protocols that transform lessons, assignments, and assessments into opportunities for students to explore and enact the values they want to bring to their work, relationships, and lives.
BKF923

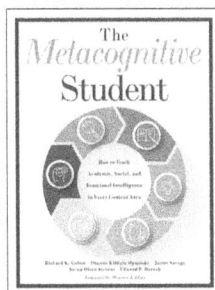

The Metacognitive Student
Richard K. Cohen, Deanne Kildare Opatosky, James Savage, Susan Olsen Stevens, and Edward P. Darrah
What if there was one strategy you could use to support students academically, socially, and emotionally? It exists—and it's simple, straightforward, and practical. Dive deep into structured SELf-questioning and learn how to empower students to develop into strong, healthy, and confident thinkers.
BKF954

Solution Tree | Press *a division of* Solution Tree

Visit SolutionTree.com or call 800.733.6786 to order.

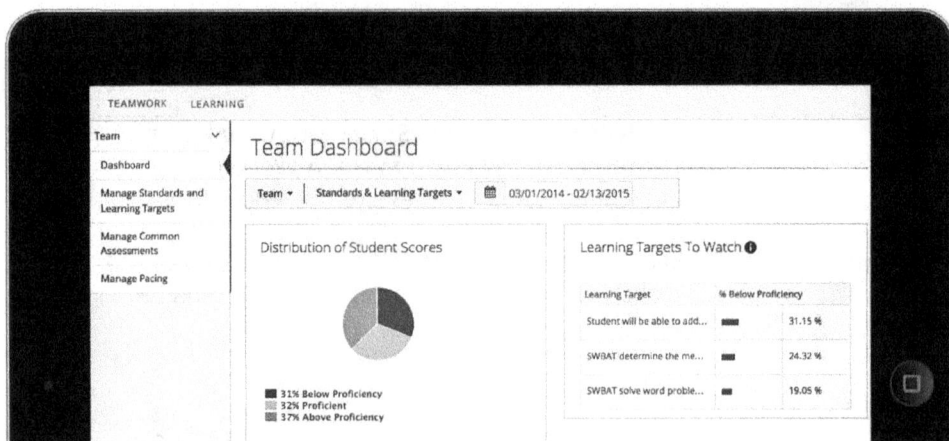